To Middle

Happy Birthday, Jesse

& Dad

Tolkien Miscellany

A Tolkien Miscellany

J.R.R. Tolkien

Quality Paperback Book Club
New York

First SFBC Science Fiction Printing: June 2002

Published by arrangement with:
Houghton Mifflin Company
215 Park Avenue South
New York, NY 10003

Visit the SFBC at *http://www.sfbc.com*

ISBN # 0-7394-2736-9

PRINTED IN THE UNITED STATES OF AMERICA.

CONTENTS

A Tolkien Miscellany

SMITH OF WOOTTON MAJOR

WITH ILLUSTRATIONS BY
PAULINE BAYNES

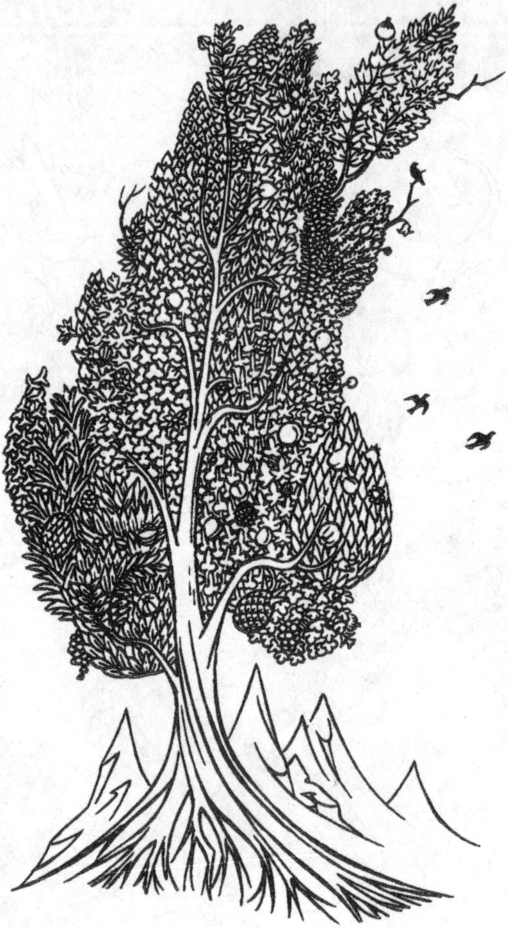

THERE was a village once, not very long ago for those with long memories, nor very far away for those with long legs. Wootton Major it was called because it was larger than Wootton Minor, a few miles away deep in the trees; but it was not very large, though it was at that time prosperous, and a fair number of folk lived in it, good, bad, and mixed, as is usual.

It was a remarkable village in its way, being well known in the country round about for the skill of its workers in various crafts, but most of all for its cooking. It had a large Kitchen which belonged to the Village Council, and the Master Cook was an important person. The Cook's House and the Kitchen adjoined the Great Hall, the largest and oldest building in the place and the most beautiful. It was built of good stone and good oak and was well tended, though it was no longer painted or gilded as it had been once upon a time. In the Hall the villagers held their meetings and debates, and their public feasts, and their family gatherings. So the Cook was kept busy, since for all these occasions he had to provide suitable fare. For the festivals, of which there were many in the course of a year, the fare that was thought suitable was plentiful and rich.

There was one festival to which all looked forward, for it was the only one held in winter. It went on for a week, and on its last day at sundown there was a merrymaking called The Feast of Good Children, to which not many were invited. No doubt some who deserved to be asked were overlooked, and some who did not were invited by mistake; for that is the way of things, however careful those who arrange such matters may try to be. In any case it was largely by chance of birthday that any child came in for the Twenty-four Feast, since that was only held once in twenty-four years, and only twenty-four children were invited. For that occasion the Master Cook was expected to do his best, and in addition to many other good things it was the custom for him to make the Great Cake. By the excellence (or otherwise) of this his name was chiefly remembered, for a Master Cook seldom if ever lasted long enough in office to make a second Great Cake.

There came a time, however, when the reigning Master Cook, to everyone's surprise, since it had never happened before, suddenly announced that he needed a holiday; and he went away, no one knew where; and when he came back some months later he seemed rather changed. He had been a kind man who liked to see other people enjoying themselves, but he was himself serious, and said very little. Now he was merrier, and often said and did most laughable things; and at feasts he would himself sing gay songs, which was not expected of Master Cooks. Also he brought back with him an Apprentice; and that astonished the Village.

It was not astonishing for the Master Cook to have an apprentice. It was usual. The Master chose one in due time, and he taught him all that he could; and as they both grew older the apprentice took on more of the important work, so that when the Master retired or died there he was, ready to take over the office and become Master Cook in his turn. But this Master had never chosen an apprentice. He had always said 'time enough yet', or 'I'm keeping my eyes open and I'll choose one when I find one to suit me'. But now he brought with him a mere boy, and not one from the village. He was more lithe than the Wootton lads and quicker, soft-spoken and very polite, but ridiculously young for the work, barely in his teens by the look of him. Still, choosing his apprentice was the Master Cook's affair, and no one had the right to interfere in it; so the boy remained and stayed in the Cook's House until he was old enough to find lodgings for himself. People soon became used to seeing him about, and he made a few friends. They and the Cook called him Alf, but to the rest he was just Prentice.

The next surprise came only three years later. One spring morning the Master Cook took off his tall white hat, folded up his clean aprons, hung up his white coat, took a stout ash stick and a small bag, and departed. He said goodbye to the apprentice. No one else was about.

'Goodbye for now, Alf', he said. 'I leave you to manage things as best you can, which is always very well. I expect it will turn out all right. If we meet again, I hope to hear all about it. Tell them that I've gone on another holiday, but this time I shan't be coming back again'.

There was quite a stir in the village when Prentice gave this message to people who came to the Kitchen. 'What a thing to do!' they said. 'And without warning or farewell! What are we going to do without any Master Cook? He has left no one to take his place'. In all their discussions no one ever thought of making young Prentice into Cook. He had grown a bit taller but still looked like a boy, and he had only served for three years.

In the end for lack of anyone better they appointed a man of the village, who could cook well enough in a small way. When he was younger he had helped the Master at busy times, but the Master had never taken to him and would not have him as apprentice. He was now a solid sort of man with a wife and children, and careful with money. 'At any rate he won't go off without notice', they said, 'and poor cooking is better than none. It is seven years till the next Great Cake, and by that time he should be able to manage it'.

Nokes, for that was his name, was very pleased with the turn things had taken. He had always wished to become Master Cook, and had never doubted that he could manage it. For some time, when he was alone in the Kitchen, he used to put on the tall white hat and look at himself in a polished frying pan and say: 'How do you do, Master. That hat suits you properly, might have been made for you. I hope things go well with you'.

Things went well enough; for at first Nokes did his best, and he had Prentice to help him. Indeed he learned a lot from him by watching him slyly, though that Nokes never admitted. But in due course the time for the Twenty-four Feast drew near, and Nokes had to think about making the Great Cake. Secretly he was worried about it, for although with seven years' practice he could turn out passable cakes and pastries for ordinary occasions, he knew that his Great Cake would be eagerly awaited, and would have to satisfy severe critics. Not only the children. A smaller cake of the same materials and baking had to be provided for those who came to help at the feast. Also it was expected that the Great Cake should have something novel and surprising about it and not be a mere repetition of the one before.

His chief notion was that it should be very sweet and rich; and he decided that it should be entirely covered in sugar-icing (at which Prentice had a clever hand). 'That will make it pretty and fairylike', he thought. Fairies and sweets were two of the very few notions he had about the tastes of children. Fairies he thought one grew out of; but of sweets he remained very fond. 'Ah! fairylike', he said, 'that gives me an idea'; and so it came into his head that he would stick a little doll on a pinnacle in the middle of the Cake, dressed all in white, with a little wand in her hand ending in a tinsel star, and *Fairy Queen* written in pink icing round her feet.

But when he began preparing the materials for the cake-making he found that he had only dim memories of what should go *inside* a Great Cake; so he looked in some old books of recipes left behind by previous cooks. They puzzled him, even when he could make out their handwriting, for they mentioned many things that he had not heard of, and some that he had forgotten and now had no time to get; but he thought he might try one or two of the spices that the books spoke of. He scratched his head and remembered an old black box with several different compartments in which the last Cook had once kept spices and other things for special cakes. He had not looked at it since he took over, but after a search he found it on a high shelf in the store-room.

He took it down and blew the dust off the lid; but when he opened it he found that very little of the spices was left, and they were dry and musty. But in one compartment in the corner he discovered a small star, hardly as big as one of our sixpences, black-looking as if it was made of silver but was tarnished. 'That's funny!' he said as he held it up to the light.

'No, it isn't!' said a voice behind him, so suddenly that he jumped. It was the voice of Prentice, and he had never spoken to the Master in that tone before. Indeed he seldom spoke to Nokes at all unless he was spoken to first. Very right and proper in a youngster; he might be clever with icing but he had a lot to learn yet: that was Nokes's opinion.

'What do you mean, young fellow?' he said, not much pleased. 'If it isn't funny what is it?'

'It is *fay*', said Prentice. 'It comes from Faery'.

Then the Cook laughed. 'All right, all right', he said. 'It means much the same; but call it that if you like. You'll grow up some day. Now you can get on with stoning the raisins. If you notice any funny fairy ones, tell me'.

'What are you going to do with the star, Master?' said Prentice.

'Put it into the Cake, of course', said the Cook. 'Just the thing, especially if it's *fairy*', he sniggered. 'I daresay you've been to children's parties yourself, and not so long ago either, where little trinkets like this were stirred into the mixture, and little coins and what not. Anyway we do that in this village: it amuses the children'.

'But this isn't a trinket, Master, it's a fay-star', said Prentice.

'So you've said already', snapped the Cook. 'Very well, I'll tell the children. It'll make them laugh'.

'I don't think it will, Master', said Prentice. 'But it's the right thing to do, quite right'.

'Who do you think you're talking to?' said Nokes.

In time the Cake was made and baked and iced, mostly by Prentice. 'As you are so set on fairies, I'll let you make the Fairy Queen', Nokes said to him.

'Very good, Master', he answered. 'I'll do it if you are too busy. But it was your idea and not mine'.

'It's my place to have ideas, and not yours', said Nokes.

At the Feast the Cake stood in the middle of the long table, inside a ring of twenty-four red candles. Its top rose into a small white mountain, up the sides of which grew little trees glittering as if with frost; on its summit stood a tiny white figure on one foot like a snow-maiden dancing, and in her hand was a minute wand of ice sparkling with light.

The children looked at it with wide eyes, and one or two clapped their hands, crying: 'Isn't it pretty and fairylike!' That delighted the Cook, but the apprentice looked displeased. They were both present: the Master to cut up the Cake when the time came, and the apprentice to sharpen the knife and hand it to him.

At last the Cook took the knife and stepped up to the table. 'I should tell you, my dears', he said, 'that inside this lovely icing there is a cake made of many nice things to eat; but also stirred well in there are many pretty little things, trinkets and little coins and what not, and I'm told that it is lucky to find one in your slice. There are twenty-four in the Cake, so there should be one for each of you, if the Fairy Queen plays fair. But she doesn't always do so: she's a tricky little creature. You ask Mr. Prentice'. The apprentice turned away and studied the faces of the children.

'No! I'm forgetting', said the Cook. 'There's twenty-five this evening. There's also a little silver star, a special magic one, or so Mr. Prentice says. So be careful! If you break one of your pretty front teeth on it, the magic star won't mend it. But I expect it's a specially lucky thing to find, all the same'.

It was a good cake, and no one had any fault to find with it, except that it was no bigger than was needed. When it was all cut up there was a large slice for each of the children, but nothing left over: no coming again. The slices soon disappeared, and every now and then a trinket or a coin was discovered. Some found one, and some found two, and

several found none; for that is the way luck goes, whether there is a doll with a wand on the cake or not. But when the Cake was all eaten, there was no sign of any magic star.

'Bless me!' said the Cook. 'Then it can't have been made of silver after all; it must have melted. Or perhaps Mr. Prentice was right and it was really magical, and it's just vanished and gone back to Fairyland. Not a nice trick to play, I don't think'. He looked at Prentice with a smirk, and Prentice looked at him with dark eyes and did not smile at all.

All the same, the silver star was indeed a fay-star: the apprentice was not one to make mistakes about things of that sort. What had happened was that one of the boys at the Feast had swallowed it without ever noticing it, although he had found a silver coin in his slice and had given it to Nell, the little girl next to him: she looked so disappointed at finding nothing lucky in hers. He sometimes wondered what had really become of the star, and did not know that it had remained with him, tucked away in some place where it could not be felt; for that was what it was intended to do. There it waited for a long time, until its day came.

The Feast had been in mid-winter, but it was now June, and the night was hardly dark at all. The boy got up before dawn, for he did not wish to sleep: it was his tenth birthday. He looked out of the window, and the world seemed quiet and expectant. A little breeze, cool and fragrant, stirred the waking trees. Then the dawn came, and far away he heard the dawn-song of the birds beginning, growing as it came towards him, until it rushed over him, filling all the land round the house, and passed on like a wave of music into the West, as the sun rose above the rim of the world.

'It reminds me of Faery', he heard himself say; 'but in Faery the people sing too'. Then he began to sing, high and clear, in strange words that he seemed to know by heart; and in that moment the star fell out of his mouth and he caught it on his open hand. It was bright silver now, glistening in the sunlight; but it quivered and rose a little, as if it was about to fly away. Without thinking he clapped his hand to his head, and there the star stayed in the middle of his forehead, and he wore it for many years.

Few people in the village noticed it though it was not invisible to attentive eyes; but it became part of his face, and it did not usually shine

at all. Some of its light passed into his eyes; and his voice, which had begun to grow beautiful as soon as the star came to him, became ever more beautiful as he grew up. People liked to hear him speak, even if it was no more than a 'good morning'.

He became well known in his country, not only in his own village but in many others round about, for his good workmanship. His father was a smith, and he followed him in his craft and bettered it. Smithson he was called while his father was still alive, and then just Smith. For by that time he was the best smith between Far Easton and the Westwood, and he could make all kinds of things of iron in his smithy. Most of them, of course, were plain and useful, meant for daily needs: farm tools, carpenters' tools, kitchen tools and pots and pans, bars and bolts and hinges, pot-hooks, firedogs, and horseshoes, and the like. They were strong and lasting, but they also had a grace about them, being shapely in their kinds, good to handle and to look at.

But some things, when he had time, he made for delight; and they were beautiful, for he could work iron into wonderful forms that looked as light and delicate as a spray of leaves and blossom, but kept the stern strength of iron, or seemed even stronger. Few could pass by one of the gates or lattices that he made without stopping to admire it; no one could pass through it once it was shut. He sang when he was making things of this sort; and when Smith began to sing those nearby stopped their own work and came to the smithy to listen.

That was all that most people knew about him. It was enough indeed and more than most men and women in the village achieved, even those who were skilled and hard-working. But there was more to know. For Smith became acquainted with Faery, and some regions of it he knew as well as any mortal can; though since too many had become like Nokes, he spoke of this to few people, except his wife and his children. His wife was Nell, to whom he gave the silver coin, and his daughter was Nan, and his son was Ned Smithson. From them it could not have been kept secret anyway, for they sometimes saw the star shining on his forehead, when he came back from one of the long walks he would take alone now and then in the evening, or when he returned from a journey.

From time to time he would go off, sometimes walking, sometimes riding, and it was generally supposed that it was on business; and sometimes it was, and sometimes it was not. At any rate not to get orders for work, or to buy pig-iron and charcoal and other supplies, though he attended to such things with care and knew how to turn an honest penny

into two-pence, as the saying went. But he had business of its own kind in Faery, and he was welcome there; for the star shone bright on his brow, and he was as safe as a mortal can be in that perilous country. The Lesser Evils avoided the star, and from the Greater Evils he was guarded.

For that he was grateful, for he soon became wise and understood that the marvels of Faery cannot be approached without danger, and that many of the Evils cannot be challenged without weapons of power too great for any mortal to wield. He remained a learner and explorer, not a warrior; and though in time he could have forged weapons that in his own world would have had power enough to become the matter of great tales and be worth a king's ransom, he knew that in Faery they would have been of small account. So among all the things that he made it is not remembered that he ever forged a sword or a spear or an arrow-head.

In Faery at first he walked for the most part quietly among the lesser folk and the gentler creatures in the woods and meads of fair valleys, and by the bright waters in which at night strange stars shone and at dawn the gleaming peaks of far mountains were mirrored. Some of his briefer visits he spent looking only at one tree or one flower; but later in longer journeys he had seen things of both beauty and terror that he could not clearly remember nor report to his friends, though he knew that they dwelt deep in his heart. But some things he did not forget, and they remained in his mind as wonders and mysteries that he often re-called.

When he first began to walk far without a guide he thought he would discover the further bounds of the land; but great mountains rose before him, and going by long ways round about them he came at last to a desolate shore. He stood beside the Sea of Windless Storm where the blue waves like snow-clad hills roll silently out of Unlight to the long strand, bearing the white ships that return from battles on the Dark Marches of which men know nothing. He saw a great ship cast high upon the land, and the waters fell back in foam without a sound. The elven mariners were tall and terrible; their swords shone and their spears glinted and a piercing light was in their eyes. Suddenly they lifted up their voices in a song of triumph, and his heart was shaken with fear, and he fell upon his face, and they passed over him and went away into the echoing hills.

* * *

Afterwards he went no more to that strand, believing that he was in an island realm beleaguered by the Sea, and he turned his mind towards the mountains, desiring to come to the heart of the kingdom. Once in these wanderings he was overtaken by a grey mist and strayed long at a loss, until the mist rolled away and he found that he was in a wide plain. Far off there was a great hill of shadow, and out of that shadow, which was its root, he saw the King's Tree springing up, tower upon tower, into the sky, and its light was like the sun at noon; and it bore at once leaves and flowers and fruits uncounted, and not one was the same as any other that grew on the Tree.

He never saw that Tree again, though he often sought for it. On one such journey climbing into the Outer Mountains he came to a deep dale among them, and at its bottom lay a lake, calm and unruffled though a breeze stirred the woods that surrounded it. In that dale the light was like a red sunset, but the light came up from the lake. From a low cliff that overhung it he looked down, and it seemed that he could see to an immeasurable depth; and there he beheld strange shapes of flame bending and branching and wavering like great weeds in a sea-dingle, and fiery creatures went to and fro among them. Filled with wonder he went down to the water's edge and tried it with his foot, but it was not water: it was harder than stone and sleeker than glass. He stepped on it and he fell heavily, and a ringing boom ran across the lake and echoed in its shores.

At once the breeze rose to a wild Wind, roaring like a great beast, and it swept him up and flung him on the shore, and it drove him up the slopes whirling and falling like a dead leaf. He put his arms about the stem of a young birch and clung to it, and the Wind wrestled fiercely with them, trying to tear him away; but the birch was bent down to the ground by the blast and enclosed him in its branches. When at last the Wind passed on he rose and saw that the birch was naked. It was stripped of every leaf, and it wept, and tears fell from its branches like rain. He set his hand upon its white bark, saying: 'Blessed be the birch! What can I do to make amends or give thanks?' He felt the answer of the tree pass up from his hand: 'Nothing', it said. 'Go away! The Wind is hunting you. You do not belong here. Go away and never return!'

As he climbed back out of that dale he felt the tears of the birch trickle down his face and they were bitter on his lips. His heart was saddened as he went on his long road, and for some time he did not enter Faery again. But he could not forsake it, and when he returned his desire was still stronger to go deep into the land.

* * *

At last he found a road through the Outer Mountains, and he went on till he came to the Inner Mountains, and they were high and sheer and daunting. Yet in the end he found a pass that he could scale, and upon a day of days greatly daring he came through a narrow cleft and looked down, though he did not know it, into the Vale of Evermorn where the green surpasses the green of the meads of Outer Faery as they surpass ours in our springtime. There the air is so lucid that eyes can see the red tongues of birds as they sing on the trees upon the far side of the valley, though that is very wide and the birds are no greater than wrens.

On the inner side the mountains went down in long slopes filled with the sound of bubbling waterfalls, and in great delight he hastened on. As he set foot upon the grass of the Vale he heard elven voices singing, and on a lawn beside a river bright with lilies he came upon many maidens dancing. The speed and the grace and the ever-changing modes of their movements enchanted him, and he stepped forward towards their ring. Then suddenly they stood still, and a young maiden with flowing hair and kilted skirt came out to meet him.

She laughed as she spoke to him, saying: 'You are becoming bold, Starbrow, are you not? Have you no fear what the Queen might say, if she knew of this? Unless you have her leave'. He was abashed, for he became aware of his own thought and knew that she read it: that the star on his forehead was a passport to go wherever he wished; and now he knew that it was not. But she smiled as she spoke again: 'Come! Now that you are here you shall dance with me'; and she took his hand and led him into the ring.

There they danced together, and for a while he knew what it was to have the swiftness and the power and the joy to accompany her. For a while. But soon as it seemed they halted again, and she stooped and took up a white flower from before her feet, and she set it in his hair. 'Farewell now!' she said. 'Maybe we shall meet again, by the Queen's leave'.

He remembered nothing of the journey home from that meeting, until he found himself riding along the roads in his own country; and in some villages people stared at him in wonder and watched him till he rode out of sight. When he came to his own house his daughter ran out and greeted him with delight—he had returned sooner than was expected, but none too soon for those that awaited him. 'Daddy!' she cried. 'Where have you been? Your star is shining bright!'

When he crossed the threshold the star dimmed again; but Nell took him by the hand and led him to the hearth, and there she turned and looked at him. 'Dear Man', she said, 'where have you been and what have you seen? There is a flower in your hair'. She lifted it gently from his head, and it lay on her hand. It seemed like a thing seen from a great distance, yet there it was, and a light came from it that cast shadows on the walls of the room, now growing dark in the evening. The shadow of the man before her loomed up and its great head was bowed over her. 'You look like a giant, Dad', said his son, who had not spoken before.

The flower did not wither nor grow dim; and they kept it as a secret and a treasure. The smith made a little casket with a key for it, and there it lay and was handed down for many generations in his kin; and those who inherited the key would at times open the casket and look long at the Living Flower, till the casket closed again: the time of its shutting was not theirs to choose.

The years did not halt in the village. Many now had passed. At the Children's Feast when he received the star the smith was not yet ten years old. Then came another Twenty-four Feast, by which time Alf had become Master Cook and had chosen a new apprentice, Harper. Twelve years later the smith had returned with the Living Flower; and now another Children's Twenty-four Feast was due in the winter to come. One day in that year Smith was walking in the woods of Outer Faery, and it was autumn. Golden leaves were on the boughs and red leaves were on the ground. Footsteps came behind him, but he did not heed them or turn round, for he was deep in thought.

On that visit he had received a summons and had made a far journey. Longer it seemed to him than any he had yet made. He was guided and guarded, but he had little memory of the ways that he had taken; for often he had been blindfolded by mist or by shadow, until at last he came to a high place under a night-sky of innumerable stars. There he was brought before the Queen herself. She wore no crown and had no throne. She stood there in her majesty and her glory, and all about her was a great host shimmering and glittering like the stars above; but she was taller than the points of their great spears, and upon her head there burned a white flame. She made a sign for him to approach, and trembling he stepped forward. A high clear trumpet sounded, and behold! they were alone.

He stood before her, and he did not kneel in courtesy, for he was dismayed and felt that for one so lowly all gestures were in vain. At length he looked up and beheld her face and her eyes bent gravely upon him; and he was troubled and amazed, for in that moment he knew her again: the fair maid of the Green Vale, the dancer at whose feet the flowers sprang. She smiled seeing his memory, and drew towards him; and they spoke long together, for the most part without words, and he learned many things in her thought, some of which gave him joy, and others filled him with grief. Then his mind turned back retracing his life, until he came to the day of the Children's Feast and the coming of the star, and suddenly he saw again the little dancing figure with its wand, and in shame he lowered his eyes from the Queen's beauty.

But she laughed again as she had laughed in the Vale of Evermorn. 'Do not be grieved for me, Starbrow', she said. 'Nor too much ashamed of your own folk. Better a little doll, maybe, than no memory of Faery at all. For some the only glimpse. For some the awaking. Ever since that day you have desired in your heart to see me, and I have granted your wish. But I can give you no more. Now at farewell I will make you my messenger. If you meet the King, say to him: *The time has come. Let him choose*'.

'But Lady of Faery', he stammered, 'where then is the King?' For he had asked this question many times of the people of Faery, and they had all said the same: 'He has not told us'.

And the Queen answered: 'If he has not told you, Starbrow, then I may not. But he makes many journeys and may be met in unlikely places. Now kneel of your courtesy'.

Then he knelt, and she stooped and laid her hand on his head, and a great stillness came upon him; and he seemed to be both in the World and in Faery, and also outside them and surveying them, so that he was at once in bereavement, and in ownership, and in peace. When after a while the stillness passed he raised his head and stood up. The dawn was in the sky and the stars were pale, and the Queen was gone. Far off he heard the echo of a trumpet in the mountains. The high field where he stood was silent and empty: and he knew that his way now led back to bereavement.

That meeting-place was now far behind him, and here he was, walking among the fallen leaves, pondering all that he had seen and learned. The footsteps came nearer. Then suddenly a voice said at his side: 'Are you going my way, Starbrow?'

He started and came out of his thoughts, and he saw a man beside him. He was tall, and he walked lightly and quickly; he was dressed all in dark green and wore a hood that partly overshadowed his face. The smith was puzzled, for only the people of Faery called him 'Starbrow', but he could not remember ever having seen this man there before; and yet he felt uneasily that he should know him. 'What way are you going then?' he said.

'I am going back to your village now', the man answered, 'and I hope that you are also returning'.

'I am indeed', said the smith. 'Let us walk together. But now something has come back to my mind. Before I began my homeward journey a Great Lady gave me a message, but we shall soon be passing from Faery, and I do not think that I shall ever return. Will you?'

'Yes, I shall. You may give the message to me'.

'But the message was to the King. Do you know where to find him?'

'I do. What was the message?'

'The Lady only asked me to say to him: *The time has come. Let him choose*'.

'I understand. Trouble yourself no further'.

They went on then side by side in silence save for the rustle of the leaves about their feet; but after a few miles while they were still within the bounds of Faery the man halted. He turned towards the smith and threw back his hood. Then the smith knew him. He was Alf the Prentice, as the smith still called him in his own mind, remembering always the day when as a youth Alf had stood in the Hall, holding the bright knife for the cutting of the Cake, and his eyes had gleamed in the light of the candles. He must be an old man now, for he had been Master Cook for many years; but here standing under the eaves of the Outer Wood he looked like the apprentice of long ago, though more masterly: there was no grey in his hair nor line on his face, and his eyes gleamed as if they reflected a light.

'I should like to speak to you, Smith Smithson, before we go back to your country', he said. The smith wondered at that, for he himself had often wished to talk to Alf, but had never been able to do so. Alf had always greeted him kindly and had looked at him with friendly eyes, but had seemed to avoid talking to him alone. He was looking now at the smith with friendly eyes; but he lifted his hand and with his forefinger touched the star on his brow. The gleam left his eyes, and then the smith knew that it had come from the star, and that it must have been shining brightly but now was dimmed. He was surprised and drew away angrily.

'Do you not think, Master Smith', said Alf, 'that it is time for you to give this thing up?'

'What is that to you, Master Cook?' he answered. 'And why should I do so? Isn't it mine? It came to me, and may a man not keep things that come to him so, at the least as a remembrance?'

'Some things. Those that are free gifts and given for remembrance. But others are not so given. They cannot belong to a man for ever, nor be treasured as heirlooms. They are lent. You have not thought, perhaps, that someone else may need this thing. But it is so. Time is pressing'.

Then the smith was troubled, for he was a generous man, and he remembered with gratitude all that the star had brought to him. 'Then what should I do?' he asked. 'Should I give it to one of the Great in Faery? Should I give it to the King?' And as he said this a hope sprang in his heart that on such an errand he might once more enter Faery.

'You could give it to me', said Alf, 'but you might find that too hard. Will you come with me to my store-room and put it back in the box where your grandfather laid it?'

'I did not know that,' said the smith.

'No one knew but me. I was the only one with him'.

'Then I suppose that you know how he came by the star, and why he put it in the box?'

'He brought it from Faery: that you know without asking', Alf answered. 'He left it behind in the hope that it might come to you, his only grandchild. So he told me, for he thought that I could arrange that. He was your mother's father. I do not know whether she told you much about him, if indeed she knew much to tell. Rider was his name, and he was a great traveller: he had seen many things and could do many things before he settled down and became Master Cook. But he went away when you were only two years old—and they could find no one better to follow him than Nokes, poor man. Still, as we expected, I became Master in time. This year I shall make another Great Cake: the only Cook, as far as is remembered, ever to make a second one. I wish to put the star in it'.

'Very well, you shall have it', said the smith. He looked at Alf as if he was trying to read his thought. 'Do you know who will find it?'

'What is that to you, Master Smith?'

'I should like to know, if you do, Master Cook. It might make it easier for me to part with a thing so dear to me. My daughter's child is too young'.

'It might and it might not. We shall see', said Alf.

They said no more, and they went on their way until they passed out of Faery and came back at last to the village. Then they walked to the

Hall; and in the world the sun was now setting and a red light was in the windows. The gilded carvings on the great door glowed, and strange faces of many colours looked down from the water-spouts under the roof. Not long ago the Hall had been re-glazed and re-painted, and there had been much debate on the Council about it. Some disliked it and called it 'new-fangled', but some with more knowledge knew that it was a return to old custom. Still, since it had cost no one a penny and the Master Cook must have paid for it himself, he was allowed to have his own way. But the smith had not seen it in such a light before, and he stood and looked at the Hall in wonder, forgetting his errand.

He felt a touch on his arm, and Alf led him round to a small door at the back. He opened it and led the smith down a dark passage into the store-room. There he lit a tall candle, and unlocking a cupboard he took down from a shelf the black box. It was polished now and adorned with silver scrolls.

He raised the lid and showed it to the smith. One small compartment was empty; the others were now filled with spices, fresh and pungent, and the smith's eyes began to water. He put his hand to his forehead, and the star came away readily, but he felt a sudden stab of pain, and tears ran down his face. Though the star shone brightly again as it lay in his hand, he could not see it, except as a blurred dazzle of light that seemed far away.

'I cannot see clearly', he said. 'You must put it in for me'. He held out his hand, and Alf took the star and laid it in its place, and it went dark.

The smith turned away without another word and groped his way to the door. On the threshold he found that his sight had cleared again. It was evening and the Even-star was shining in a luminous sky close to the Moon. As he stood for a moment looking at their beauty, he felt a hand on his shoulder and turned.

'You gave me the star freely', said Alf. 'If you still wish to know to which child it will go, I will tell you'.

'I do indeed'.

'It shall go to any one that you appoint'.

The smith was taken aback and did not answer at once. 'Well', he said hesitating, 'I wonder what you may think of my choice. I believe you have little reason to love the name of Nokes, but, well, his little great-grandson, Nokes of Townsend's Tim, is coming to the Feast. Nokes of Townsend is quite different'.

'I have observed that', said Alf. 'He had a wise mother'.

'Yes, my Nell's sister. But apart from the kinship I love little Tim. Though he's not an obvious choice'.

Alf smiled. 'Neither were you', he said. 'But I agree. Indeed I had already chosen Tim'.

'Then why did you ask me to choose?'

'The Queen wished me to do so. If you had chosen differently I should have given way'.

The smith looked long at Alf. Then suddenly he bowed low. 'I understand at last, sir', he said. 'You have done us too much honour'.

'I have been repaid', said Alf. 'Go home now in peace!'

When the smith reached his own house on the western outskirts of the village he found his son by the door of the forge. He had just locked it, for the day's work was done, and now he stood looking up the white road by which his father used to return from his journeys. Hearing footsteps, he turned in surprise to see him coming from the village, and he ran forward to meet him. He put his arms about him in loving welcome.

'I've been hoping for you since yesterday, Dad', he said. Then looking into his father's face he said anxiously: 'How tired you look! You have walked far, maybe?'

'Very far indeed, my son. All the way from Daybreak to Evening'.

They went into the house together, and it was dark except for the fire flickering on the hearth. His son lit candles, and for a while they sat by the fire without speaking; for a great weariness and bereavement was on the smith. At last he looked round, as if coming to himself, and he said: 'Why are we alone?'

His son looked hard at him. 'Why? Mother's over at Minor, at Nan's. It's the little lad's second birthday. They hoped you would be there too'.

'Ah yes. I ought to have been. I should have been, Ned, but I was delayed; and I have had matters to think of that put all else out of mind for a time. But I did not forget Tomling'.

He put his hand in his breast and drew out a little wallet of soft leather. 'I have brought him something. A trinket old Nokes maybe would call it—but it comes out of Faery, Ned'. Out of the wallet he took a little thing of silver. It was like the smooth stem of a tiny lily from the top of which came three delicate flowers, bending down like shapely bells. And bells they were, for when he shook them gently each flower rang with a small clear note. At the sweet sound the candles flickered and then for a moment shone with a white light.

Ned's eyes were wide with wonder. 'May I look at it, Dad?' he said.

He took it with careful fingers and peered into the flowers. 'The work is a marvel!' he said. 'And, Dad, there is a scent in the bells: a scent that reminds me of, reminds me, well of something I've forgotten'.

'Yes, the scent comes for a little while after the bells have rung. But don't fear to handle it, Ned. It was made for a babe to play with. He can do it no harm, and he'll take none from it'.

The smith put the gift back in the wallet and stowed it away. 'I'll take it over to Wootton Minor myself tomorrow', he said. 'Nan and her Tom, and Mother, will forgive me, maybe. As for Tomling, his time has not come yet for the counting of days . . . and of weeks, and of months, and of years'.

'That's right. You go, Dad. I'd be glad to go with you; but it will be some time before I can get over to Minor. I couldn't have gone today, even if I hadn't waited here for you. There's a lot of work in hand, and more coming in'.

'No, no, Smith's son! Make it a holiday! The name of grandfather hasn't weakened my arms yet a while. Let the work come! There'll be two pairs of hands to tackle it now, all working days. I shall not be going on journeys again, Ned: not on long ones, if you understand me'.

'It's that way is it, Dad? I wondered what had become of the star. That's hard'. He took his father's hand. 'I'm grieved for you; but there's good in it too, for this house. Do you know, Master Smith, there is much you can teach me yet, if you have the time. And I do not mean only the working of iron'.

They had supper together, and long after they had finished they still sat at the table, while the smith told his son of his last journey in Faery, and of other things that came to his mind—but about the choice of the next holder of the star he said nothing.

At last his son looked at him, and 'Father', he said, 'do you remember the day when you came back with the Flower? And I said that you looked like a giant by your shadow. The shadow was the truth. So it was the Queen herself that you danced with. Yet you have given up the star. I hope it may go to someone as worthy. The child should be grateful'.

'The child won't know', said the smith. 'That's the way with such gifts. Well, there it is. I have handed it on and come back to hammer and tongs'.

It is a strange thing, but old Nokes, who had scoffed at his apprentice, had never been able to put out of his mind the disappearance of the star in the Cake, although that event had happened so many years ago. He had grown fat and lazy, and retired from his office when he was sixty (no great age in the village). He was now near the end of his eighties, and was of enormous bulk, for he still ate heavily and doted on sugar. Most of his days, when not at table, he spent in a big chair by the window of his cottage, or by the door if it was fine weather. He liked talking, since he still had many opinions to air; but lately his talk mostly turned to the one Great Cake that he had made (as he was now firmly convinced), for whenever he fell asleep it came into his dreams. Prentice sometimes stopped for a word or two. So the old cook still called him, and he expected himself to be called Master. That Prentice was careful to do; which was a point in his favour, though there were others that Nokes was more fond of.

One afternoon Nokes was nodding in his chair by the door after his dinner. He woke with a start to find Prentice standing by and looking down at him. 'Hullo!' he said. 'I'm glad to see you, for that cake's been on my mind again. I was thinking of it just now in fact. It was the best cake I ever made, and that's saying something. But perhaps you have forgotten it'.

'No, Master. I remember it very well. But what is troubling you? It was a good cake, and it was enjoyed and praised'.

'Of course. I made it. But that doesn't trouble me. It's the little trinket, the star. I cannot make up my mind what became of it. Of course it wouldn't melt. I only said that to stop the children from being frightened. I have wondered if one of them did not swallow it. But is that likely? You might swallow one of those little coins and not notice it, but not that star. It was small but it had sharp points'.

'Yes, Master. But do you really know what the star was made of? Don't trouble your mind about it. Someone swallowed it, I assure you'.

'Then who? Well, I've a long memory, and that day sticks in it somehow. I can recall all the children's names. Let me think. It must have been Miller's Molly! She was greedy and bolted her food. She's as fat as a sack now'.

'Yes, there are some folk who get like that, Master. But Molly did not bolt her cake. She found two trinkets in her slice'.

'Oh, did she? Well, it was Cooper's Harry then. A barrel of a boy with a big mouth like a frog's'.

'I should have said, Master, that he was a nice boy with a large friendly grin. Anyway he was so careful that he took his slice to pieces before he ate it. He found nothing but cake'.

'Then it must have been that little pale girl, Draper's Lily. She used to swallow pins as a baby and came to no harm'.

'Not Lily, Master. She only ate the paste and the sugar, and gave the inside to the boy that sat next to her'.

'Then I give up. Who was it? You seem to have been watching very closely. If you're not making it all up'.

'It was the Smith's son, Master; and I think it was good for him'.

'Go on!' laughed old Nokes. 'I ought to have known you were having a game with me. Don't be ridiculous! Smith was a quiet slow boy then. He makes more noise now: a bit of a songster, I hear; but he's cautious. No risks for him. Chews twice before he swallows, and always did, if you take my meaning'.

'I do, Master. Well, if you won't believe it was Smith, I can't help you. Perhaps it doesn't matter much now. Will it ease your mind if I tell you that the star is back in the box now? Here it is!'

Prentice was wearing a dark green cloak, which Nokes now noticed for the first time. From its folds he produced the black box and opened it under the old cook's nose. 'There is the star, Master, down in the corner'.

Old Nokes began coughing and sneezing, but at last he looked into the box. 'So it is!' he said. 'At least it looks like it'.

'It is the same one, Master. I put it there myself a few days ago. It will go back in the Great Cake this winter'.

'A-ha!' said Nokes, leering at Prentice; and then he laughed till he shook like a jelly. 'I see, I see! Twenty-four children and twenty-four lucky bits, and the star was one extra. So you nipped it out before the baking and kept it for another time. You were always a tricky fellow: nimble one might say. And thrifty: wouldn't waste a bee's knee of butter. Ha, ha, ha! So that was the way of it. I might have guessed. Well, that's cleared up. Now I can have a nap in peace'. He settled down in his chair. 'Mind that prentice-man of yours plays you no tricks! The artful don't know all the arts, they say'. He closed his eyes.

'Goodbye, Master!' said Prentice, shutting the box with such a snap that the cook opened his eyes again. 'Nokes', he said, 'your knowledge is so great that I have only twice ventured to tell you anything. I told you that the star came from Faery; and I have told you that it went to the smith. You laughed at me. Now at parting I will tell you one thing more. Don't laugh again! You are a vain old fraud, fat, idle and sly. I did most of your work. Without thanks you learned all that you could from me—except respect for Faery, and a little courtesy. You have not even enough to bid me good day'.

'If it comes to courtesy', said Nokes, 'I see none in calling your elders and betters by ill names. Take your Fairy and your nonsense somewhere else! Good day to you, if that's what you're waiting for. Now go along with you!' He flapped his hand mockingly. 'If you've got one of your fairy friends hidden in the Kitchen, send him to me and I'll have a look at him. If he waves his little wand and makes me thin again, I'll think better of him', he laughed.

'Would you spare a few moments for the King of Faery?' the other answered. To Nokes's dismay he grew taller as he spoke. He threw back his cloak. He was dressed like a Master Cook at a Feast, but his white garments shimmered and glinted, and on his forehead was a great jewel like a radiant star. His face was young but stern.

'Old man', he said, 'you are at least not my elder. As to my better: you have often sneered at me behind my back. Do you challenge me now openly?' He stepped forward, and Nokes shrank from him, trembling. He tried to shout for help but found that he could hardly whisper.

'No, sir!' he croaked. 'Don't do me a harm! I'm only a poor old man'.

The King's face softened. 'Alas, yes! You speak the truth. Do not be afraid! Be at ease! But will you not expect the King of Faery to do something for you before he leaves you? I grant you your wish. Farewell! Now go to sleep!'

He wrapped his cloak about him again and went away towards the Hall; but before he was out of sight the old cook's goggling eyes had shut and he was snoring.

When the old cook woke again the sun was going down. He rubbed his eyes and shivered a little, for the autumn air was chilly. 'Ugh! What a dream!' he said. 'It must have been that pork at dinner'.

From that day he became so afraid of having more bad dreams of that sort that he hardly dared eat anything for fear that it might upset him, and his meals became very short and plain. He soon became lean, and his clothes and his skin hung on him in folds and creases. The children called him old Rag-and-Bones. Then for a time he found that he could get about the village again and walk with no more help than a stick; and he lived many years longer than he would otherwise have done. Indeed it is said that he just made his century: the only memorable thing he ever achieved. But till his last year he could be heard saying to any that would listen to his tale: 'Alarming, you might call it; but a silly dream, when you come to think of it. King o' Fairy! Why, he hadn't no wand. And if you stop eating you grow thinner. That's natural. Stands to reason. There ain't no magic in it'.

* * *

The time for the Twenty-four Feast came round. Smith was there to sing songs and his wife to help with the children. Smith looked at them as they sang and danced, and he thought that they were more beautiful and lively than they had been in his boyhood—for a moment it crossed his mind to wonder what Alf might have been doing in his spare time. Any one of them seemed fit to find the star. But his eyes were mostly on Tim: a rather plump little boy, clumsy in the dances, but with a sweet voice in the singing. At table he sat silent watching the sharpening of the knife and the cutting of the Cake. Suddenly, he piped up: 'Dear Mr. Cook, only cut me a small slice please. I've eaten so much already, I feel rather full'.

'All right, Tim', said Alf. 'I'll cut you a special slice. I think you'll find it go down easily'.

Smith watched as Tim ate his cake slowly, but with evident pleasure; though when he found no trinket or coin in it he looked disappointed. But soon a light began to shine in his eyes, and he laughed and became merry, and sang softly to himself. Then he got up and began to dance all alone with an odd grace that he had never shown before. The children all laughed and clapped.

'All is well then', thought Smith. 'So you are my heir. I wonder what strange places the star will lead you to? Poor old Nokes. Still I suppose he will never know what a shocking thing has happened in his family'.

He never did. But one thing happened at that Feast that pleased him mightily. Before it was over the Master Cook took leave of the children and of all the others that were present.

'I will say goodbye now', he said. 'In a day or two I shall be going away. Master Harper is quite ready to take over. He is a very good cook, and as you know he comes from your own village. I shall go back home. I do not think you will miss me'.

The children said goodbye cheerfully, and thanked the Cook prettily for his beautiful Cake. Only little Tim took his hand and said quietly, 'I'm sorry'.

In the village there were in fact several families that did miss Alf for some time. A few of his friends, especially Smith and Harper, grieved at his going, and they kept the Hall gilded and painted in memory of Alf. Most people, however, were content. They had had him for a very long time and were not sorry to have a change. But old Nokes thumped his stick on the floor and said roundly: 'He's gone at last! And I'm glad for one. I never liked him. He was artful. Too nimble, you might say'.

FARMER GILES OF HAM

Aegidii Ahenobarbi Julii Agricole de Hammo
Domini de Domito
Aule Draconarie Comitis
Regnie Minimi Regis et Basilei
mira facinora et mirabilis exortus

or in the vulgar tongue

The Rise and Wonderful Adventures
of Farmer Giles, Lord of Tame
Count of Worminghall and
King of the Little Kingdom

EMBELLISHED BY
PAULINE BAYNES

FOREWORD

OF THE history of the Little Kingdom few fragments have survived; but by chance an account of its origin has been preserved: a legend, perhaps, rather than an account; for it is evidently a late compilation, full of marvels, derived not from sober annals, but from the popular lays to which its author frequently refers. For him the events that he records lay already in a distant past; but he seems, nonetheless, to have lived himself in the lands of the Little Kingdom. Such geographical knowledge as he shows (it is not his strong point) is of that country, while of regions outside it, north or west, he is plainly ignorant.

An excuse for presenting a translation of this curious tale, out of its very insular Latin into the modern tongue of the United Kingdom, may be found in the glimpse that it affords of life in a dark period of the history of Britain, not to mention the light that it throws on the origin of some difficult place-names. Some may find the character and adventures of its hero attractive in themselves.

The boundaries of the Little Kingdom, either in time or space, are not easy to determine from the scanty evidence. Since Brutus came to Britain many kings and realms have come and gone. The partition under Locrin, Camber, and Albanac, was only the first of many shifting divisions. What with the love of petty independence on the one hand, and on the other the greed of kings for wider realms, the years were filled with swift alternations of war and peace, of mirth and woe, as historians of the reign of Arthur tell us: a time of unsettled frontiers, when men might rise or fall suddenly, and songwriters had abundant material and eager audiences. Somewhere in those long years, after the days of King Coel maybe, but before Arthur or the Seven Kingdoms of the English, we must place the events here related; and their scene is the valley of the Thames, with an excursion north-west to the walls of Wales.

The capital of the Little Kingdom was evidently, as is ours, in its south-east corner, but its confines are vague. It seems never to have reached far up the Thames into the West, nor beyond Otmoor to the North; its eastern borders are dubious. There are indications in a fragmentary legend of Georgius son of Giles and his page Suovetaurilius (Suet) that at one time an outpost against the Middle Kingdom was maintained at Farthingho. But that situation does not concern this story, which is now presented without alteration or further comment, though the original grandiose title has been suitably reduced to *Farmer Giles of Ham*.

AEgidius de Hammo was a man who lived in the midmost parts of the Island of Britain. In full his name was AEgidius Ahenobarbus Julius Agricola de Hammo; for people were richly endowed with names in those days, now long ago, when this island was still happily divided into many kingdoms. There was more time then, and folk were fewer, so that most men were distinguished. However, those days are now over, so I will in what follows give the man his name shortly, and in the vulgar form: he was Farmer Giles of Ham, and he had a red beard. Ham was only a village, but villages were proud and independent still in those days.

Farmer Giles had a dog. The dog's name was Garm. Dogs had to be content with short names in the vernacular: the Book-latin was reserved for their betters. Garm could not talk even dog-latin; but he could use the vulgar tongue (as could most dogs of his day) either to bully or to brag or to wheedle in. Bullying was for beggars and trespassers, bragging for other dogs, and wheedling for his master. Garm was both proud and afraid of Giles, who could bully and brag better than he could.

The time was not one of hurry or bustle. But bustle has very little to do with business. Men did their work without it; and they got through a deal both of work and of talk. There was plenty to talk about, for memorable events occurred very frequently. But at the moment when this tale begins nothing memorable had, in fact, happened in Ham for quite a long time. Which suited Farmer Giles down to the ground: he was a slow sort of fellow, rather set in his ways, and taken up with his own affairs. He had his hands full (he said) keeping the wolf from the door: that is, keeping himself as fat and comfortable as his father before him. The dog was busy helping him. Neither of them gave much thought to the Wide World outside their fields, the village, and the nearest market.

But the Wide World was there. The forest was not far off, and away west and north were the Wild Hills, and the dubious marches of the mountain-country. And among other things still at large there were giants: rude and uncultured folk, and troublesome at times. There was one giant in particular, larger and more stupid than his fellows. I find no mention of his name in the histories, but it does not matter. He was very large, his walking-stick was like a tree, and his tread was heavy. He brushed elms aside like tall grasses; and he was the ruin of roads and the desolation of gardens, for his great feet made holes in them as deep as wells; if he stumbled into a house, that was the end of it. And all this damage he did wherever he went, for his head was far above the roofs of houses and left his feet to look after themselves. He was near-sighted and also rather deaf. Fortunately he lived far off in the Wild, and seldom visited the lands inhabited by men, at least not on purpose. He had a great tumbledown house away up in the mountains; but he had very few friends, owing to his deafness and his stupidity, and the scarcity of giants. He used to go out walking in the Wild Hills and in the empty regions at the feet of the mountains, all by himself.

One fine summer's day this giant went out for a walk, and wandered aimlessly along, doing a great deal of damage in the woods. Suddenly he noticed that the sun was setting, and felt that his supper-time was drawing near; but he discovered that he was in a part of the country that he did not know at all and had lost his way. Making a wrong guess at the right direction he walked and he walked until it was dark night. Then he sat down and waited for the moon to rise. Then he walked and walked in the moonlight, striding out with a will, for he was anxious to get home. He had left his best copper pot on the fire, and feared that the bottom would be burned. But his back was to the mountains, and he was already in the lands inhabited by men. He was, indeed, now drawing near to the farm of AEgidius Ahenobarbus Julius Agricola and the village called (in the vulgar tongue) Ham.

It was a fine night. The cows were in the fields, and Farmer Giles's dog had got out and gone for a walk on his own account. He had a fancy for moonshine, and rabbits. He had no idea, of course, that a giant was also out for a walk. That would have given him a good reason for going out without leave, but a still better reason for staying quiet in the kitchen. At about two o'clock the giant arrived in Farmer Giles's fields, broke the hedges, trampled on the crops, and flattened the mowing-grass. In five minutes he had done more damage than the royal fox-hunt could have done in five days.

Garm heard a thump-thump coming along the riverbank, and he ran to the west side of the low hill on which the farmhouse stood, just to see what was happening. Suddenly he saw the giant stride right across the river and tread upon Galathea, the farmer's favourite cow, squashing the poor beast as flat as the farmer could have squashed a blackbeetle.

That was more than enough for Garm. He gave a yelp of fright and bolted home. Quite forgetting that he was out without leave, he came and barked and yammered underneath his master's bedroom window.

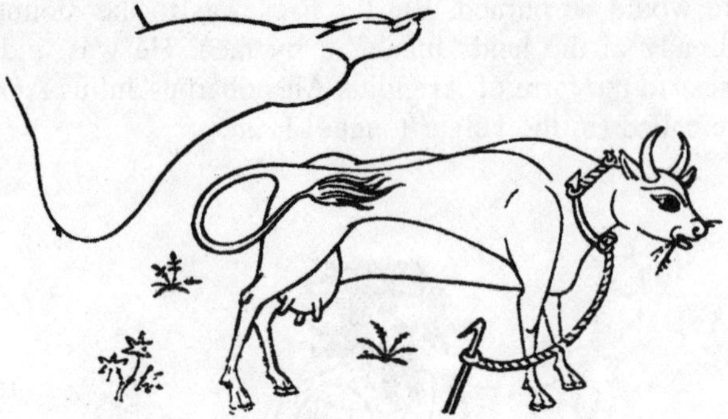

There was no answer for a long time. Farmer Giles was not easily wakened.

'Help! help! help!' cried Garm.

The window opened suddenly and a well-aimed bottle came flying out.

'Ow!' said the dog, jumping aside with practised skill. 'Help! help! help!'

Out popped the farmer's head. 'Drat you, dog! What be you a-doing?' said he.

'Nothing,' said the dog.

'I'll give you nothing! I'll flay the skin off you in the morning,' said the farmer, slamming the window.

'Help! help! help!' cried the dog.

Out came Giles's head again. 'I'll kill you, if you make another sound,' he said. 'What's come to you, you fool?'

'Nothing,' said the dog; 'but something's come to you.'

'What d'you mean?' said Giles, startled in the midst of his rage. Never before had Garm answered him saucily.

'There's a giant in your fields, an enormous giant; and he's coming this way,' said the dog. 'Help! help! He is trampling on your sheep. He has stamped on poor Galathea, and she's as flat as a doormat. Help! help! He's bursting all your hedges, and he's crushing all your crops. You must be bold and quick, master, or you will soon have nothing left. Help!' Garm began to howl.

'Shut up!' said the farmer, and he shut the window. 'Lord-a-mercy!' he said to himself; and though the night was warm, he shivered and shook.

'Get back to bed and don't be a fool!' said his wife. 'And drown that dog in the morning. There is no call to believe what a dog says; they'll tell any tale, when caught truant or thieving.'

'May be, Agatha,' said he, 'and may be not. But there's something going on in my fields, or Garm's a rabbit. That dog was frightened. And why should he come yammering in the night when he could sneak in at the back door with the milk in the morning?'

'Don't stand there arguing!' said she. 'If you believe the dog, then take his advice: be bold and quick!'

'Easier said than done,' answered Giles; for, indeed, he believed quite half of Garm's tale. In the small hours of the night giants seem less unlikely.

Still, property is property; and Farmer Giles had a short way with trespassers that few could outface. So he pulled on his breeches, and went down into the kitchen and took his blunderbuss from the wall. Some may well ask what a blunderbuss was. Indeed, this very question,

it is said, was put to the Four Wise Clerks of Oxenford, and after thought they replied: 'A blunderbuss is a short gun with a large bore firing many balls or slugs, and capable of doing execution within a limited range without exact aim. (Now superseded in civilised countries by other fire-arms.)'

However, Farmer Giles's blunderbuss had a wide mouth that opened like a horn, and it did not fire balls or slugs, but anything that he could spare to stuff in. And it did not do execution, because he seldom loaded it, and never let it off. The sight of it was usually enough for his purpose. And this country was not yet civilised, for the blunderbuss was not superseded: it was indeed the only kind of gun that there was, and rare at that. People preferred bows and arrows and used gunpowder mostly for fireworks.

Well then, Farmer Giles took down the blunderbuss, and he put in a good charge of powder, just in case extreme measures should be required; and into the wide mouth he stuffed old nails and bits of wire, pieces of broken pot, bones and stones and other rubbish. Then he drew on his top-boots and his overcoat, and he went out through the kitchen garden.

The moon was low behind him, and he could see nothing worse than the long black shadows of bushes and trees; but he could hear a dreadful stamping-stumping coming up the side of the hill. He did not feel either bold or quick, whatever Agatha might say; but he was more anxious about his property than his skin. So, feeling a bit loose about the belt, he walked towards the brow of the hill.

Suddenly up over the edge of it the giant's face appeared, pale in the moonlight, which glittered in his large round eyes. His feet were still

far below, making holes in the fields. The moon dazzled the giant and he did not see the farmer; but Farmer Giles saw him and was scared out of his wits. He pulled the trigger without thinking, and the blunderbuss went off with a staggering bang. By luck it was pointed more or less at the giant's large ugly face. Out flew the rubbish, and the stones and the bones, and the bits of crock and wire, and half a dozen nails. And since the range was indeed limited, by chance and no choice of the farmer's many of these things struck the giant: a piece of pot went in his eye, and a large nail stuck in his nose.

'Blast!' said the giant in his vulgar fashion. 'I'm stung!' The noise had made no impression on him (he was rather deaf), but he did not like the nail. It was a long time since he had met any insect fierce enough to pierce his thick skin; but he had heard tell that away East, in the Fens, there were dragonflies that could bite like hot pincers. He thought that he must have run into something of the kind.

'Nasty unhealthy parts, evidently,' said he. 'I shan't go any further this way tonight.'

So he picked up a couple of sheep off the hill-side, to eat when he got home, and went back over the river, making off about nor-nor-west at a great pace. He found his way home again in the end, for he was at last going in the right direction; but the bottom was burned off his copper pot.

As for Farmer Giles, when the blunderbuss went off it knocked him over flat on his back; and there he lay looking at the sky and wondering if the giant's feet would miss him as they passed by. But nothing happened, and the stamping-stumping died away in the distance. So he got up, rubbed his shoulder, and picked up the blunderbuss. Then suddenly he heard the sound of people cheering.

Most of the people of Ham had been looking out of their windows; a few had put on their clothes and come out (after the giant had gone away). Some were now running up the hill shouting.

The villagers had heard the horrible thump-thump of the giant's feet, and most of them had immediately got under the bed-clothes; some had got under the beds. But Garm was both proud and frightened of his master. He thought him terrible and splendid, when he was angry; and he naturally thought that any giant would think the same. So, as soon as he saw Giles come out with the blunderbuss (a sign of great wrath as a rule), he rushed off to the village, barking and crying:

'Come out! Come out! Come out! Get up! Get up! Come and see my great master! He is bold and quick. He is going to shoot a giant for trespassing. Come out!'

The top of the hill could be seen from most of the houses. When the people and the dog saw the giant's face rise above it, they quailed and held their breath, and all but the dog among them thought that this would prove a matter too big for Giles to deal with. Then the blunderbuss went bang, and the giant turned suddenly and went away, and in their amazement and their joy they clapped and cheered, and Garm nearly barked his head off.

'Hooray!' they shouted. 'That will learn him! Master AEgidius has given him what for. Now he will go home and die, and serve him right and proper.' Then they all cheered again together. But even as they cheered, they took note for their own profit that after all this blunderbuss could really be fired. There had been some debate in the village inns on that point; but now the matter was settled. Farmer Giles had little trouble with trespassers after that.

When all seemed safe some of the bolder folk came right up the hill and shook hands with Farmer Giles. A few—the parson, and the blacksmith, and the miller, and one or two other persons of importance—slapped him on the back. That did not please him (his shoulder was very sore), but he felt obliged to invite them into his house. They sat round in the kitchen drinking his health and loudly praising him. He made no effort to hide his yawns, but as long as the drink lasted they took no notice. By the time they had all had one or two (and the farmer two or three), he began to feel quite bold; when they had all had two or three (and he himself five or six), he felt as bold as his dog thought him. They parted good friends; and he slapped their backs heartily. His hands were large, red, and thick; so he had his revenge.

* * *

Next day he found that the news had grown in the telling, and he had become an important local figure. By the middle of the next week the news had spread to all the villages within twenty miles. He had become the Hero of the Countryside. Very pleasant he found it. Next market day he got enough free drink to float a boat: that is to say, he nearly had his fill, and came home singing old heroic songs.

At last even the King got to hear of it. The capital of that realm, the Middle Kingdom of the island in those happy days, was some twenty leagues distant from Ham, and they paid little heed at court, as a rule, to the doings of rustics in the provinces. But so prompt an expulsion of a giant so injurious seemed worthy of note and of some little courtesy. So in due course—that is, in about three months, and on the feast of St Michael—the King sent a magnificent letter. It was written in red upon white parchment, and expressed the royal approbation of 'our loyal subject and well-beloved AEgidius Ahenobarbus Julius Agricola de Hammo'.

The letter was signed with a red blot; but the court scribe had added:

Ego Augustus Bonifacius Ambrosius Aurelianus Antoninus Pius et Magnificus, dux rex, tyrannus, et Basileus Mediterranearum Partium, subscribo;

and a large red seal was attached. So the document was plainly genuine. It afforded great pleasure to Giles, and was much admired, especially when it was discovered that one could get a seat and a drink by the farmer's fire by asking to look at it.

Better than the testimonial was the accompanying gift. The King sent

a belt and a long sword. To tell the truth the King had never used the sword himself. It belonged to the family and had been hanging in his armoury time out of mind. The armourer could not say how it came there, or what might be the use of it. Plain heavy swords of that kind were out of fashion at court just then, so the King thought it the very thing for a present to a rustic. But Farmer Giles was delighted, and his local reputation became enormous.

Giles much enjoyed the turn of events. So did his dog. He never got his promised whipping. Giles was a just man according to his lights; in his heart he gave a fair share of the credit to Garm, though he never went so far as to mention it. He continued to throw hard words and hard things at the dog when he felt inclined, but he winked at many little outings. Garm took to walking far afield. The farmer went about with a high step, and luck smiled on him. The autumn and early winter work went well. All seemed set fair—until the dragon came.

In those days dragons were already getting scarce in the island. None had been seen in the midland realm of Augustus Bonifacius for many a year. There were, of course, the dubious marches and the uninhabited mountains, westward and northward, but they were a long way off. In those parts once upon a time there had dwelt a number of dragons of one kind and another, and they had made raids far and wide. But the Middle Kingdom was in those days famous for the daring of the King's

knights, and so many stray dragons had been killed, or had returned with grave damage, that the others gave up going that way.

It was still the custom for Dragon's Tail to be served up at the King's Christmas Feast; and each year a knight was chosen for the duty of hunting. He was supposed to set out upon St Nicholas' Day and come home with a dragon's tail not later than the eve of the feast. But for many years now the Royal Cook had made a marvellous confection, a

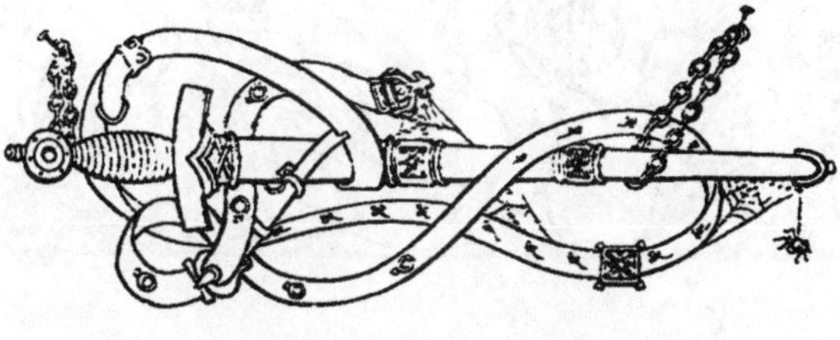

Mock Dragon's Tail of cake and almond-paste, with cunning scales of hard icing-sugar. The chosen knight then carried this into the hall on Christmas Eve, while the fiddles played and the trumpets rang. The Mock Dragon's Tail was eaten after dinner on Christmas Day, and everybody said (to please the cook) that it tasted much better than Real Tail.

That was the situation when a real dragon turned up again. The giant

was largely to blame. After his adventure he used to go about in the mountains visiting his scattered relations more than had been his custom, and much more than they liked. For he was always trying to borrow a large copper pot. But whether he got the loan of one or not, he would sit and talk in his long-winded lumbering fashion about the excellent country down away East, and all the wonders of the Wide World. He had got it into his head that he was a great and daring traveller.

'A nice land,' he would say, 'pretty flat, soft to the feet, and plenty

to eat for the taking: cows, you know, and sheep all over the place, easy to spot, if you look carefully.'

'But what about the people?' said they.

'I never saw any,' said he. 'There was not a knight to be seen or heard, my dear fellows. Nothing worse than a few stinging flies by the river.'

'Why don't you go back and stay there?' said they.

'Oh well, there's no place like home, they say,' said he. 'But maybe

I shall go back one day when I have a mind. And anyway I went there once, which is more than most folk can say. Now about that copper pot.'

'And these rich lands,' they would hurriedly ask, 'these delectable regions full of undefended cattle, which way do they lie? And how far off?'

'Oh,' he would answer, 'away east or sou'east. But it's a long journey.' And then he would give such an exaggerated account of the distance that he had walked, and the woods, hills, and plains that he had crossed, that none of the other less long-legged giants ever set out. Still, the talk got about.

Then the warm summer was followed by a hard winter. It was bitter cold in the mountains and food was scarce. The talk got louder. Lowland sheep and kine from the deep pastures were much discussed. The dragons pricked up their ears. They were hungry, and these rumours were attractive.

'So knights are mythical!' said the younger and less experienced dragons. 'We always thought so.'

'At least they may be getting rare,' thought the older and wiser worms; 'far and few and no longer to be feared.'

There was one dragon who was deeply moved. Chrysophylax Dives was his name, for he was of ancient and imperial lineage, and very rich. He was cunning, inquisitive, greedy, well-armoured, but not over bold. But at any rate he was not in the least afraid of flies or insects of any sort or size; and he was mortally hungry.

So one winter's day, about a week before Christmas, Chrysophylax spread his wings and took off. He landed quietly in the middle of the night plump in the heart of the midland realm of Augustus Bonifacius rex et basileus. He did a deal of damage in a short while, smashing and burning, and devouring sheep, cattle, and horses.

This was in a part of the land a long way from Ham, but Garm got the fright of his life. He had gone off on a long expedition, and taking advantage of his master's favour he had ventured to spend a night or two away from home. He was following an engaging scent along the eaves of a wood, when he turned a corner and came suddenly upon a new and alarming smell; he ran indeed slap into the tail of Chrysophylax Dives, who had just landed. Never did a dog turn his own tail round and bolt home swifter than Garm. The dragon, hearing his yelp, turned and snorted; but Garm was already far out of range. He ran all the rest of the night, and arrived home about breakfast-time.

'Help! help! help!' he cried outside the back door.

Giles heard, and did not like the sound of it. It reminded him that unexpected things may happen, when all seems to be going well.

'Wife, let that dratted dog in,' said he, 'and take a stick to him!'

Garm came bundling into the kitchen with his eyes starting and his tongue hanging out. 'Help!' he cried.

'Now what have you been a-doing this time?' said Giles, throwing a sausage at him.

'Nothing,' panted Garm, too flustered to give heed to the sausage.

'Well, stop doing it, or I'll skin you,' said the farmer.

'I've done no wrong. I didn't mean no harm,' said the dog. 'But I came on a dragon accidental-like, and it frightened me.'

The farmer choked in his beer. 'Dragon?' said he. 'Drat you for a good-for-nothing nosey-parker! What d'you want to go and find a dragon for, at this time of the year, and me with my hands full? Where was it?'

'Oh! North over the hills and far away, beyond the Standing Stones and all,' said the dog.

'Oh, away there!' said Giles, mighty relieved. 'They're queer folk in those parts, I've heard tell, and aught might happen in their land. Let them get on with it! Don't come worriting me with such tales. Get out!'

Garm got out, and spread the news all over the village. He did not forget to mention that his master was not scared in the least. 'Quite cool he was, and went on with his breakfast.'

People chatted about it pleasantly at their doors. 'How like old times!'

they said. 'Just as Christmas is coming, too. So seasonable. How pleased the King will be! He will be able to have Real Tail this Christmas.'

But more news came in next day. The dragon, it appeared, was exceptionally large and ferocious. He was doing terrible damage.

'What about the King's knights?' people began to say.

Others had already asked the same question. Indeed, messengers were now reaching the King from the villages most afflicted by Chrysophylax, and they said to him as loudly and as often as they dared: 'Lord, what of your knights?'

But the knights did nothing; their knowledge of the dragon was still quite unofficial. So the King brought the matter to their notice, fully and formally, asking for necessary action at their early convenience. He was greatly displeased when he found that their convenience would not be early at all, and was indeed daily postponed.

Yet the excuses of the knights were undoubtedly sound. First of all, the Royal Cook had already made the Dragon's Tail for that Christmas, being a man who believed in getting things done in good time. It would not do at all to offend him by bringing in a real tail at the last minute. He was a very valuable servant.

'Never mind the Tail! Cut his head off and put an end to him!' cried the messengers from the villages most nearly affected.

But Christmas had arrived, and most unfortunately a grand tournament had been arranged for St John's Day: knights of many realms had been invited and were coming to compete for a valuable prize. It was obviously unreasonable to spoil the chances of the Midland Knights by sending their best men off on a dragon-hunt before the tournament was over.

After that came the New Year Holiday.

But each night the dragon had moved; and each move had brought him nearer to Ham. On the night of New Year's Day people could see a blaze in the distance. The dragon had settled in a wood about ten miles away, and it was burning merrily. He was a hot dragon when he felt in the mood.

After that people began to look at Farmer Giles and whisper behind his back. It made him very uncomfortable; but he pretended not to notice it. The next day the dragon came several miles nearer. Then Farmer Giles himself began to talk loudly of the scandal of the King's knights.

'I should like to know what they do to earn their keep,' said he.

'So should we!' said everyone in Ham.

But the miller added: 'Some men still get knighthood by sheer merit, I am told. After all, our good AEgidius here is already a knight in a manner of speaking. Did not the King send him a red letter and a sword?'

'There's more to knighthood than a sword,' said Giles. 'There's dubbing and all that, or so I understand. Anyway I've my own business to attend to.'

'Oh! but the King would do the dubbing, I don't doubt, if he were asked,' said the miller. 'Let us ask him, before it is too late!'

'Nay!' said Giles. 'Dubbing is not for my sort. I am a farmer and proud of it: a plain honest man and honest men fare ill at court, they say. It is more in your line, Master Miller.'

The parson smiled: not at the farmer's retort, for Giles and the miller were always giving one another as good as they got, being bosom enemies, as the saying was in Ham. The parson had suddenly been struck with a notion that pleased him, but he said no more at that time. The miller was not so pleased, and he scowled.

'Plain certainly, and honest perhaps,' said he. 'But do you have to go to court and be a knight before you kill a dragon? Courage is all that is needed, as only yesterday I heard Master AEgidius declare. Surely he has as much courage as any knight?'

All the folk standing by shouted: 'Of course not!' and 'Yes indeed! Three cheers for the Hero of Ham!'

Then Farmer Giles went home feeling very uncomfortable. He was finding that a local reputation may require keeping up, and that may prove awkward. He kicked the dog, and hid the sword in a cupboard in the kitchen. Up till then it had hung over the fireplace.

The next day the dragon moved to the neighbouring village of Quercetum (Oakley in the vulgar tongue). He ate not only sheep and cows and one or two persons of tender age, but he ate the parson too. Rather rashly the parson had sought to dissuade him from his evil ways. Then there was a terrible commotion. All the people of Ham came up the hill headed by their own parson; and they waited on Farmer Giles.

'We look to you!' they said; and they remained standing round and looking, until the farmer's face was redder than his beard.

'When are you going to start?' they asked.

'Well, I can't start today, and that's a fact,' said he. 'I've a lot on hand with my cowman sick and all. I'll see about it.'

They went away; but in the evening it was rumoured that the dragon had moved even nearer, so they all came back.

'We look to you, Master AEgidius,' they said.

'Well,' said he, 'it's very awkward for me just now. My mare has gone lame, and the lambing has started. I'll see about it as soon as may be.'

So they went away once more, not without some grumbling and whispering. The miller was sniggering. The parson stayed behind, and could not be got rid of. He invited himself to supper, and made some pointed remarks. He even asked what had become of the sword and insisted on seeing it.

It was lying in a cupboard on a shelf hardly long enough for it, and as soon as Farmer Giles brought it out in a flash it leaped from the sheath, which the farmer dropped as if it had been hot. The parson sprang to his feet, upsetting his beer. He picked the sword up carefully and tried to put it back in the sheath; but it would not go so much as a foot in, and it jumped clean out again, as soon as he took his hand off the hilt.

'Dear me! This is very peculiar!' said the parson, and he took a good look at both scabbard and blade. He was a lettered man, but the farmer could only spell out large uncials with difficulty, and was none too sure of the reading even of his own name. That is why he had never given any heed to the strange letters that could dimly be seen on sheath and sword. As for the King's armourer, he was so accustomed to runes, names, and other signs of power and significance upon swords and scabbards that he had not bothered his head about them; he thought them out of date, anyway.

But the parson looked long, and he frowned. He had expected to find some lettering on the sword or on the scabbard, and that was indeed the idea that had come to him the day before; but now he was surprised at what he saw, for letters and signs there were, to be sure, but he could not make head or tail of them.

'There is an inscription on this sheath, and some, ah, epigraphical signs are visible also upon the sword,' he said.

'Indeed?' said Giles. 'And what may that amount to?'

'The characters are archaic and the language barbaric,' said the parson, to gain time. 'A little closer inspection will be required.' He begged the loan of the sword for the night, and the farmer let him have it with pleasure.

When the parson got home he took down many learned books from his shelves, and he sat up far into the night. Next morning it was discovered that the dragon had moved nearer still. All the people of Ham barred their doors and shuttered their windows; and those that had cellars went down into them and sat shivering in the candle-light.

But the parson stole out and went from door to door; and he told, to all who would listen through a crack or a keyhole, what he had discovered in his study.

'Our good AEgidius,' he said, 'by the King's grace is now the owner of Caudimordax, the famous sword that in popular romances is more vulgarly called Tailbiter.'

Those that heard this name usually opened the door. They all knew the renown of Tailbiter, for that sword had belonged to Bellomarius, the greatest of all the dragon-slayers of the realm. Some accounts made him the maternal great-great-grandfather of the King. The songs and tales of his deeds were many, and if forgotten at court, were still remembered in the villages.

'This sword,' said the parson, 'will not stay sheathed, if a dragon is within five miles; and without doubt in a brave man's hands no dragon can resist it.'

Then people began to take heart again; and some unshuttered the windows and put their heads out. In the end the parson persuaded a few to come and join him; but only the miller was really willing. To see Giles in a real fix seemed to him worth the risk.

They went up the hill, not without anxious looks north across the river. There was no sign of the dragon. Probably he was asleep; he had been feeding very well all the Christmastime.

The parson (and the miller) hammered on the farmer's door. There was no answer, so they hammered louder. At last Giles came out. His face was very red. He also had sat up far into the night, drinking a good deal of ale; and he had begun again as soon as he got up.

They all crowded round him, calling him Good AEgidius, Bold Ahenobarbus, Great Julius, Staunch Agricola, Pride of Ham, Hero of the Countryside. And they spoke of Caudimordax, Tailbiter, The Sword that would not be Sheathed, Death or Victory, The Glory of the Yeomanry, Backbone of the Country, and the Good of one's Fellow Men, until the farmer's head was hopelessly confused.

'Now then! One at a time!' he said, when he got a chance. 'What's all this, what's all this? It's my busy morning, you know.'

So they let the parson explain the situation. Then the miller had the pleasure of seeing the farmer in as tight a fix as he could wish. But things did not turn out quite as the miller expected. For one thing Giles had drunk a deal of strong ale. For another he had a queer feeling of pride and encouragement when he learned that his sword was actually Tailbiter. He had been very fond of tales about Bellomarius when he was a boy, and before he had learned sense he had sometimes wished that he could have a marvellous and heroic sword of his own. So it came over him all of a sudden that he would take Tailbiter and go dragon-hunting. But he had been used to bargaining all his life, and he made one more effort to postpone the event.

'What!' said he. 'Me go dragon-hunting? In my old leggings and waistcoat? Dragon-fights need some kind of armour, from all I've heard tell. There isn't any armour in this house, and that's a fact,' said he.

That was a bit awkward, they all allowed; but they sent for the blacksmith. The blacksmith shook his head. He was a slow, gloomy man, vulgarly known as Sunny Sam, though his proper name was Fabricius Cunctator. He never whistled at his work, unless some disaster (such as frost in May) had duly occurred after he had foretold it. Since he was daily foretelling disasters of every kind, few happened that he had not foretold, and he was able to take the credit of them. It was his chief pleasure; so naturally he was reluctant to do anything to avert them. He shook his head again.

'I can't make armour out of naught,' he said. 'And it's not in my line. You'd best get the carpenter to make you a wooden shield. Not that it will help you much. He's a hot dragon.'

Their faces fell; but the miller was not so easily to be turned from his plan of sending Giles to the dragon, if he would go; or of blowing the bubble of his local reputation, if he refused in the end. 'What about ring-mail?' he said. 'That would be a help; and it need not be very fine. It would be for business and not for showing off at court. What about your old leather jerkin, friend AEgidius? And there is a great pile of links and rings in the smithy. I don't suppose Master Fabricius himself knows what may be lying there.'

'You don't know what you are talking about,' said the smith, growing cheerful. 'If it's real ring-mail you mean, then you can't have it. It needs the skill of the dwarfs, with every little ring fitting into four others and all. Even if I had the craft, I should be working for weeks. And we shall all be in our graves before then,' said he, 'or leastways in the dragon.'

They all wrung their hands in dismay, and the blacksmith began to smile. But they were now so alarmed that they were unwilling to give up the miller's plan and they turned to him for counsel.

'Well,' said he, 'I've heard tell that in the old days those that could not buy bright hauberks out of the Southlands would stitch steel rings on a leather shirt and be content with that. Let's see what can be done in that line!'

So Giles had to bring out his old jerkin, and the smith was hurried back to his smithy. There they rummaged in every corner and turned over the pile of old metal, as had not been done for many a year. At the bottom they found, all dull with rust, a whole heap of small rings, fallen from some forgotten coat, such as the miller had spoken of. Sam, more unwilling and gloomy as the task seemed more hopeful, was set to work on the spot, gathering and sorting and cleaning the rings; and when (as he was pleased to point out) these were clearly insufficient for one so broad of back and breast as Master AEgidius, they made him split up old chains and hammer the links into rings as fine as his skill could contrive.

They took the smaller rings of steel and stitched them on to the breast of the jerkin, and the larger and clumsier rings they stitched on the back; and then, when still more rings were forthcoming, so hard was poor Sam driven, they took a pair of the farmer's breeches and stitched rings on to them. And up on a shelf in a dark nook of the smithy the miller found the old iron frame of a helmet, and he set the cobbler to work, covering it with leather as well as he could.

The work took them all the rest of that day, and all the next day—which was Twelfthnight and the eve of the Epiphany, but festivities were neglected. Farmer Giles celebrated the occasion with more ale than usual; but the dragon mercifully slept. For the moment he had forgotten all about hunger or swords.

Early on the Epiphany they went up the hill, carrying the strange result of their handiwork. Giles was expecting them. He had now no excuses left to offer; so he put on the mail jerkin and the breeches. The miller sniggered. Then Giles put on his topboots and an old pair of spurs; and also the leather-covered helmet. But at the last moment he clapped an old felt hat over the helmet, and over the mail coat he threw his big grey cloak.

'What is the purpose of that, Master?' they asked.

'Well,' said Giles, 'if it is your notion to go dragon-hunting jingling and dingling like Canterbury Bells, it ain't mine. It don't seem sense to me to let a dragon know that you are coming along the road sooner than need be. And a helmet's a helmet, and a challenge to battle. Let the worm see only my old hat over the hedge, and maybe I'll get nearer before the trouble begins.'

They had stitched on the rings so that they overlapped, each hanging loose over the one below, and jingle they certainly did. The cloak did something to stop the noise of them, but Giles cut a queer figure in his gear. They did not tell him so. They girded the belt round his waist with difficulty, and they hung the scabbard upon it; but he had to carry the

sword, for it would no longer stay sheathed, unless held with main strength.

The farmer called for Garm. He was a just man according to his lights. 'Dog,' he said, 'you are coming with me.'

The dog howled. 'Help! help!' he cried.

'Now stop it!' said Giles. 'Or I'll give you worse than any dragon could. You know the smell of this worm, and maybe you'll prove useful for once.'

Then Farmer Giles called for his grey mare. She gave him a queer look and sniffed at the spurs. But she let him get up; and then off they went, and none of them felt happy. They trotted through the village, and all the folk clapped and cheered, mostly from their windows. The farmer and his mare put as good a face on it as they could; but Garm had no sense of shame and slunk along with his tail down.

They crossed the bridge over the river at the end of the village. When at last they were well out of sight, they slowed to a walk. Yet all too soon they passed out of the lands belonging to Farmer Giles and to other folk of Ham and came to parts that the dragon had visited. There were broken trees, burned hedges and blackened grass, and a nasty uncanny silence.

The sun was shining bright, and Farmer Giles began to wish that he dared shed a garment or two; and he wondered if he had not taken a pint too many. 'A nice end to Christmas and all,' he thought. 'And I'll

be lucky if it don't prove the end of me too.' He mopped his face with a large handkerchief—green, not red; for red rags infuriate dragons, or so he had heard tell.

But he did not find the dragon. He rode down many lanes, wide and narrow, and over other farmers' deserted fields, and still he did not find the dragon. Garm was, of course, of no use at all. He kept just behind the mare and refused to use his nose.

They came at last to a winding road that had suffered little damage and seemed quiet and peaceful. After following it for half a mile Giles began to wonder whether he had not done his duty and all that his reputation required. He had made up his mind that he had looked long and far enough, and he was just thinking of turning back, and of his dinner, and of telling his friends that the dragon had seen him coming and simply flown away, when he turned a sharp corner.

There was the dragon, laying half across a broken hedge with his horrible head in the middle of the road. 'Help!' said Garm and bolted. The grey mare sat down plump, and Farmer Giles went off backwards into a ditch. When he put his head out, there was the dragon wide awake looking at him.

'Good morning!' said the dragon. 'You seem surprised.'

'Good morning!' said Giles. 'I am that.'

'Excuse me,' said the dragon. He had cocked a very suspicious ear when he caught the sound of rings jingling, as the farmer fell. 'Excuse my asking, but were you looking for me, by any chance?'

'No, indeed!' said the farmer. 'Who'd a' thought of seeing you here? I was just going for a ride.'

He scrambled out of the ditch in a hurry and backed away towards the grey mare. She was now on her feet again and was nibbling some grass at the wayside, seeming quite unconcerned.

'Then we meet by good luck,' said the dragon. 'The pleasure is mine. Those are your holiday clothes, I suppose. A new fashion, perhaps?' Farmer Giles's felt hat had fallen off and his grey cloak had slipped open; but he brazened it out.

'Aye,' said he, 'brand-new. But I must be after that dog of mine. He's gone after rabbits, I fancy.'

'I fancy not,' said Chrysophylax, licking his lips (a sign of amusement). 'He will get home a long time before you do, I expect. But pray proceed on your way, Master—let me see, I don't think I know your name?'

'Nor I yours,' said Giles; 'and we'll leave it at that.'

'As you like,' said Chrysophylax, licking his lips again, but pretending to close his eyes. He had a wicked heart (as dragons all have), but not a very bold one (as is not unusual). He preferred a meal that he did not have to fight for; but appetite had returned after a good long sleep. The parson of Oakley had been stringy, and it was years since he had tasted a large fat man. He had now made up his mind to try this easy meat, and he was only waiting until the old fool was off his guard.

But the old fool was not as foolish as he looked, and he kept his eye on the dragon, even while he was trying to mount. The mare, however, had other ideas, and she kicked and shied when Giles tried to get up. The dragon became impatient and made ready to spring.

'Excuse me!' said he. 'Haven't you dropped something?'

An ancient trick, but it succeeded; for Giles had indeed dropped something. When he fell he had dropped Caudimordax (or vulgarly Tailbiter), and there it lay by the wayside. He stooped to pick it up; and the dragon sprang. But not as quick as Tailbiter. As soon as it was in the farmer's hand, it leaped forward with a flash, straight at the dragon's eyes.

'Hey!' said the dragon, and stopped very short. 'What have you got there?'

'Only Tailbiter, that was given to me by the King,' said Giles.

'My mistake!' said the dragon. 'I beg your pardon.' He lay and grovelled, and Farmer Giles began to feel more comfortable. 'I don't think you have treated me fair.'

'How not?' said Giles. 'And anyway why should I?'

'You have concealed your honourable name and pretended that our meeting was by chance; yet you are plainly a knight of high lineage. It used, sir, to be the custom of knights to issue a challenge in such cases, after a proper exchange of titles and credentials.'

'Maybe it used, and maybe it still is,' said Giles, beginning to feel pleased with himself. A man who has a large and imperial dragon grovelling before him may be excused if he feels somewhat uplifted. 'But you are making more mistakes than one, old worm. I am no knight. I am Farmer AEgidius of Ham, I am; and I can't abide trespassers. I've shot giants with my blunderbuss before now, for doing less damage than you have. And I issued no challenge neither.'

The dragon was disturbed. 'Curse that giant for a liar!' he thought. 'I have been sadly misled. And now what on earth does one do with a bold farmer and a sword so bright and aggressive?' He could recall no precedent for such a situation. 'Chrysophylax is my name,' said he, 'Chrysophylax the Rich. What can I do for your honour?' he added ingratiatingly, with one eye on the sword, and hoping to escape battle.

'You can take yourself off, you horny old varmint,' said Giles, also hoping to escape battle. 'I only want to be shut of you. Go right away from here, and get back to your own dirty den!' He stepped towards Chrysophylax, waving his arms as if he was scaring crows.

That was quite enough for Tailbiter. It circled flashing in the air; then down it came, smiting the dragon on the joint of the right wing, a ringing blow that shocked him exceedingly. Of course Giles knew very little about the right methods of killing a dragon, or the sword might have landed in a tenderer spot; but Tailbiter did the best it could in inexperienced hands. It was quite enough for Chrysophylax—he could not use his wing for days. Up he got and turned to fly, and found that he could not. The farmer sprang on the mare's back. The dragon began to run. So did the mare. The dragon galloped over a field puffing and blowing. So did the mare. The farmer bawled and shouted, as if he was watching

a horse race; and all the while he waved Tailbiter. The faster the dragon ran the more bewildered he became; and all the while the grey mare put her best leg foremost and kept close behind him.

On they pounded down the lanes, and through the gaps in the fences, over many fields and across many brooks. The dragon was smoking and bellowing and losing all sense of direction. At last they came suddenly to the bridge of Ham, thundered over it, and came roaring down the village street. There Garm had the impudence to sneak out of an alley and join in the chase.

All the people were at their windows or on the roofs. Some laughed and some cheered; and some beat tins and pans and kettles; and others blew horns and pipes and whistles; and the parson had the church bells rung. Such a to-do and an ongoing had not been heard in Ham for a hundred years.

Just outside the church the dragon gave up. He lay down in the middle of the road and gasped. Garm came and sniffed at his tail, but Chrysophylax was past all shame.

'Good people, and gallant warrior,' he panted, as Farmer Giles rode up, while the villagers gathered round (at a reasonable distance) with

hayforks, poles, and pokers in their hands. 'Good people, don't kill me! I am very rich. I will pay for all the damage I have done. I will pay for the funerals of all the people I have killed, especially the parson of Oakley; he shall have a noble cenotaph—though he was rather lean. I will give you each a really good present, if you will only let me go home and fetch it.'

'How much?' said the farmer.

'Well,' said the dragon, calculating quickly. He noticed that the crowd was rather large. 'Thirteen and eightpence each?'

'Nonsense!' said Giles. 'Rubbish!' said the people. 'Rot!' said the dog.

'Two golden guineas each, and children half price?' said the dragon.

'What about dogs?' said Garm. 'Go on!' said the farmer. 'We're listening.'

'Ten pounds and a purse of silver for every soul, and gold collars for the dogs?' said Chrysophylax anxiously.

'Kill him!' shouted the people, getting impatient.

'A bag of gold for everybody, and diamonds for the ladies?' said Chrysophylax hurriedly.

'Now you're talking, but not good enough,' said Farmer Giles. 'You've left dogs out again,' said Garm. 'What size of bags?' said the men. 'How many diamonds?' said their wives.

'Dear me! dear me!' said the dragon. 'I shall be ruined.'

'You deserve it,' said Giles. 'You can choose between being ruined and being killed where you lie.' He brandished Tailbiter, and the dragon cowered. 'Make up your mind!' the people cried, getting bolder and drawing nearer.

Chrysophylax blinked; but deep down inside him he laughed: a silent quiver which they did not observe. Their bargaining had begun to amuse him. Evidently they expected to get something out of it. They knew very little of the ways of the wide and wicked world—indeed, there was no one now living in all the realm who had had any actual experience in dealing with dragons and their tricks. Chrysophylax was getting his breath back, and his wits as well. He licked his lips.

'Name your own price!' he said.

Then they all began to talk at once. Chrysophylax listened with interest. Only one voice disturbed him: that of the blacksmith.

'No good'll come of it, mark my words,' said he. 'A worm won't return, say what you like. But no good will come of it, either way.'

'You can stand out of the bargain, if that's your mind,' they said to him, and went on haggling, taking little further notice of the dragon.

Chrysophylax raised his head; but if he thought of springing on them, or of slipping off during the argument he was disappointed. Farmer Giles was standing by, chewing a straw and considering; but Tailbiter was in his hand, and his eye was on the dragon.

'You lie where you be!' said he, 'or you'll get what you deserve, gold or no gold.'

The dragon lay flat. At last the parson was made spokesman and he stepped up beside Giles. 'Vile Worm!' he said. 'You must bring back to this spot all your ill-gotten wealth; and after recompensing those whom you have injured we will share it fairly among ourselves. Then, if you make a solemn vow never to disturb our land again, nor to stir up any other monster to trouble us, we will let you depart with both your head and your tail to your own home. And now you shall take such strong oaths to return (with your ransom) as even the conscience of a worm must hold binding.'

Chrysophylax accepted, after a plausible show of hesitation. He even shed hot tears, lamenting his ruin, till there were steaming puddles in the road; but no one was moved by them. He swore many oaths, solemn and astonishing, that he would return with all his wealth on the feast of St Hilarius and St Felix. That gave him eight days, and far too short a time for the journey, as even those ignorant of geography might well have reflected. Nonetheless they let him go, and escorted him as far as the bridge.

'To our next meeting!' he said, as he passed over the river. 'I am sure we shall all look forward to it.'

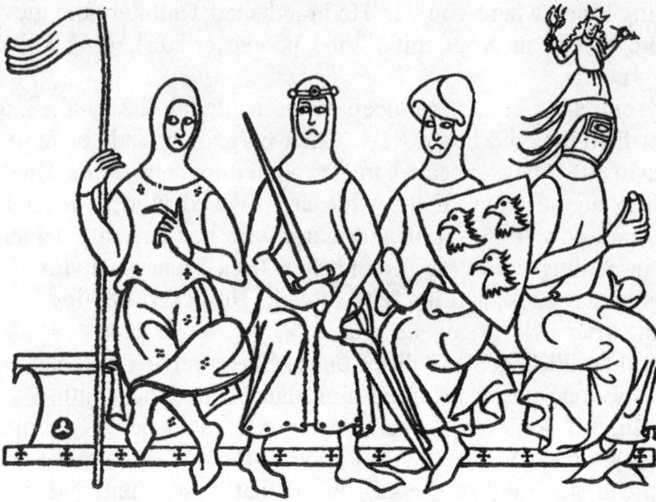

'We shall indeed,' they said. They were, of course, very foolish. For though the oaths he had taken should have burdened his conscience with sorrow and a great fear of disaster, he had, alas! no conscience at all. And if this regrettable lack in one of imperial lineage was beyond the comprehension of the simple, at the least the parson with his book-learning might have guessed it. Maybe he did. He was a grammarian, and could doubtless see further into the future than others.

The blacksmith shook his head as he went back to his smithy. 'Ominous names,' he said. 'Hilarius and Felix! I don't like the sound of them.'

The King, of course, quickly heard the news. It ran through the realm like fire and lost nothing in the telling. The King was deeply moved, for various reasons, not the least being financial; and he made up his mind to ride at once in person to Ham, where such strange things seemed to happen.

He arrived four days after the dragon's departure, coming over the bridge on his white horse, with many knights and trumpeters, and a large baggage-train. All the people had put on their best clothes and lined the street to welcome him. The cavalcade came to a halt in the open space before the church gate. Farmer Giles knelt before the King, when he was presented; but the King told him to rise, and actually patted him on the back. The knights pretended not to observe this familiarity.

The King ordered the whole village to assemble in Farmer Giles's large pasture beside the river; and when they were all gathered together (including Garm, who felt that he was concerned), Augustus Bonifacius rex et basileus was graciously pleased to address them.

He explained carefully that the wealth of the miscreant Chrysophylax all belonged to himself as lord of the land. He passed rather lightly over his claim to be considered suzerain of the mountain-country (which was debatable); but 'we make no doubt in any case,' said he, 'that all the treasure of this worm was stolen from our ancestors. Yet we are, as all know, both just and generous, and our good liege AEgidius shall be suitably rewarded; nor shall any of our loyal subjects in this place go without some token of our esteem, from the parson to the youngest child. For we are well pleased with Ham. Here at least a sturdy and uncorrupted folk still retain the ancient courage of our race.' The knights were talking among themselves about the new fashion in hats.

The people bowed and curtsied, and thanked him humbly. But they wished now that they had closed with the dragon's offer of ten pounds all round, and kept the matter private. They knew enough, at any rate, to feel sure that the King's esteem would not rise to that. Garm noticed that there was no mention of dogs. Farmer Giles was the only one of them who was really content. He felt sure of some reward, and was mighty glad anyway to have come safely out of a nasty business with his local reputation higher than ever.

The King did not go away. He pitched his pavilions in Farmer Giles's field, and waited for January the fourteenth, making as merry as he could in a miserable village far from the capital. The royal retinue ate up nearly all the bread, butter, eggs, chickens, bacon and mutton, and drank up every drop of old ale there was in the place in the next three days. Then they began to grumble at short commons. But the King paid handsomely for everything (in tallies to be honoured later by the Exchequer, which he hoped would shortly be richly replenished); so the folk of Ham were well satisfied, not knowing the actual state of the Exchequer.

January the fourteenth came, the feast of Hilarius and of Felix, and everybody was up and about early. The knights put on their armour. The farmer put on his coat of home-made mail, and they smiled openly, until they caught the King's frown. The farmer also put on Tailbiter, and it went into its sheath as easy as butter, and stayed there. The parson looked hard at the sword, and nodded to himself. The blacksmith laughed.

Midday came. People were too anxious to eat much. The afternoon passed slowly. Still Tailbiter showed no sign of leaping from the scabbard. None of the watchers on the hill, nor any of the small boys who had climbed to the tops of tall trees, could see anything by air or by land that might herald the return of the dragon.

The blacksmith walked about whistling; but it was not until evening fell and the stars came out that the other folk of the village began to suspect that the dragon did not mean to come back at all. Still they recalled his many solemn and astonishing oaths and kept on hoping. When, however, midnight struck and the appointed day was over, their disappointment was deep. The blacksmith was delighted.

'I told you so,' he said. But they were still not convinced.

'After all he was badly hurt,' said some.

'We did not give him enough time,' said others. 'It is a powerful

long way to the mountains, and he would have a lot to carry. Maybe he has had to get help.'

But the next day passed and the next. Then they all gave up hope. The King was in a red rage. The victuals and drink had run out, and the knights were grumbling loudly. They wished to go back to the merriments of court. But the King wanted money.

He took leave of his loyal subjects, but he was short and sharp about it; and he cancelled half the tallies on the Exchequer. He was quite cold to Farmer Giles and dismissed him with a nod.

'You will hear from us later,' he said, and rode off with his knights and his trumpeters.

The more hopeful and simple-minded thought that a message would soon come from the court to summon Master AEgidius to the King, to be knighted at the least. In a week the message came, but it was of different sort. It was written and signed in triplicate: one copy for Giles; one for the parson; and one to be nailed on the church door. Only the copy addressed to the parson was of any use, for the court-hand was peculiar and as dark to the folk of Ham as the Book-latin. But the parson rendered it into the vulgar tongue and read it from the pulpit. It was short and to the point (for a royal letter); the King was in a hurry.

'We Augustus B. A. A. P and M. rex et cetera make known that we have determined, for the safety of our realm and for the keeping of our honour, that the worm or dragon styling himself Chrysophylax the Rich shall be sought out and condignly punished for his misdemeanours, torts, felonies, and foul perjury. All the knights of our Royal household are hereby commanded to arm and make ready to ride upon this quest, so soon as Master Aegidius A. J. Agricola shall arrive at this our court. Inasmuch as the said Aegidius has proved himself a trusty man and well able to deal with giants, dragons, and other enemies of the King's peace, now therefore we command him to ride forth at once, and to join the company of our knights with all speed.'

People said this was a high honour and next door to being dubbed. The miller was envious. 'Friend AEgidius is rising in the world,' said he. 'I hope he will know us when he gets back.'

'Maybe he never will,' said the blacksmith.

'That's enough from you, old horse-face!' said the farmer, mighty put out. 'Honour be blowed! If I get back even the miller's company will be welcome. Still, it is some comfort to think that I shall be missing you both for a bit.' And with that he left them.

You cannot offer excuses to the King as you can to your neighbours; so lambs or no lambs, ploughing or none, milk or water, he had to get up on his grey mare and go. The parson saw him off.

'I hope you are taking some stout rope with you?' he said.

'What for?' said Giles. 'To hang myself?'

'Nay! Take heart, Master AEgidius!' said the parson. 'It seems to me that you have a luck that you can trust. But take also a long rope, for you may need it, unless my foresight deceives me. And now farewell, and return safely!'

'Aye! And come back and find all my house and land in a pickle. Blast dragons!' said Giles. Then, stuffing a great coil of rope in a bag by his saddle, he climbed up and rode off.

He did not take the dog, who had kept well out of sight all the morning. But when he was gone, Garm slunk home and stayed there, and howled all the night, and was beaten for it, and went on howling.

'Help, ow help!' he cried. 'I'll never see dear master again, and he was so terrible and splendid. I wish I had gone with him, I do.'

'Shut up!' said the farmer's wife, 'or you'll never live to see if he comes back or he don't.'

The blacksmith heard the howls. 'A bad omen,' he said cheerfully.

Many days passed and no news came. 'No news is bad news,' he said, and burst into song.

* * *

When Farmer Giles got to court he was tired and dusty. But the knights, in polished mail and with shining helmets on their heads, were all standing by their horses. The King's summons and the inclusion of the farmer had annoyed them, and so they insisted on obeying orders literally, setting off the moment that Giles arrived. The poor farmer had barely time to swallow a sop in a draught of wine before he was off on the road again. The mare was offended. What she thought of the King was luckily unexpressed, as it was highly disloyal.

It was already late in the day. 'Too late in the day to start a dragon-hunt,' thought Giles. But they did not go far. The knights were in no hurry, once they had started. They rode along at their leisure, in a straggling line, knights, esquires, servants, and ponies trussed with baggage; and Farmer Giles jogging behind on his tired mare.

When evening came, they halted and pitched their tents. No provision had been made for Farmer Giles and he had to borrow what he could. The mare was indignant, and she forswore her allegiance to the house of Augustus Bonifacius.

The next day they rode on, and all the day after. On the third day they descried in the distance the dim and inhospitable mountains. Before long they were in regions where the lordship of Augustus Bonifacius was not universally acknowledged. They rode then with more care and kept closer together.

On the fourth day they reached the Wild Hills and the borders of the dubious lands where legendary creatures were reputed to dwell. Suddenly one of those riding ahead came upon ominous footprints in the sand by a stream. They called for the farmer.

'What are these, Master AEgidius?' they said.

'Dragon-marks,' said he.

'Lead on!' said they.

So now they rode west with Farmer Giles at their head, and all the rings were jingling on his leather coat. That mattered little; for all the knights were laughing and talking, and a minstrel rode with them singing a lay. Every now and again they took up the refrain of the song and sang it all together, very loud and strong. It was encouraging, for the song was good—it had been made long before in days when battles were more common than tournaments; but it was unwise. Their coming was now known to all the creatures of that land, and the dragons were cocking their ears in all the caves of the West. There was no longer any chance of their catching old Chrysophylax napping.

As luck (or the grey mare herself) would have it, when at last they drew under the very shadow of the dark mountains, Farmer Giles's mare went lame. They had now begun to ride along steep and stony paths, climbing upwards with toil and ever-growing disquiet. Bit by bit she dropped back in the line, stumbling and limping and looking so patient and sad that at last Farmer Giles was obliged to get off and walk. Soon they found themselves right at the back among the pack-ponies; but no one took any notice of them. The knights were discussing points of precedence and etiquette, and their attention was distracted. Otherwise they would have observed that dragon-marks were now obvious and numerous.

They had come, indeed, to the places where Chrysophylax often roamed, or alighted after taking his daily exercise in the air. The lower hills, and the slopes on either side of the path, had a scorched and trampled look. There was little grass, and the twisted stumps of heather and gorse stood up black amid wide patches of ash and burned earth. The region had been a dragons' playground for many a year. A dark mountain-wall loomed up before them.

Farmer Giles was concerned about his mare; but he was glad of the excuse for no longer being so conspicuous. It had not pleased him to be riding at the head of such a cavalcade in these dreary and dubious places. A little later he was gladder still, and had reason to thank his fortune (and his mare). For just about midday—it being then the Feast of Candlemas, and the seventh day of their riding—Tailbiter leaped out of its sheath, and the dragon out of his cave.

Without warning or formality he swooped out to give battle. Down he came upon them with a rush and a roar. Far from his home he had not shown himself over bold, in spite of his ancient and imperial lineage. But now he was filled with a great wrath; for he was fighting at his own gate, as it were, and with all his treasure to defend. He came round a shoulder of the mountain like a ton of thunderbolts, with a noise like a gale and a gust of red lightning.

The argument concerning precedence stopped short. All the horses shied to one side or the other, and some of the knights fell off. The ponies and the baggage and the servants turned and ran at once. They had no doubt as to the order of precedence.

Suddenly there came a rush of smoke that smothered them all, and right in the midst of it the dragon crashed into the head of the line. Several of the knights were killed before they could even issue their formal challenge to battle, and several others were bowled over, horses and all. As for the remainder, their steeds took charge of them, and turned round and fled, carrying their masters off, whether they wished it or no. Most of them wished it indeed.

But the old grey mare did not budge. Maybe she was afraid of breaking her legs on the steep stony path. Maybe she felt too tired to run away. She knew in her bones that dragons on the wing are worse behind you than before you, and you need more speed than a race-horse for flight to be useful. Besides, she had seen this Chrysophylax before, and remembered chasing him over field and brook in her own country, till he lay down tame in the village high-street. Anyway she stuck her legs out wide, and she snorted. Farmer Giles went as pale as his face could manage, but he stayed by her side; for there seemed nothing else to do.

And so it was that the dragon, charging down the line, suddenly saw straight in front of him his old enemy with Tailbiter in his hand. It was the last thing he expected. He swerved aside like a great bat and collapsed on the hillside close to the road. Up came the grey mare, quite forgetting to walk lame. Farmer Giles, much encouraged, had scrambled hastily on her back.

'Excuse me,' said he, 'but were you looking for me, by any chance?'

'No, indeed!' said Chrysophylax. 'Who would have thought of seeing you here? I was just flying about.'

'Then we meet by good luck,' said Giles, 'and the pleasure is mine; for I was looking for *you*. What's more, I have a bone to pick with you, several bones in a manner of speaking.'

The dragon snorted. Farmer Giles put up his arm to ward off the hot gust, and with a flash Tailbiter swept forward, dangerously near the dragon's nose.

'Hey!' said he, and stopped snorting. He began to tremble and backed away, and all the fire in him was chilled. 'You have not, I hope, come to kill me, good master?' he whined.

'Nay! nay!' said the farmer. 'I said naught about killing.' The grey mare sniffed.

'Then what, may I ask, are you doing with all these knights?' said Chrysophylax. 'Knights always kill dragons, if we don't kill them first.'

'I'm doing nothing with them at all. They're naught to me,' said Giles. 'And anyway, they are all dead now or gone. What about what you said last Epiphany?'

'What about it?' said the dragon anxiously.

'You're nigh on a month late,' said Giles, 'and payment is overdue. I've come to collect it. You should beg my pardon for all the bother I have been put to.'

'I do indeed!' said he. 'I wish you had not troubled to come.'

'It'll be every bit of your treasure this time, and no market-tricks,' said Giles, 'or dead you'll be, and I shall hang your skin from our church steeple as a warning.'

'It's cruel hard!' said the dragon.

'A bargain's a bargain,' said Giles.

'Can't I keep just a ring or two, and a mite of gold, in consideration of cash payment?' said he.

'Not a brass button!' said Giles. And so they kept on for a while, chaffering and arguing like folk at a fair. Yet the end of it was as you might expect; for whatever else might be said, few had ever outlasted Farmer Giles at a bargaining.

The dragon had to walk all the way back to his cave, for Giles stuck to his side with Tailbiter held mighty close. There was a narrow path that wound up and round the mountain, and there was barely room for the two of them. The mare came just behind and she looked rather thoughtful.

It was five miles, if it was a step, and stiff going; and Giles trudged along, puffing and blowing, but never taking his eye off the worm. At last on the west side of the mountain they came to the mouth of the cave. It was large and black and forbidding, and its brazen doors swung on great pillars of iron. Plainly it had been a place of strength and pride in days long forgotten; for dragons do not build such works nor delve such mines, but dwell rather, when they may, in the tombs and treasuries of mighty men and giants of old. The doors of this deep house were set wide, and in their shadow they halted. So far Chrysophylax had had no chance to escape, but coming now to his own gate he sprang forward and prepared to plunge in.

Farmer Giles hit him with the flat of the sword. 'Woa!' said he. 'Before you go in, I've something to say to you. If you ain't outside again in quick time with something worth bringing, I shall come in after you and cut off your tail to begin with.'

The mare sniffed. She could not imagine Farmer Giles going down alone into a dragon's den for any money on earth. But Chrysophylax was quite prepared to believe it, with Tailbiter looking so bright and sharp and all. And maybe he was right, and the mare, for all her wisdom, had not yet understood the change in her master. Farmer Giles was backing his luck, and after two encounters was beginning to fancy that no dragon could stand up to him.

Anyway, out came Chrysophylax again in mighty quick time, with twenty pounds (troy) of gold and silver, and a chest of rings and necklaces and other pretty stuff.

'There!' said he.

'Where?' said Giles. 'That's not half enough, if that's what you mean. Nor half what you've got, I'll be bound.'

'Of course not!' said the dragon, rather perturbed to find that the farmer's wits seemed to have become brighter since that day in the village. 'Of course not! But I can't bring it all out at once.'

'Nor at twice, I'll wager,' said Giles. 'In you go again, and out again double quick, or I'll give you a taste of Tailbiter!'

'No!' said the dragon, and in he popped and out again double quick. 'There!' said he, putting down an enormous load of gold and two chests of diamonds.

'Now try again!' said the farmer. 'And try harder!'

'It's hard, cruel hard,' said the dragon, as he went back in again.

But by this time the grey mare was getting a bit anxious on her own account. 'Who's going to carry all this heavy stuff home, I wonder?' thought she; and she gave such a long sad look at all the bags and the boxes that the farmer guessed her mind.

'Never you worry, lass!' said he. 'We'll make the old worm do the carting.'

'Mercy on us!' said the dragon, who overheard these words as he came out of the cave for the third time with the biggest load of all, and

a mort of rich jewels like green and red fire. 'Mercy on us! If I carry all this, it will be near the death of me, and a bag more I never could manage, not if you killed me for it.'

'Then there is more still, is there?' said the farmer.

'Yes,' said the dragon, 'enough to keep me respectable.' He spoke near the truth for a rare wonder, and wisely as it turned out. 'If you will leave me what remains,' said he very wily, 'I'll be your friend for ever. And I will carry all this treasure back to your honour's own house and not to the King's. And I will help you to keep it, what is more,' said he.

Then the farmer took out a toothpick with his left hand, and he thought very hard for a minute. Then 'Done with you!' he said, showing a laudable discretion. A knight would have stood out for the whole hoard and got a curse laid upon it. And as likely as not, if Giles had driven the worm to despair, he would have turned and fought in the end, Tailbiter or no Tailbiter. In which case Giles, if not slain himself, would have been obliged to slaughter his transport and leave the best part of his gains in the mountains.

Well, that was the end of it. The farmer stuffed his pockets with jewels, just in case anything went wrong; and he gave the grey mare a small load to carry. All the rest he bound on the back of Chrysophylax in boxes and bags, till he looked like a royal pantechnicon. There was no chance of his flying, for his load was too great, and Giles had tied down his wings.

'Mighty handy this rope has turned out in the end!' he thought, and he remembered the parson with gratitude.

So off now the dragon trotted, puffing and blowing, with the mare at his tail, and the farmer holding out Caudimordax very bright and threatening. He dared try no tricks.

In spite of their burdens the mare and the dragon made better speed going back than the cavalcade had made coming. For Farmer Giles was in a hurry—not the least reason being that he had little food in his bags.

Also he had no trust in Chrysophylax after his breaking of oaths so solemn and binding, and he wondered much how to get through a night without death or great loss. But before that night fell he ran again into luck; for they overtook half a dozen of the servants and ponies that had departed in haste and were now wandering at a loss in the Wild Hills. They scattered in fear and amazement, but Giles shouted after them.

'Hey, lads!' said he. 'Come back! I have a job for you, and good wages while this packet lasts.'

So they entered his service, being glad of a guide, and thinking that their wages might indeed come more regular now than had been usual. Then they rode on, seven men, six ponies, one mare, and a dragon; and Giles began to feel like a lord and stuck out his chest. They halted as seldom as they could. At night Farmer Giles roped the dragon to four pickets, one to each leg, with three men to watch him in turn. But the grey mare kept half an eye open, in case the men should try any tricks on their own account.

After three days they were back over the borders of their own country; and their arrival caused such wonder and uproar as had seldom been seen between the two seas before. In the first village that they stopped at food and drink was showered on them free, and half the young lads wanted to join in the procession. Giles chose out a dozen likely young fellows. He promised them good wages, and bought them such mounts as he could get. He was beginning to have ideas.

After resting a day he rode on again, with his new escort at his heels. They sang songs in his honour: rough and ready, but they sounded good in his ears. Some folk cheered and others laughed. It was a sight both merry and wonderful.

Soon Farmer Giles took a bend southward, and steered towards his own home, and never went near the court of the King nor sent any message. But the news of the return of master AEgidius spread like fire from the West; and there was great astonishment and confusion. For he came hard on the heels of a royal proclamation bidding all the towns and villages to go into mourning for the fall of the brave knights in the pass of the mountains.

Wherever Giles went the mourning was cast aside, and bells were set ringing, and people thronged by the wayside shouting and waving their caps and their scarves. But they booed the poor dragon, till he began bitterly to regret the bargain he had made. It was most humiliating for one of ancient and imperial lineage. When they got back to Ham all the dogs barked at him scornfully. All except Garm: he had eyes, ears, and nose only for his master. Indeed, he went quite off his head, and turned somersaults all along the street.

Ham, of course, gave the farmer a wonderful welcome; but probably nothing pleased him more than finding the miller at a loss for a sneer and the blacksmith quite out of countenance.

'This is not the end of the affair, mark my words!' said he; but he could not think of anything worse to say and hung his head gloomily. Farmer Giles, with his six men and his dozen likely lads and the dragon and all, went on up the hill, and there they stayed quiet for a while. Only the parson was invited to the house.

The news soon reached the capital, and forgetting the official mourning, and their business as well, people gathered in the streets. There was much shouting and noise.

The King was in his great house, biting his nails and tugging his beard. Between grief and rage (and financial anxiety) his mood was so grim that no one dared speak to him. But at last the noise of the town came to his ears; it did not sound like mourning or weeping.

'What is all the noise about?' he demanded. 'Tell the people to go indoors and mourn decently! It sounds more like a goose-fair.'

'The dragon has come back, lord,' they answered.

'What!' said the King. 'Summon our knights, or what is left of them!'

'There is no need, lord,' they answered. 'With Master AEgidius behind him the dragon is tame as tame. Or so we are informed. The news has not long come in, and reports are conflicting.'

'Bless our Soul!' said the King, looking greatly relieved. 'And to think that we ordered a Dirge to be sung for the fellow the day after tomorrow! Cancel it! Is there any sign of our treasure?'

'Reports say that there is a veritable mountain of it, lord,' they answered.

'When will it arrive?' said the King eagerly. 'A good man this AEgidius—send him in to us as soon as he comes!'

There was some hesitation in replying to this. At last someone took courage and said: 'Your pardon, lord, but we hear that the farmer has turned aside towards his own home. But doubtless he will hasten here in suitable raiment at the earliest opportunity.'

'Doubtless,' said the King. 'But confound his raiment! He had no business to go home without reporting. We are much displeased.'

The earliest opportunity presented itself, and passed, and so did many later ones. In fact, Farmer Giles had been back for a good week or more, and still no word or news of him came to the court.

On the tenth day the King's rage exploded. 'Send for the fellow!' he said; and they sent. It was a day's hard riding to Ham, each way.

'He will not come, lord!' said a trembling messenger two days later.

'Lightning of Heaven!' said the King. 'Command him to come on Tuesday next, or he shall be cast into prison for life!'

'Your pardon, lord, but he still will not come,' said a truly miserable messenger returning alone on the Tuesday.

'Ten Thousand Thunders!' said the King. 'Take this fool to prison instead! Now send some men to fetch the churl in chains!' he bellowed to those that stood by.

'How many men?' they faltered. 'There's a dragon, and . . . and Tailbiter, and—'

'And broomstales and fiddlesticks!' said the King. Then he ordered his white horse, and summoned his knights (or what was left of them) and a company of men-at-arms, and he rode off in fiery anger. All the people ran out of their houses in surprise.

But Farmer Giles had now become more than the Hero of the Countryside: he was the Darling of the Land; and folk did not cheer the knights and men-at-arms as they went by, though they still took off their hats to the King. As he drew nearer to Ham the looks grew more sullen; in some villages the people shut their doors and not a face could be seen.

Then the King changed from hot wrath to cold anger. He had a grim look as he rode up at last to the river beyond which lay Ham and the house of the farmer. He had a mind to burn the place down. But there was Farmer Giles on the bridge, sitting on the grey mare with Tailbiter in his hand. No one else was to be seen, except Garm, who was lying in the road.

'Good morning, lord!' said Giles, as cheerful as day, not waiting to be spoken to.

The King eyed him coldly. 'Your manners are unfit for our presence,' said he; 'but that does not excuse you from coming when sent for.'

'I had not thought of it, lord, and that's a fact,' said Giles. 'I had matters of my own to mind, and had wasted time enough on your errands.'

'Ten Thousand Thunders!' cried the King in a hot rage again. 'To the devil with you and your insolence! No reward will you get after this; and you will be lucky if you escape hanging. And hanged you shall be, unless you beg our pardon here and now, and give us back our sword.'

'Eh?' said Giles. 'I have got my reward, I reckon. Finding's keeping, and keeping's having, we say here. And I reckon Tailbiter is better with me than with your folk. But what are all these knights and men for, by any chance?' he asked. 'If you've come on a visit, you'd be welcome with fewer. If you want to take me away, you'll need a lot more.'

The King choked, and the knights went very red and looked down their noses. Some of the men-at-arms grinned, since the King's back was turned to them.

'Give me my sword!' shouted the King, finding his voice, but forgetting his plural.

'Give us your crown!' said Giles: a staggering remark, such as had never before been heard in all the days of the Middle Kingdom.

'Lightning of Heaven! Seize him and bind him!' cried the King, justly enraged beyond bearing. 'What do you hang back for? Seize him or slay him!'

The men-at-arms strode forward.

'Help! help! help!' cried Garm.

Just at that moment the dragon got up from under the bridge. He had lain there concealed under the far bank, deep in the river. Now he let off a terrible steam, for he had drunk many gallons of water. At once there was a thick fog, and only the red eyes of the dragon to be seen in it.

'Go home, you fools!' he bellowed. 'Or I will tear you to pieces. There are knights lying cold in the mountain-pass, and soon there will be more in the river. All the King's horses and all the King's men!' he roared.

Then he sprang forward and struck a claw into the King's white horse; and it galloped away like the ten thousand thunders that the King men-

tioned so often. The other horses followed as swiftly: some had met this dragon before and did not like the memory. The men-at-arms legged it as best they could in every direction save that of Ham.

The white horse was only scratched, and he was not allowed to go far. After a while the King brought him back. He was master of his own horse at any rate; and no one could say that he was afraid of any man or dragon on the face of the earth. The fog was gone when he got back, but so were all his knights and his men. Now things looked very different with the King all alone to talk to a stout farmer with Tailbiter and a dragon as well.

But talk did no good. Farmer Giles was obstinate. He would not yield, and he would not fight, though the King challenged him to single combat there and then.

'Nay, lord!' said he, laughing. 'Go home and get cool! I don't want to hurt you; but you had best be off, or I won't be answerable for the worm. Good day!'

And that was the end of the Battle of the Bridge of Ham. Never a penny of all the treasure did the King get, nor any word of apology from Farmer Giles, who was beginning to think mighty well of himself. What is more, from that day the power of the Middle Kingdom came to an end in that neighbourhood. For many a mile round about men took Giles for their lord. Never a man could the King with all his titles get to ride against the rebel AEgidius; for he had become the Darling of the Land, and the matter of song; and it was impossible to suppress all the lays that celebrated his deeds. The favourite one dealt with the meeting on the bridge in a hundred mock-heroic couplets.

Chrysophylax remained long in Ham, much to the profit of Giles; for the man who has a tame dragon is naturally respected. He was housed in the tithebarn, with the leave of the parson, and there he was guarded by the twelve likely lads. In this way arose the first of the titles of Giles: Dominus de Domito Serpente, which is in the vulgar Lord of the Tame Worm, or shortly of Tame. As such he was widely honoured; but he still paid a nominal tribute to the King: six oxtails and a pint of bitter, delivered on St Matthias' Day, that being the date of the meeting on the bridge. Before long, however, he advanced the Lord to Earl, and the belt of the Earl of Tame was indeed of great length.

After some years he became Prince Julius AEgidius and the tribute ceased. For Giles, being fabulously rich, had built himself a hall of great magnificence, and gathered great strength of men-at-arms. Very bright and gay they were, for their gear was the best that money could buy. Each of the twelve likely lads became a captain. Garm had a gold collar, and while he lived roamed at his will, a proud and happy dog, insufferable to his fellows; for he expected all other dogs to accord him the respect due to the terror and splendour of his master. The grey mare passed to her days' end in peace and gave no hint of her reflections.

In the end Giles became a king, of course, the King of the Little Kingdom. He was crowned in Ham in the name of AEgidius Draconarius; but he was more often known as Old Giles Worming. For the vulgar tongue came into fashion at his court, and none of his speeches were in the Book-latin. His wife made a queen of great size and majesty, and she kept a tight hand on the household accounts. There was no getting round Queen Agatha—at least it was a long walk.

Thus Giles became at length old and venerable and had a white beard

down to his knees, and a very respectable court (in which merit was often rewarded), and an entirely new order of knighthood. These were the Wormwardens, and a dragon was their ensign: the twelve likely lads were the senior members.

It must be admitted that Giles owed his rise in a large measure to luck, though he showed some wits in the use of it. Both the luck and the wits remained with him to the end of his days, to the great benefit of his friends and his neighbours. He rewarded the parson very handsomely; and even the blacksmith and the miller had their bit. For Giles could afford to be generous. But after he became king he issued a strong law against unpleasant prophecy, and made milling a royal monopoly. The blacksmith changed to the trade of an undertaker; but the miller became an obsequious servant of the crown. The parson became a bishop, and set up his see in the church of Ham, which was suitably enlarged.

Now those who live still in the lands of the Little Kingdom will observe in this history the true explanation of the names that some of its towns and villages bear in our time. For the learned in such matters inform us that Ham, being made the chief town of the new realm, by a natural confusion between the Lord of Ham and the Lord of Tame became known by the latter name, which it retains to this day; for Thame with an *h* is a folly without warrant. Whereas in memory of the dragon, upon whom their fame and fortune were founded, the Draconarii built themselves a great house, four miles northwest of Tame, upon the spot where Giles and Chrysophylax first made acquaintance. That place became known throughout the kingdom as Aula Draconaria, or in the vulgar Worminghall, after the king's name and his standard.

The face of the land has changed since that time, and kingdoms have come and gone; woods have fallen, and rivers have shifted, and only the hills remain, and they are worn down by the rain and the wind. But still that name endures; though men now call it Wunnle (or so I am told); for villages have fallen from their pride. But in the days of which this tale speaks Worminghall it was, and a Royal Seat, and the dragon-standard flew above the trees; and all things went well there and merrily, while Tailbiter was above ground.

Envoy

Chrysophylax begged often for his liberty; and he proved expensive to feed, since he continued to grow, as dragons will, like trees, as long as there is life in them. So it came to pass, after some years, when Giles felt himself securely established, that he let the poor worm go back home. They parted with many expressions of mutual esteem, and a pact of non-aggression upon either side. In his bad heart of hearts the dragon felt as kindly disposed towards Giles as a dragon can feel towards anyone. After all there was Tailbiter: his life might easily have been taken, and all his hoard too. As it was, he still had a mort of treasure at home in his cave (as indeed Giles suspected).

He flew back to the mountains, slowly and laboriously, for his wings were clumsy with long disuse, and his size and his armour were greatly increased. Arriving home, he at once routed out a young dragon who had had the temerity to take up residence in his cave while Chrysophylax was away. It is said that the noise of the battle was heard throughout Venedotia. When, with great satisfaction, he had devoured his defeated opponent, he felt better, and the scars of his humiliation were assuaged, and he slept for a long while. But at last, waking suddenly, he set off in search of that tallest and stupidest of the giants, who had started all the trouble one summer's night long before. He gave him a piece of his mind, and the poor fellow was very much crushed.

'A blunderbuss, was it?' said he, scratching his head. 'I thought it was horseflies!'

finis

or in the vulgar

THE END

TREE AND LEAF

INTRODUCTORY NOTE

THESE two things, *On Fairy-stories* and *Leaf by Niggle*, are here reprinted and issued together. They are no longer easy to obtain, but they may still be found interesting, especially by those to whom *The Lord of the Rings* has given pleasure. Though one is an "essay" and the other a "story", they are related: by the symbols of Tree and Leaf, and by both touching in different ways on what is called in the essay "sub-creation." Also they were written in the same period (1938-39), when *The Lord of the Rings* was beginning to unroll itself and to unfold the prospects of labour and exploration in yet unknown country as daunting to me as to the hobbits. At about that time we had reached Bree, and I had then no more notion than they had of what had become of Gandalf or who Strider was; and I had begun to despair of surviving to find out.

The essay was originally composed as an Andrew Lang Lecture and was in a shorter form delivered in the University of St. Andrews in 1938.[1] It was eventually published, with a little enlargement, as one of the items in *Essays presented to Charles Williams,* Oxford University Press, 1947, now out of print. It is here reproduced with only a few minor alterations.

The story was not published until 1947 (*Dublin Review*). It has not been changed since it reached manuscript form, very swiftly, one day when I awoke with it already in mind. One of its sources was a great-limbed poplar tree that I could see even lying in bed. It was suddenly lopped and mutilated by its owner, I do not know why. It is cut down now, a less barbarous punishment for any crimes it may have been accused of, such as being large and alive. I do not think it had any friends, or any mourners, except myself and a pair of owls.

J. R. R. TOLKIEN

[1]Not 1940 as incorrectly stated in 1947.

ON FAIRY-STORIES

I PROPOSE to speak about fairy-stories, though I am aware that this is a rash adventure. Faërie is a perilous land, and in it are pitfalls for the unwary and dungeons for the overbold. And overbold I may be accounted, for though I have been a lover of fairy-stories since I learned to read, and have at times thought about them, I have not studied them professionally. I have been hardly more than a wandering explorer (or trespasser) in the land, full of wonder but not of information.

The realm of fairy-story is wide and deep and high and filled with many things: all manner of beasts and birds are found there; shoreless seas and stars uncounted; beauty that is an enchantment, and an ever-present peril; both joy and sorrow as sharp as swords. In that realm a man may, perhaps, count himself fortunate to have wandered, but its very richness and strangeness tie the tongue of a traveller who would report them. And while he is there it is dangerous for him to ask too many questions, lest the gates should be shut and the keys be lost.

There are, however, some questions that one who is to speak about fairy-stories must expect to answer, or attempt to answer, whatever the folk of Faërie may think of his impertinence. For instance: What are fairy-stories? What is their origin? What is the use of them? I will try to give answers to these questions, or such hints of answers to them as I have gleaned—primarily from the stories themselves, the few of all their multitude that I know.

FAIRY-STORY

What is a fairy-story? In this case you will turn to the *Oxford English Dictionary* in vain. It contains no reference to the combination *fairy-*

story, and is unhelpful on the subject of *fairies* generally. In the Supplement, *fairy-tale* is recorded since the year 1750, and its leading sense is said to be (*a*) a tale about fairies, or generally a fairy legend; with developed senses, (*b*) an unreal or incredible story, and (*c*) a falsehood.

The last two senses would obviously make my topic hopelessly vast. But the first sense is too narrow. Not too narrow for an essay; it is wide enough for many books, but too narrow to cover actual usage. Especially so, if we accept the lexicographer's definition of *fairies*: "supernatural beings of diminutive size, in popular belief supposed to possess magical powers and to have great influence for good or evil over the affairs of man."

Supernatural is a dangerous and difficult word in any of its senses, looser or stricter. But to fairies it can hardly be applied, unless *super* is taken merely as a superlative prefix. For it is man who is, in contrast to fairies, supernatural (and often of diminutive stature); whereas they are natural, far more natural than he. Such is their doom. The road to fairyland is not the road to Heaven; nor even to Hell, I believe, though some have held that it may lead thither indirectly by the Devil's tithe.

O see ye not yon narrow road
So thick beset wi' thorns and briers?
That is the path of Righteousness,
Though after it but few inquires.

And see ye not yon braid, braid road
That lies across the lily leven?
That is the path of Wickedness,
Though some call it the Road to Heaven.

And see ye not yon bonny road
That winds about yon fernie brae?
That is the road to fair Elfland,
Where thou and I this night maun gae.

As for *diminutive size*: I do not deny that the notion is a leading one in modern use. I have often thought that it would be interesting to try to find out how that has come to be so; but my knowledge is not sufficient for a certain answer. Of old there were indeed some inhabitants of Faërie that were small (though hardly diminutive), but smallness was not characteristic of that people as a whole. The diminutive being, elf or fairy, is (I guess) in England largely a sophisticated product of literary fancy.[1] It is perhaps not unnatural that in England, the land where the love of the delicate and fine has often reappeared in art, fancy should in this matter turn towards the dainty and diminutive, as in France it went to court and put on powder and diamonds. Yet I suspect that this flower-and-butterfly minuteness was also a product of "rationalization," which transformed the glamour of Elfland into mere finesse, and invisibility into a fragility that could hide in a cowslip or shrink behind a blade of grass. It seems to become fashionable soon after the great voyages had begun to make the world seem too narrow to hold both men and elves; when the magic land of Hy Breasail in the West had become the mere Brazils, the land of red-dye-wood.[2] In any case it was largely a literary business in which William Shakespeare and Michael Drayton played a part.[3] Drayton's *Nymphidia* is one ancestor of that long line of flower-fairies and fluttering sprites with antennae that I so disliked as a child, and which my children in their turn detested. Andrew Lang had similar feelings. In the preface to the *Lilac Fairy Book* he refers to the tales of tiresome contemporary authors: "they always begin with a little boy or girl who goes out and meets the fairies of polyanthuses and gardenias and appleblossom. . . . These fairies try to be funny and fail; or they try to preach and succeed."

But the business began, as I have said, long before the nineteenth century, and long ago achieved tiresomeness, certainly the tiresomeness of trying to be funny and failing. Drayton's *Nymphidia* is, considered as a fairy-story (a story about fairies), one of the worst ever written. The palace of Oberon has walls of spider's legs,

And windows of the eyes of cats,
And for the roof, instead of slats,
Is covered with the wings of bats.

The knight Pigwiggen rides on a frisky earwig, and sends his love, Queen Mab, a bracelet of emmets' eyes, making an assignation in a cowslip-flower. But the tale that is told amid all this prettiness is a dull

[1]I am speaking of developments before the growth of interest in the folk-lore of other countries. The English words, such as *elf*, have long been influenced by French (from which *fay* and *faërie, fairy* are derived); but in later times, through their use in translation, both *fairy* and *elf* have acquired much of the atmosphere of German, Scandinavian, and Celtic tales, and many characteristics of the *huldu-fólk*, the *daoine-sithe*, and the *tylwyth teg*.

[2]For the probability that the Irish *Hy Breasail* played a part in the naming of Brazil see Nansen, *In Northern Mists*, ii, 223–30.

[3]Their influence was not confined to England. German *Elf, Elfe* appears to be derived from *A Midsummer-night's Dream*, in Wieland's translation (1764).

story of intrigue and sly go-betweens; the gallant knight and angry husband fall into the mire, and their wrath is stilled by a draught of the waters of Lethe. It would have been better if Lethe had swallowed the whole affair. Oberon, Mab, and Pigwiggen may be diminutive elves or fairies, as Arthur, Guinevere, and Lancelot are not; but the good and evil story of Arthur's court is a "fairy-story" rather than this tale of Oberon.

Fairy, as a noun more or less equivalent to *elf*, is a relatively modern word, hardly used until the Tudor period. The first quotation in the *Oxford Dictionary* (the only one before A.D. 1450) is significant. It is taken from the poet Gower: *as he were a faierie*. But this Gower did not say. He wrote *as he were of faierie*, "as if he were come from Faërie." Gower was describing a young gallant who seeks to bewitch the hearts of the maidens in church.

> *His croket kembd and thereon set*
> *A Nouche with a chapelet,*
> *Or elles one of grene leves*
> *Which late com out of the greves,*
> *Al for he sholde seme freissh;*
> *And thus he loketh on the fleissh,*
> *Riht as an hauk which hath a sihte*
> *Upon the foul ther he schal lihte,*
> *And as he were of faierie*
> *He scheweth him tofore here yhe.*[4]

This is a young man of mortal blood and bone; but he gives a much better picture of the inhabitants of Elfland than the definition of a "fairy" under which he is, by a double error, placed. For the trouble with the real folk of Faërie is that they do not always look like what they are; and they put on the pride and beauty that we would fain wear ourselves. At least part of the magic that they wield for the good or evil of man is power to play on the desires of his body and his heart. The Queen of Elfland, who carried off Thomas the Rhymer upon her milk-white steed swifter than the wind, came riding by the Eildon Tree as a lady, if one of enchanting beauty. So that Spenser was in the true tradition when he called the knights of his Faërie by the name of Elfe. It belonged to such knights as Sir Guyon rather than to Pigwiggen armed with a hornet's sting.

Now, though I have only touched (wholly inadequately) on *elves* and

[4]*Confessio Amantis*, v. 7065 ff.

fairies, I must turn back; for I have digressed from my proper theme: fairy-stories. I said the sense "stories about fairies" was too narrow.[5] It is too narrow, even if we reject the diminutive size, for fairy-stories are not in normal English usage stories *about* fairies or elves, but stories about Fairy, that is *Faërie*, the realm or state in which fairies have their being. *Faërie* contains many things besides elves and fays, and besides dwarfs, witches, trolls, giants, or dragons: it holds the seas, the sun, the moon, the sky; and the earth, and all things that are in it: tree and bird, water and stone, wine and bread, and ourselves, mortal men, when we are enchanted.

Stories that are actually concerned primarily with "fairies," that is with creatures that might also in modern English be called "elves," are relatively rare, and as a rule not very interesting. Most good "fairy-stories" are about the *aventures* of men in the Perilous Realm or upon its shadowy marches. Naturally so; for if elves are true, and really exist independently of our tales about them, then this also is certainly true: elves are not primarily concerned with us, nor we with them. Our fates are sundered, and our paths seldom meet. Even upon the borders of Faërie we encounter them only at some chance crossing of the ways.[6]

The definition of a fairy-story—what it is, or what it should be—does not, then, depend on any definition or historical account of elf or fairy, but upon the nature of *Faërie*: the Perilous Realm itself, and the air that blows in that country. I will not attempt to define that, nor to describe it directly. It cannot be done. Faërie cannot be caught in a net of words; for it is one of its qualities to be indescribable, though not imperceptible. It has many ingredients, but analysis will not necessarily discover the secret of the whole. Yet I hope that what I have later to say about the other questions will give some glimpses of my own imperfect vision of it. For the moment I will say only this: a "fairy-story" is one which touches on or uses Faërie, whatever its own main purpose may be: satire, adventure, morality, fantasy. Faërie itself may perhaps most nearly be translated by Magic[7]—but it is magic of a peculiar mood and power, at the furthest pole from the vulgar devices of the laborious, scientific, magician. There is one proviso: if there is any satire present

[5]Except in special cases such as collections of Welsh or Gaelic tales. In these the stories about the "Fair Family" or the Shee-folk are sometimes distinguished as "fairy-tales" from "folk-tales" concerning other marvels. In this use "fairy-tales" or "fairy-lore" are usually short accounts of the appearances of "fairies" or their intrusions upon the affairs of men. But this distinction is a product of translation.

[6]This is true also, even if they are only creations of Man's mind, "true" only as reflecting in a particular way one of Man's visions of Truth.

[7]See further below, p. 128.

in the tale, one thing must not be made fun of, the magic itself. That must in that story be taken seriously, neither laughed at nor explained away. Of this seriousness the medieval *Sir Gawain and the Green Knight* is an admirable example.

But even if we apply only these vague and ill-defined limits, it becomes plain that many, even the learned in such matters, have used the term "fairy-tale" very carelessly. A glance at those books of recent times that claim to be collections of "fairy-stories" is enough to show that tales about fairies, about the fair family in any of its houses, or even about dwarfs and goblins, are only a small part of their content. That, as we have seen, was to be expected. But these books also contain many tales that do not use, do not even touch upon, Faërie at all; that have in fact no business to be included.

I will give one or two examples of the expurgations I would perform. This will assist the negative side of definition. It will also be found to lead on to the second question: what are the origins of fairy-stories?

The number of collections of fairy-stories is now very great. In English none probably rival either the popularity, or the inclusiveness, or the general merits of the twelve books of twelve colours which we owe to Andrew Lang and to his wife. The first of these appeared more than seventy years ago (1889), and is still in print. Most of its contents pass the test, more or less clearly. I will not analyse them, though an analysis might be interesting, but I note in passing that of the stories in this *Blue Fairy Book* none are primarily about "fairies," few refer to them. Most of the tales are taken from French sources: a just choice in some ways at that time, as perhaps it would be still (though not to my taste, now or in childhood). At any rate, so powerful has been the influence of Charles Perrault, since his *Contes de ma Mère l'Oye* were first Englished in the eighteenth century, and of such other excerpts from the vast storehouse of the *Cabinet des Fées* as have become well known, that still, I suppose, if you asked a man to name at random a typical "fairy-story," he would be most likely to name one of these French things: such as *Puss-in-Boots, Cinderella*, or *Little Red Riding Hood*. With some people *Grimm's Fairy Tales* might come first to mind.

But what is to be said of the appearance in the *Blue Fairy Book* of *A Voyage to Lilliput?* I will say this: it is *not* a fairy-story, neither as its author made it, nor as it here appears "condensed" by Miss May Kendall. It has no business in this place. I fear that it was included merely because Lilliputians are small, even diminutive—the only way in which they are at all remarkable. But smallness is in Faërie, as in our world, only an accident. Pygmies are no nearer to fairies than are Patagonians. I do not rule this story out because of its satirical intent:

there is satire, sustained or intermittent, in undoubted fairy-stories, and satire may often have been intended in traditional tales where we do not now perceive it. I rule it out, because the vehicle of the satire, brilliant invention though it may be, belongs to the class of travellers' tales. Such tales report many marvels, but they are marvels to be seen in this mortal world in some region of our own time and space; distance alone conceals them. The tales of Gulliver have no more right of entry than the yarns of Baron Munchausen; or than, say, *The First Men in the Moon* or *The Time-Machine*. Indeed, for the Eloi and the Morlocks there would be a better claim than for the Lilliputians. Lilliputians are merely men peered down at, sardonically, from just above the house-tops. Eloi and Morlocks live far away in an abyss of time so deep as to work an enchantment upon them; and if they are descended from ourselves, it may be remembered that an ancient English thinker once derived the *ylfe*, the very elves, through Cain from Adam.[8] This enchantment of distance, especially of distant time, is weakened only by the preposterous and incredible Time Machine itself. But we see in this example one of the main reasons why the borders of fairy-story are inevitably dubious. The magic of Faërie is not an end in itself, its virtue is in its operations: among these are the satisfaction of certain primordial human desires. One of these desires is to survey the depths of space and time. Another is (as will be seen) to hold communion with other living things. A story may thus deal with the satisfaction of these desires, with or without the operation of either machine or magic, and in proportion as it succeeds it will approach the quality and have the flavour of fairy-story.

Next, after travellers' tales, I would also exclude, or rule out of order, any story that uses the machinery of Dream, the dreaming of actual human sleep, to explain the apparent occurrence of its marvels. At the least, even if the reported dream was in other respects in itself a fairy-story, I would condemn the whole as gravely defective: like a good picture in a disfiguring frame. It is true that Dream is not unconnected with Faërie. In dreams strange powers of the mind may be unlocked. In some of them a man may for a space wield the power of Faërie, that power which, even as it conceives the story, causes it to take living form and colour before the eyes. A real dream may indeed sometimes be a fairy-story of almost elvish ease and skill—while it is being dreamed. But if a waking writer tells you that his tale is only a thing imagined in his sleep, he cheats deliberately the primal desire at the heart of Faërie: the realization, independent of the conceiving mind, of

[8]*Beowulf*, 111–12.

imagined wonder. It is often reported of fairies (truly or lyingly, I do not know) that they are workers of illusion, that they are cheaters of men by "fantasy"; but that is quite another matter. That is their affair. Such trickeries happen, at any rate, inside tales in which the fairies are not themselves illusions; behind the fantasy real wills and powers exist, independent of the minds and purposes of men.

It is at any rate essential to a genuine fairy-story, as distinct from the employment of this form for lesser or debased purposes, that it should be presented as "true." The meaning of "true" in this connexion I will consider in a moment. But since the fairy-story deals with "marvels," it cannot tolerate any frame or machinery suggesting that the whole story in which they occur is a figment or illusion. The tale itself may, of course, be so good that one can ignore the frame. Or it may be successful and amusing as a dream-story. So are Lewis Carroll's *Alice* stories, with their dream-frame and dream-transitions. For this (and other reasons) they are not fairy-stories.[9]

There is another type of marvellous tale that I would exclude from the title "fairy-story," again certainly not because I do not like it: namely pure "Beast-fable." I will choose an example from Lang's Fairy Books: *The Monkey's Heart*, a Swahili tale which is given in the *Lilac Fairy Book*. In this story a wicked shark tricked a monkey into riding on his back, and carried him half-way to his own land, before he revealed the fact that the sultan of that country was sick and needed a monkey's heart to cure his disease. But the monkey outwitted the shark, and induced him to return by convincing him that the heart had been left behind at home, hanging in a bag on a tree.

The beast-fable has, of course, a connexion with fairy-stories. Beasts and birds and other creatures often talk like men in real fairy-stories. In some part (often small) this marvel derives from one of the primal "desires" that lie near the heart of Faërie: the desire of men to hold communion with other living things. But the speech of beasts in a beast-fable, as developed into a separate branch, has little reference to that desire, and often wholly forgets it. The magical understanding by men of the proper languages of birds and beasts and trees, that is much nearer to the true purposes of Faërie. But in stories in which no human being is concerned; or in which the animals are the heroes and heroines, and men and women, if they appear, are mere adjuncts; and above all those in which the animal form is only a mask upon a human face, a device of the satirist or the preacher, in these we have beast-fable and not fairystory: whether it be *Reynard the Fox*, or *The Nun's Priest's Tale*,

[9]See Note A at the end (p. 75).

or *Brer Rabbit*, or merely *The Three Little Pigs*. The stories of Beatrix Potter lie near the borders of Faërie, but outside it, I think, for the most part.[10] Their nearness is due largely to their strong moral element: by which I mean their inherent morality, not any allegorical *significatio*. But *Peter Rabbit*, though it contains a prohibition, and though there are prohibitions in fairyland (as, probably, there are throughout the universe on every plane and in every dimension), remains a beast-fable.

Now *The Monkey's Heart* is also plainly only a beast-fable. I suspect that its inclusion in a "Fairy Book" is due not primarily to its entertaining quality, but precisely to the monkey's heart supposed to have been left behind in a bag. That was significant to Lang, the student of folklore, even though this curious idea is here used only as a joke; for, in this tale, the monkey's heart was in fact quite normal and in his breast. None the less this detail is plainly only a secondary use of an ancient and very widespread folk-lore notion, which does occur in fairy-stories;[11] the notion that the life or strength of a man or creature may reside in some other place or thing; or in some part of the body (especially the heart) that can be detached and hidden in a bag, or under a stone, or in an egg. At one end of recorded folklore history this idea was used by George MacDonald in his fairy-story *The Giant's Heart*, which derives this central motive (as well as many other details) from well-known traditional tales. At the other end, indeed in what is probably one of the oldest stories in writing, it occurs in *The Tale of the Two Brothers* on the Egyptian D'Orsigny papyrus. There the younger brother says to the elder:

> I shall enchant my heart, and I shall place it upon the top of the flower of the cedar. Now the cedar will be cut down and my heart will fall to the ground, and thou shalt come to seek for it, even though thou pass seven years in seeking it; but when thou has found it, put it into a vase of cold water, and in very truth I shall live.[12]

But that point of interest and such comparisons as these bring us to the brink of the second question: What are the origins of "fairy-stories"? That must, of course, mean: the origin or origins of the fairy elements.

[10]*The Tailor of Gloucester* perhaps comes nearest. *Mrs. Tiggy-winkle* would be as near, but for the hinted dream-explanation. I would also include *The Wind in the Willows* in Beast-fable.

[11]Such as, for instance: *The Giant that had no Heart* in Dasent's *Popular Tales from the Norse*; or *The Sea-Maiden* in Campbell's *Popular Tales of the West Highlands* (no. iv, cf. also no. i); or more remotely *Die Kristallkugel* in Grimm.

[12]Budge, *Egyptian Reading Book*, p. xxi.

To ask what is the origin of stories (however qualified) is to ask what is the origin of language and of the mind.

ORIGINS

Actually the question: What is the origin of the fairy element? lands us ultimately in the same fundamental inquiry; but there are many elements in fairy-stories (such as this detachable heart, or swan-robes, magic rings, arbitrary prohibitions, wicked stepmothers, and even fairies themselves) that can be studied without tackling this main question. Such studies are, however, scientific (at least in intent); they are the pursuit of folklorists or anthropologists: that is of people using the stories not as they were meant to be used, but as a quarry from which to dig evidence, or information, about matters in which they are interested. A perfectly legitimate procedure in itself—but ignorance or forgetfulness of the nature of a story (as a thing told in its entirety) has often led such inquirers into strange judgements. To investigators of this sort recurring similarities (such as this matter of the heart) seem specially important. So much so that students of folk-lore are apt to get off their own proper track, or to express themselves in a misleading "shorthand": misleading in particular, if it gets out of their monographs into books about literature. They are inclined to say that any two stories that are built round the same folk-lore motive, or are made up of a generally similar combination of such motives, are "the same stories." We read that *Beowulf* "is only a version of *Dat Erdmänneken*"; that "*The Black Bull of Norroway* is *Beauty and the Beast*," or "is the same story as *Eros and Psyche*"; that the Norse *Mastermaid* (or the Gaelic *Battle of the Birds*[13] and its many congeners and variants) is "the same story as the Greek tale of Jason and Medea."

Statements of that kind may express (in undue abbreviation) some element of truth; but they are not true in a fairy-story sense, they are not true in art or literature. It is precisely the colouring, the atmosphere, the unclassifiable individual details of a story, and above all the general purport that informs with life the undissected bones of the plot, that really count. Shakespeare's *King Lear* is not the same as Layamon's story in his *Brut*. Or to take the extreme case of *Red Riding Hood:* it is of merely secondary interest that the re-told versions of this story, in which the little girl is saved by wood-cutters, is directly derived from Perrault's story in which she was eaten by the wolf. The really important

[13]See Campbell, op. cit., vol. i.

thing is that the later version has a happy ending (more or less, and if we do not mourn the grandmother overmuch), and that Perrault's version had not. And that is a very profound difference, to which I shall return.

Of course, I do not deny, for I feel strongly, the fascination of the desire to unravel the intricately knotted and ramified history of the branches on the Tree of Tales. It is closely connected with the philologists' study of the tangled skein of Language, of which I know some small pieces. But even with regard to language it seems to me that the essential quality and aptitudes of a given language in a living monument is both more important to seize and far more difficult to make explicit than its linear history. So with regard to fairy stories, I feel that it is more interesting, and also in its way more difficult, to consider what they are, what they have become for us, and what values the long alchemic processes of time have produced in them. In Dasent's words I would say: "We must be satisfied with the soup that is set before us, and not desire to see the bones of the ox out of which it has been boiled."[14] Though, oddly enough, Dasent by "the soup" meant a mishmash of bogus pre-history founded on the early surmises of Comparative Philology; and by "desire to see the bones" he meant a demand to see the workings and the proofs that led to these theories. By "the soup" I mean the story as it is served up by its author or teller, and by "the bones" its sources or material—even when (by rare luck) those can be with certainty discovered. But I do not, of course, forbid criticism of the soup as soup.

I shall therefore pass lightly over the question of origins. I am too unlearned to deal with it in any other way; but it is the least important of the three questions for my purpose, and a few remarks will suffice. It is plain enough that fairy-stories (in wider or in narrower sense) are very ancient indeed. Related things appear in very early records; and they are found universally, wherever there is language. We are therefore obviously confronted with a variant of the problem that the archaeologist encounters, or the comparative philologist: with the debate between *independent evolution* (or rather *invention*) of the similar; *inheritance* from a common ancestry; and *diffusion* at various times from one or more centres. Most debates depend on an attempt (by one or both sides) at over-simplification; and I do not suppose that this debate is an exception. The history of fairy-stories is probably more complex than the physical history of the human race, and as complex as the history of human language. All three things: independent invention, inheritance,

[14]*Popular Tales from the Norse*, p. xviii.

and diffusion, have evidently played their part in producing the intricate web of Story. It is now beyond all skill but that of the elves to unravel it.[15] Of these three *invention* is the most important and fundamental, and so (not surprisingly) also the most mysterious. To an inventor, that is to a storymaker, the other two must in the end lead back. *Diffusion* (borrowing in space) whether of an artefact or a story, only refers the problem of origin elsewhere. At the centre of the supposed diffusion there is a place where once an inventor lived. Similarly with *inheritance* (borrowing in time): in this way we arrive at last only at an ancestral inventor. While if we believe that sometimes there occurred the independent striking out of similar ideas and themes or devices, we simply multiply the ancestral inventor but do not in that way the more clearly understand his gift.

Philology has been dethroned from the high place it once had in this court of inquiry. Max Müller's view of mythology as a "disease of language" can be abandoned without regret. Mythology is not a disease at all, though it may like all human things become diseased. You might as well say that thinking is a disease of the mind. It would be more near the truth to say that languages, especially modern European languages, are a disease of mythology. But Language cannot, all the same, be dismissed. The incarnate mind, the tongue, and the tale are in our world coeval. The human mind, endowed with the powers of generalization and abstraction, sees not only *green-grass*, discriminating it from other things (and finding it fair to look upon), but sees that it is *green* as well as being *grass*. But how powerful, how stimulating to the very faculty that produced it, was the invention of the adjective: no spell or incantation in Faërie is more potent. And that is not surprising: such incantations might indeed be said to be only another view of adjectives, a part of speech in a mythical grammar. The mind that thought of *light, heavy, grey, yellow, still, swift*, also conceived of magic that would make heavy things light and able to fly, turn grey lead into yellow gold, and the still rock into a swift water. If it could do the one, it could do the other; it inevitably did both. When we can take green from grass, blue from heaven, and red from blood, we have already an enchanter's power—upon one plane; and the desire to wield that power in the world external to our minds awakes. It does not follow that we shall use that

[15]Except in particularly fortunate cases; or in a few occasional details. It is indeed easier to unravel a single *thread*—an incident, a name, a motive—than to trace the history of any *picture* defined by many threads. For with the picture in the tapestry a new element has come in: the picture is greater than, and not explained by, the sum of the component threads. Therein lies the inherent weakness of the analytic (or "scientific") method: it finds out much about things that occur in stories, but little or nothing about their effect in any given story.

power well upon any plane. We may put a deadly green upon a man's face and produce a horror; we may make the rare and terrible blue moon to shine; or we may cause woods to spring with silver leaves and rams to wear fleeces of gold, and put hot fire into the belly of the cold worm. But in such "fantasy," as it is called, new form is made; Faërie begins; Man becomes a subcreator.

An essential power of Faërie is thus the power of making immediately effective by the will the visions of "fantasy." Not all are beautiful or even wholesome, not at any rate the fantasies of fallen Man. And he has stained the elves who have this power (in verity or fable) with his own stain. This aspect of "mythology"—sub-creation, rather than either representation or symbolic interpretation of the beauties and terrors of the world—is, I think, too little considered. Is that because it is seen rather in Faërie than upon Olympus? Because it is thought to belong to the "lower mythology" rather than to the "higher"? There has been much debate concerning the relations of these things, of *folk-tale* and *myth*; but, even if there had been no debate, the question would require some notice in any consideration of origins, however brief.

At one time it was a dominant view that all such matter was derived from "nature-myths." The Olympians were *personifications* of the sun, of dawn, of night, and so on, and all the stories told about them were originally *myths* (*allegories* would have been a better word) of the greater elemental changes and processes of nature. Epic, heroic legend, saga, then localized these stories in real places and humanized them by attributing them to ancestral heroes, mightier than men and yet already men. And finally these legends, dwindling down, became folk-tales, *Märchen*, fairy-stories—nursery-tales.

That would seem to be the truth almost upside down. The nearer the so-called "nature myth," or allegory, of the large processes of nature is to its supposed archetype, the less interesting it is, and indeed the less is it of a myth capable of throwing any illumination whatever on the world. Let us assume for the moment, as this theory assumes, that nothing actually exists corresponding to the "gods" of mythology: no personalities, only astronomical or meteorological objects. Then these natural objects can only be arrayed with a personal significance and glory by a gift, the gift of a person, of a man. Personality can only be derived from a person. The gods may derive their colour and beauty from the high splendours of nature, but it was Man who obtained these for them, abstracted them from sun and moon and cloud; their personality they get direct from him; the shadow or flicker of divinity that is upon them they receive through him from the invisible world, the Supernatural. There is no fundamental distinction between the higher and lower mythologies. Their peoples live, if they live at all, by the same life, just as in the mortal world do kings and peasants.

Let us take what looks like a clear case of Olympian nature-myth: the Norse god Thórr. His name is Thunder, of which Thórr is the Norse form; and it is not difficult to interpret his hammer, Miöllnir, as lightning. Yet Thórr has (as far as our late records go) a very marked character, or personality, which cannot be found in thunder or in lightning, even though some details can, as it were, be related to these natural phenomena: for instance, his red beard, his loud voice and violent temper, his blundering and smashing strength. None the less it is asking a question without much meaning, if we inquire: Which came first, nature-allegories about personalized thunder in the mountains, splitting rocks and trees; or stories about an irascible, not very clever, redbeard farmer, of a strength beyond common measure, a person (in all but mere stature) very like the Northern farmers, the *bœndr* by whom Thórr was chiefly beloved? To a picture of such a man Thórr may be held to have "dwindled," or from it the god may be held to have been enlarged. But I doubt whether either view is right—not by itself, not if you insist that one of these things must precede the other. It is more reasonable to suppose that the farmer popped up in the very moment when Thunder got a voice and face; that there was a distant growl of thunder in the hills every time a storyteller heard a farmer in a rage.

Thórr must, of course, be reckoned a member of the higher aristocracy of mythology: one of the rulers of the world. Yet the tale that is told of him in *Thrymskvitha* (in the Elder Edda) is certainly just a fairy-story. It is old, as far as Norse poems go, but that is not far back (say A.D. 900 or a little earlier, in this case). But there is no real reason for supposing that this tale is "unprimitive," at any rate in quality: that is, because it is of folk-tale kind and not very dignified. If we could go backwards in time, the fairy-story might be found to change in details, or to give way to other tales. But there would always be a "fairy-tale" as long as there was any Thórr. When the fairy-tale ceased, there would be just thunder, which no human ear had yet heard.

Something really "higher" is occasionally glimpsed in mythology: Divinity, the right to power (as distinct from its possession), the due of worship; in fact "religion." Andrew Lang said, and is by some still commended for saying,[16] that mythology and religion (in the strict sense of that word) are two distinct things that have become inextricably en-

[16]For example, by Christopher Dawson in *Progress and Religion.*

tangled, though mythology is in itself almost devoid of religious significance.[17]

Yet these things have in fact become entangled—or maybe they were sundered long ago and have since groped slowly, through a labyrinth of error, through confusion, back towards re-fusion. Even fairy-stories as a whole have three faces: the Mystical towards the Supernatural; the Magical towards Nature; and the Mirror of scorn and pity towards Man. The essential face of Faërie is the middle one, the Magical. But the degree in which the others appear (if at all) is variable, and may be decided by the individual story-teller. The Magical, the fairy-story, may be used as a *Mirour de l'Omme*; and it may (but not so easily) be made a vehicle of Mystery. This at least is what George MacDonald attempted, achieving stories of power and beauty when he succeeded, as in *The Golden Key* (which he called a fairy-tale); and even when he partly failed, as in *Lilith* (which he called a romance).

For a moment let us return to the "Soup" that I mentioned above. Speaking of the history of stories and especially of fairy-stories we may say that the Pot of Soup, the Cauldron of Story, has always been boiling, and to it have continually been added new bits, dainty and undainty. For this reason, to take a casual example, the fact that a story resembling the one known as *The Goosegirl* (*Die Gänsemagd* in Grimm) is told in the thirteenth century of Bertha Broadfoot, mother of Charlemagne, really proves nothing either way: neither that the story was (in the thirteenth century) descending from Olympus or Asgard by way of an already legendary king of old, on its way to become a *Hausmärchen*; nor that it was on its way up. The story is found to be widespread, unattached to the mother of Charlemagne or to any historical character. From this fact by itself we certainly cannot deduce that it is not true of Charlemagne's mother, though that is the kind of deduction that is most frequently made from that kind of evidence. The opinion that the story is not true of Bertha Broadfoot must be founded on something else: on features in the story which the critic's philosophy does not allow to be possible in "real life," so that he would actually disbelieve the tale, even if it were found nowhere else; or on the existence of good historical evidence that Bertha's actual life was quite different, so that he would disbelieve the tale, even if his philosophy allowed that it was perfectly

[17]This is borne out by the more careful and sympathetic study of "primitive" peoples: that is, peoples still living in an inherited paganism, who are not, as we say, civilized. The hasty survey finds only their wilder tales; a closer examination finds their cosmological myths; only patience and inner knowledge discovers their philosophy and religion: the truly worshipful, of which the "gods" are not necessarily an embodiment at all, or only in a variable measure (often decided by the individual).

possible in "real life." No one, I fancy, would discredit a story that the Archbishop of Canterbury slipped on a banana skin merely because he found that a similar comic mishap had been reported of many people, and especially of elderly gentlemen of dignity. He might disbelieve the story, if he discovered that in it an angel (or even a fairy) had warned the Archbishop that he would slip if he wore gaiters on a Friday. He might also disbelieve the story, if it was stated to have occurred in the period between, say, 1940 and 1945. So much for that. It is an obvious point, and it has been made before; but I venture to make it again (although it is a little beside my present purpose), for it is constantly neglected by those who concern themselves with the origins of tales.

But what of the banana skin? Our business with it really only begins when it has been rejected by historians. It is more useful when it has been thrown away. The historian would be likely to say that the banana-skin story "became attached to the Archbishop," as he does say on fair evidence that "the Goosegirl *Märchen* became attached to Bertha." That way of putting it is harmless enough, in what is commonly known as "history." But is it really a good description of what is going on and has gone on in the history of story-making? I do not think so. I think it would be nearer the truth to say that the Archbishop became attached to the banana skin, or that Bertha was turned into the Goosegirl. Better still: I would say that Charlemagne's mother and the Archbishop were put into the Pot, in fact got into the Soup. They were just new bits added to the stock. A considerable honour, for in that soup were many things older, more potent, more beautiful, comic, or terrible than they were in themselves (considered simply as figures of history).

It seems fairly plain that Arthur, once historical (but perhaps as such not of great importance), was also put into the Pot. There he was boiled for a long time, together with many other older figures and devices, of mythology and Faërie, and even some other stray bones of history (such as Alfred's defence against the Danes), until he emerged as a King of Faërie. The situation is similar in the great Northern "Arthurian" court of the Shield-Kings of Denmark, the *Scyldingas* of ancient English tradition. King Hrothgar and his family have many manifest marks of true history, far more than Arthur; yet even in the older (English) accounts of them they are associated with many figures and events of fairy-story: they have been in the Pot. But I refer now to the remnants of the oldest recorded English tales of Faërie (or its borders), in spite of the fact that they are little known in England, not to discuss the turning of the bear-boy into the knight Beowulf, or to explain the intrusion of the ogre Grendel into the royal hall of Hrothgar. I wish to point to something else that these traditions contain: a singularly suggestive example of the relation of the "fairy-tale element" to gods and kings and nameless men, illustrating (I believe) the view that this element does not rise or fall, but is there, in the Cauldron of Story, waiting for the great figures of Myth and History, and for the yet nameless He or She, waiting for the moment when they are cast into the simmering stew, one by one or all together, without consideration of rank or precedence.

The great enemy of King Hrothgar was Froda, King of the Heathobards. Yet of Hrothgar's daughter Freawaru we hear echoes of a strange tale—not a usual one in Northern heroic legend: the son of the enemy of her house, Ingeld son of Froda, fell in love with her and wedded her, disastrously. But that is extremely interesting and significant. In the background of the ancient feud looms the figure of that god whom the Norsemen called Frey (the Lord) or Yngvi-frey, and the Angles called Ing: a god of the ancient Northern mythology (and religion) of Fertility and Corn. The enmity of the royal houses was connected with the sacred site of a cult of that religion. Ingeld and his father bear names belonging to it. Freawaru herself is named "Protection of the Lord (of Frey)." Yet one of the chief things told later (in Old Icelandic) about Frey is the story in which he falls in love from afar with the daughter of the enemies of the gods, Gerdr, daughter of the giant Gymir, and weds her. Does this prove that Ingeld and Freawaru, or their love, are "merely mythical"? I think not. History often resembles "Myth," because they are both ultimately of the same stuff. If indeed Ingeld and Freawaru never lived, or at least never loved, then it is ultimately from nameless man and woman that they get their tale, or rather into whose tale they have entered. They have been put into the Cauldron, where so many potent things lie simmering agelong on the fire, among them Love-at-first-sight. So too of the god. If no young man had ever fallen in love by chance meeting with a maiden, and found old enmities to stand between him and his love, then the god Frey would never have seen Gerdr the giant's daughter from the high-seat of Odin. But if we speak of a Cauldron, we must not wholly forget the Cooks. There are many things in the Cauldron, but the Cooks do not dip in the ladle quite blindly. Their selection is important. The gods are after all gods, and it is a matter of some moment what stories are told of them. So we must freely admit that a tale of love is more likely to be told of a prince in history, indeed is more likely actually to happen in an historical family whose traditions are those of Golden Frey and the Vanir, rather than those of Odin the Goth, the Necromancer, glutter of the crows, Lord of the Slain. Small wonder that *spell* means both a story told, and a formula of power over living men.

But when we have done all that research—collection and comparison of the tales of many lands—can do; when we have explained many of the elements commonly found embedded in fairy-stories (such as stepmothers, enchanted bears and bulls, cannibal witches, taboos on names, and the like) as relics of ancient customs once practised in daily life, or of beliefs once held as beliefs and not as "fancies"—there remains still a point too often forgotten: that is the effect produced *now* by these old things in the stories as they are.

For one thing they are now *old*, and antiquity has an appeal in itself. The beauty and horror of *The Juniper Tree* (*Von dem Machandelboom*), with its exquisite and tragic beginning, the abominable cannibal stew, the gruesome bones, the gay and vengeful bird-spirit coming out of a mist that rose from the tree, has remained with me since childhood; and yet always the chief flavour of that tale lingering in the memory was not beauty or horror, but distance and a great abyss of time, not measurable even by *twe tusend Johr*. Without the stew and the bones—which children are now too often spared in mollified versions of Grimm[18]—that vision would largely have been lost. I do not think I was harmed by the horror *in the fairy-tale setting*, out of whatever dark beliefs and practices of the past it may have come. Such stories have now a mythical or total (unanalysable) effect, an effect quite independent of the findings of Comparative Folk-lore, and one which it cannot spoil or explain; they open a door on Other Time, and if we pass through, though only for a moment, we stand outside our own time, outside Time itself, maybe.

If we pause, not merely to note that such old elements have been preserved, but to think *how* they have been preserved, we must conclude, I think, that it has happened, often if not always, precisely because of this literary effect. It cannot have been we, or even the brothers Grimm, that first felt it. Fairy-stories are by no means rocky matrices out of which the fossils cannot be prised except by an expert geologist. The ancient elements can be knocked out, or forgotten and dropped out, or replaced by other ingredients with the greatest ease: as any comparison of a story with closely related variants will show. The things that are there must often have been retained (or inserted) because the oral narrators, instinctively or consciously, felt their literary "significance."[19] Even where a prohibition in a fairy-story is guessed to be derived from some taboo once practised long ago, it has probably been preserved in the later stages of the tale's history because of the great mythical significance of prohibition. A sense of that significance may indeed have

[18]They should not be spared it—unless they are spared the whole story until their digestions are stronger.

[19]*See* Note B at end (p. 141–142)

lain behind some of the taboos themselves. Thou shalt not—or else thou shalt depart beggared into endless regret. The gentlest "nursery-tales" know it. Even Peter Rabbit was forbidden a garden, lost his blue coat, and took sick. The Locked Door stands as an eternal Temptation.

CHILDREN

I will now turn to children, and so come to the last and most important of the three questions: what, if any, are the values and functions of fairy-stories *now?* It is usually assumed that children are the natural or the specially appropriate audience for fairy-stories. In describing a fairy-story which they think adults might possibly read for their own entertainment, reviewers frequently indulge in such waggeries as: "this book is for children from the ages of six to sixty." But I have never yet seen the puff of a new motor-model that began thus: "this toy will amuse infants from seventeen to seventy"; though that to my mind would be much more appropriate. Is there any *essential* connexion between children and fairy-stories? Is there any call for comment, if an adult reads them for himself? *Reads* them as tales, that is, not *studies* them as curios. Adults are allowed to collect and study anything, even old theatre programmes or paper bags.

Among those who still have enough wisdom not to think fairy-stories pernicious, the common opinion seems to be that there is a natural connexion between the minds of children and fairy-stories, of the same order as the connexion between children's bodies and milk. I think this is an error; at best an error of false sentiment, and one that is therefore most often made by those who, for whatever private reason (such as childlessness), tend to think of children as a special kind of creature, almost a different race, rather than as normal, if immature, members of a particular family, and of the human family at large.

Actually, the association of children and fairy-stories is an accident of our domestic history. Fairy-stories have in the modern lettered world been relegated to the "nursery," as shabby or old-fashioned furniture is relegated to the play-room, primarily because the adults do not want it, and do not mind if it is misused.[20] It is not the choice of the children

[20]In the case of stories and other nursery lore, there is also another factor. Wealthier families employed women to look after their children, and the stories were provided by these nurses, who were sometimes in touch with rustic and traditional lore forgotten by their "betters." It is long since this source dried up, at any rate in England; but it once had some importance. But again there is no proof of the special fitness of children as the recipients of this vanishing "folk-lore." The nurses might just as well (or better) have been left to choose the pictures and furniture.

which decides this. Children as a class—except in a common lack of experience they are not one—neither like fairy-stories more, nor understand them better than adults do; and no more than they like many other things. They are young and growing, and normally have keen appetites, so the fairy-stories as a rule go down well enough. But in fact only some children, and some adults, have any special taste for them; and when they have it, it is not exclusive, nor even necessarily dominant.[21] It is a taste, too, that would not appear, I think, very early in childhood without artificial stimulus; it is certainly one that does not decrease but increases with age, if it is innate.

It is true that in recent times fairy-stories have usually been written or "adapted" for children. But so may music be, or verse, or novels, or history, or scientific manuals. It is a dangerous process, even when it is necessary. It is indeed only saved from disaster by the fact that the arts and sciences are not as a whole relegated to the nursery; the nursery and schoolroom are merely given such tastes and glimpses of the adult thing as seem fit for them in adult opinion (often much mistaken). Any one of these things would, if left altogether in the nursery, become gravely impaired. So would a beautiful table, a good picture, or a useful machine (such as a microscope), be defaced or broken, if it were left long unregarded in a schoolroom. Fairy-stories banished in this way, cut off from a full adult art, would in the end be ruined; indeed in so far as they have been so banished, they have been ruined.

The value of fairy-stories is thus not, in my opinion, to be found by considering children in particular. Collections of fairy-stories are, in fact, by nature attics and lumber-rooms, only by temporary and local custom play-rooms. Their contents are disordered, and often battered, a jumble of different dates, purposes, and tastes; but among them may occasionally be found a thing of permanent virtue: an old work of art, not too much damaged, that only stupidity would ever have stuffed away.

Andrew Lang's *Fairy Books* are not, perhaps, lumber-rooms. They are more like stalls in a rummage-sale. Someone with a duster and a fair eye for things that retain some value has been round the attics and box-rooms. His collections are largely a by-product of his adult study of mythology and folk-lore; but they were made into and presented as books for children.[22] Some of the reasons that Lang gave are worth considering.

[21]See Note C at end (p. 142–143).

[22]By Lang and his helpers. It is not true of the majority of the contents in their original (or oldest surviving) forms.

The introduction to the first of the series speaks of "children to whom and for whom they are told." "They represent," he says, "the young age of man true to his early loves, and have his unblunted edge of belief, a fresh appetite for marvels." " 'Is it true?' " he says, "is the great question children ask."

I suspect that *belief* and *appetite for marvels* are here regarded as identical or as closely related. They are radically different, though the appetite for marvels is not at once or at first differentiated by a growing human mind from its general appetite. It seems fairly clear that Lang was using *belief* in its ordinary sense: belief that a thing exists or can happen in the real (primary) world. If so, then I fear that Lang's words, stripped of sentiment, can only imply that the teller of marvellous tales to children must, or may, or at any rate does trade on their *credulity*, on the lack of experience which makes it less easy for children to distinguish fact from fiction in particular cases, though the distinction in itself is fundamental to the sane human mind, and to fairy-stories.

Children are capable, of course, of *literary belief*, when the story-maker's art is good enough to produce it. That state of mind has been called "willing suspension of disbelief." But this does not seem to me a good description of what happens. What really happens is that the story-maker proves a successful "sub-creator." He makes a Secondary World which your mind can enter. Inside it, what he relates is "true": it accords with the laws of that world. You therefore believe it, while you are, as it were, inside. The moment disbelief arises, the spell is broken; the magic, or rather art, has failed. You are then out in the Primary World again, looking at the little abortive Secondary World from outside. If you are obliged, by kindliness or circumstance, to stay, then disbelief must be suspended (or stifled), otherwise listening and looking would become intolerable. But this suspension of disbelief is a substitute for the genuine thing, a subterfuge we use when condescending to games or make-believe, or when trying (more or less willingly) to find what virtue we can in the work of an art that has for us failed.

A real enthusiast for cricket is in the enchanted state: Secondary Belief. I, when I watch a match, am on the lower level. I can achieve (more or less) willing suspension of disbelief, when I am held there and supported by some other motive that will keep away boredom: for instance, a wild, heraldic, preference for dark blue rather than light. This suspension of disbelief may thus be a somewhat tired, shabby, or sentimental state of mind, and so lean to the "adult." I fancy it is often the state of adults in the presence of a fairy-story. They are held there and supported by sentiment (memories of childhood, or notions of what childhood ought to be like); they think they ought to like the tale. But if they really liked it, for itself, they would not have to suspend disbelief: they would believe—in this sense.

Now if Lang had meant anything like this there might have been some truth in his words. It may be argued that it is easier to work the spell with children. Perhaps it is, though I am not sure of this. The appearance that it is so is often, I think, an adult illusion produced by children's humility, their lack of critical experience and vocabulary, and their voracity (proper to their rapid growth). They like or try to like what is given to them: if they do not like it, they cannot well express their dislike or give reasons for it (and so may conceal it); and they like a great mass of different things indiscriminately, without troubling to analyse the planes of their belief. In any case I doubt if this potion—the enchantment of the effective fairy-story—is really one of the kind that becomes "blunted" by use, less potent after repeated draughts.

" 'Is it true?' is the great question children ask," Lang said. They do ask that question, I know; and it is not one to be rashly or idly answered.[23] But that question is hardly evidence of "unblunted belief," or even of the desire for it. Most often it proceeds from the child's desire to know which kind of literature he is faced with. Children's knowledge of the world is often so small that they cannot judge, off-hand and without help, between the fantastic, the strange (that is rare or remote facts), the nonsensical, and the merely "grown-up" (that is ordinary things of their parents' world, much of which still remains unexplored). But they recognize the different classes, and may like all of them at times. Of course the borders between them are often fluctuating or confused; but that is not only true for children. We all know the differences in kind, but we are not always sure how to place anything that we hear. A child may well believe a report that there are ogres in the next county; many grown-up persons find it easy to believe of another country; and as for another planet, very few adults seem able to imagine it as peopled, if at all, by anything but monsters of iniquity.

Now I was one of the children whom Andrew Lang was addressing—I was born at about the same time as the *Green Fairy Book*—the children for whom he seemed to think that fairy-stories were the equivalent of the adult novel, and of whom he said: "Their taste remains like the taste of their naked ancestors thousands of years ago; and they seem to like fairy-tales better than history, poetry, geography, or arithmetic."[24]

[23]Far more often they have asked me: "Was he good? Was he wicked?" That is, they were more concerned to get the Right side and the Wrong side clear. For that is a question equally important in History and in Faërie.

[24]Preface to the *Violet Fairy Book.*

But do we really know much about these "naked ancestors," except that they were certainly not naked? Our fairy-stories, however old certain elements in them may be, are certainly not the same as theirs. Yet if it is assumed that we have fairy-stories because they did, then probably we have history, geography, poetry, and arithmetic because they liked these things too, as far as they could get them, and in so far as they had yet separated the many branches of their general interest in everything.

And as for children of the present day, Lang's description does not fit my own memories, or my experience of children. Lang may have been mistaken about the children he knew, but if he was not, then at any rate children differ considerably, even within the narrow borders of Britain, and such generalizations which treat them as a class (disregarding their individual talents, and the influences of the countryside they live in, and their upbringing) are delusory. I had no special "wish to believe." I wanted to know. Belief depended on the way in which stories were presented to me, by older people, or by the authors, or on the inherent tone and quality of the tale. But at no time can I remember that the enjoyment of a story was dependent on belief that such things could happen, or had happened, in "real life." Fairy-stories were plainly not primarily concerned with possibility, but with desirability. If they awakened *desire*, satisfying it while often whetting it unbearably, they succeeded. It is not necessary to be more explicit here, for I hope to say something later about this desire, a complex of many ingredients, some universal, some particular to modern men (including modern children), or even to certain kinds of men. I had no desire to have either dreams or adventures like *Alice*, and the account of them merely amused me. I had very little desire to look for buried treasure or fight pirates, and *Treasure Island* left me cool. Red Indians were better: there were bows and arrows (I had and have a wholly unsatisfied desire to shoot well with a bow), and strange languages, and glimpses of an archaic mode of life, and, above all, forests in such stories. But the land of Merlin and Arthur was better than these, and best of all the nameless North of Sigurd of the Völsungs, and the prince of all dragons. Such lands were pre-eminently desirable. I never imagined that the dragon was of the same order as the horse. And that was not solely because I saw horses daily, but never even the footprint of a worm.[25] The dragon had the trade-mark *Of Faërie* written plain upon him. In whatever world he had his being it was an Other-world. Fantasy, the making or glimpsing of Other-worlds, was the heart of the desire of Faërie. I desired

[25]See Note D at end (p. 143).

dragons with a profound desire. Of course, I in my timid body did not wish to have them in the neighbourhood, intruding into my relatively safe world, in which it was, for instance, possible to read stories in peace of mind, free from fear.[26] But the world that contained even the imagination of Fáfnir was richer and more beautiful, at whatever cost of peril. The dweller in the quiet and fertile plains may hear of the tormented hills and the unharvested sea and long for them in his heart. For the heart is hard though the body be soft.

All the same, important as I now perceive the fairy-story element in early reading to have been, speaking for myself as a child, I can only say that a liking for fairy-stories was not a dominant characteristic of early taste. A real taste for them awoke after "nursery" days, and after the years, few but long-seeming, between learning to read and going to school. In that (I nearly wrote "happy" or "golden," it was really a sad and troublous) time I liked many other things as well, or better: such as history, astronomy, botany, grammar, and etymology. I agreed with Lang's generalized "children" not at all in principle, and only in some points by accident: I was, for instance, insensitive to poetry, and skipped it if it came in tales. Poetry I discovered much later in Latin and Greek, and especially through being made to try and translate English verse into classical verse. A real taste for fairy-stories was wakened by philology on the threshold of manhood, and quickened to full life by war.

I have said, perhaps, more than enough on this point. At least it will be plain that in my opinion fairy-stories should not be *specially* associated with children. They are associated with them: naturally, because children are human and fairy-stories are a natural human taste (though not necessarily a universal one); accidentally, because fairy-stories are a large part of the literary lumber that in latter-day Europe has been stuffed away in attics; unnaturally, because of erroneous sentiment about children, a sentiment that seems to increase with the decline in children.

It is true that the age of childhood-sentiment has produced some delightful books (especially charming, however, to adults) of the fairy kind or near to it; but it has also produced a dreadful undergrowth of stories written or adapted to what was or is conceived to be the measure of children's minds and needs. The old stories are mollified or bowdlerized, instead of being reserved; the imitations are often merely silly, Pigwiggenry without even the intrigue; or patronizing; or (deadliest of all) covertly sniggering, with an eye on the other grown-ups present. I will

[26]This is, naturally, often enough what children mean when they ask: "Is it true?" They mean: "I like this, but is it contemporary? Am I safe in my bed?" The answer: "There is certainly no dragon in England today," is all that they want to hear.

not accuse Andrew Lang of sniggering, but certainly he smiled to himself, and certainly too often he had an eye on the faces of other clever people over the heads of his child-audience—to the very grave detriment of the *Chronicles of Pantouflia*.

Dasent replied with vigour and justice to the prudish critics of his translations from Norse popular tales. Yet he committed the astonishing folly of particularly *forbidding* children to read the last two in his collection. That a man could study fairy-stories and not learn better than that seems almost incredible. But neither criticism, rejoinder, nor prohibition would have been necessary if children had not unnecessarily been regarded as the inevitable readers of the book.

I do not deny that there is a truth in Andrew Lang's words (sentimental though they may sound): "He who would enter into the Kingdom of Faërie should have the heart of a little child." For that possession is necessary to all high adventure, into kingdoms both less and far greater than Faërie. But humility and innocence—these things "the heart of a child" must mean in such a context—do not necessarily imply an uncritical wonder, nor indeed an uncritical tenderness. Chesterton once remarked that the children in whose company he saw Maeterlinck's *Blue Bird* were dissatisfied "because it did not end with a Day of Judgement, and it was not revealed to the hero and the heroine that the Dog had been faithful and the Cat faithless." "For children," he says, "are innocent and love justice; while most of us are wicked and naturally prefer mercy."

Andrew Lang was confused on this point. He was at pains to defend the slaying of the Yellow Dwarf by Prince Ricardo in one of his own fairy-stories. "I hate cruelty," he said, ". . . but that was in fair fight, sword in hand, and the dwarf, peace to his ashes! died in harness." Yet it is not clear that "fair fight" is less cruel than "fair judgement"; or that piercing a dwarf with a sword is more just than the execution of wicked kings and evil stepmothers—which Lang abjures: he sends the criminals (as he boasts) to retirement on ample pensions. That is mercy untempered by justice. It is true that this plea was not addressed to children but to parents and guardians, to whom Lang was recommending his own *Prince Prigio* and *Prince Ricardo* as suitable for their charges.[27] It is parents and guardians who have classified fairy-stories as *Juvenilia*. And this is a small sample of the falsification of values that results.

If we use *child* in a good sense (it has also legitimately a bad one) we must not allow that to push us into the sentimentality of only using *adult* or *grown-up* in a bad sense (it has also legitimately a good one).

[27]Preface to the *Lilac Fairy Book*.

The process of growing older is not necessarily allied to growing wickeder, though the two do often happen together. Children are meant to grow up, and not to become Peter Pans. Not to lose innocence and wonder, but to proceed on the appointed journey: that journey upon which it is certainly not better to travel hopefully than to arrive, though we must travel hopefully if we are to arrive. But it is one of the lessons of fairy-stories (if we can speak of the lessons of things that do not lecture) that on callow, lumpish, and selfish youth peril, sorrow, and the shadow of death can bestow dignity, and even sometimes wisdom.

Let us not divide the human race into Eloi and Morlocks: pretty children—"elves" as the eighteenth century often idiotically called them—with their fairy-tales (carefully pruned), and dark Morlocks tending their machines. If fairy-story as a kind is worth reading at all it is worthy to be written for and read by adults. They will, of course, put more in and get more out than children can. Then, as a branch of a genuine art, children may hope to get fairy-stories fit for them to read and yet within their measure; as they may hope to get suitable introductions to poetry, history, and the sciences. Though it may be better for them to read some things, especially fairy-stories, that are beyond their measure rather than short of it. Their books like their clothes should allow for growth, and their books at any rate should encourage it.

Very well, then. If adults are to read fairy-stories as a natural branch of literature—neither playing at being children, nor pretending to be choosing for children, nor being boys who would not grow up—what are the values and functions of this kind? That is, I think, the last and most important question. I have already hinted at some of my answers. First of all: if written with art, the prime value of fairy-stories will simply be that value which, as literature, they share with other literary forms. But fairy-stories offer also, in a peculiar degree or mode, these things: Fantasy, Recovery, Escape, Consolation, all things of which children have, as a rule, less need than older people. Most of them are nowadays very commonly considered to be bad for anybody. I will consider them briefly, and will begin with *Fantasy*.

FANTASY

The human mind is capable of forming mental images of things not actually present. The faculty of conceiving the images is (or was) naturally called Imagination. But in recent times, in technical not normal language, Imagination has often been held to be something higher than the mere image-making, ascribed to the operations of Fancy (a reduced and depreciatory form of the older word Fantasy); an attempt is thus made to restrict, I should say misapply, Imagination to "the power of giving to ideal creations the inner consistency of reality."

Ridiculous though it may be for one so ill-instructed to have an opinion on this critical matter, I venture to think the verbal distinction philologically inappropriate, and the analysis inaccurate. The mental power of image-making is one thing, or aspect; and it should appropriately be called Imagination. The perception of the image, the grasp of its implications, and the control, which are necessary to a successful expression, may vary in vividness and strength: but this is a difference of degree in Imagination, not a difference in kind. The achievement of the expression, which gives (or seems to give) "the inner consistency of reality,"[28] is indeed another thing, or aspect, needing another name: Art, the operative link between Imagination and the final result, Sub-creation. For my present purpose I require a word which shall embrace both the Sub-creative Art in itself and a quality of strangeness and wonder in the Expression, derived from the Image: a quality essential to fairy-story. I propose, therefore, to arrogate to myself the powers of Humpty-Dumpty, and to use Fantasy for this purpose: in a sense, that is, which combines with its older and higher use as an equivalent of Imagination the derived notions of "unreality" (that is, of unlikeness to the Primary World), of freedom from the domination of observed "fact," in short of the fantastic. I am thus not only aware but glad of the etymological and semantic connexions of *fantasy* with *fantastic:* with images of things that are not only "not actually present," but which are indeed not to be found in our primary world at all, or are generally believed not to be found there. But while admitting that, I do not assent to the depreciative tone. That the images are of things not in the primary world (if that indeed is possible) is a virtue, not a vice. Fantasy (in this sense) is, I think, not a lower but a higher form of Art, indeed the most nearly pure form, and so (when achieved) the most potent.

Fantasy, of course, starts out with an advantage: arresting strangeness. But that advantage has been turned against it, and has contributed to its disrepute. Many people dislike being "arrested." They dislike any meddling with the Primary World, or such small glimpses of it as are familiar to them. They, therefore, stupidly and even maliciously confound Fantasy with Dreaming, in which there is no Art;[29] and with mental

[28]That is: which commands or induces Secondary Belief.

[29]This is not true of all dreams. In some Fantasy seems to take a part. But this is exceptional. Fantasy is a rational, not an irrational, activity.

disorders, in which there is not even control: with delusion and hallucination.

But the error or malice, engendered by disquiet and consequent dislike, is not the only cause of this confusion. Fantasy has also an essential drawback: it is difficult to achieve. Fantasy may be, as I think, not less but more sub-creative; but at any rate it is found in practice that "the inner consistency of reality" is more difficult to produce, the more unlike are the images and the rearrangements of primary material to the actual arrangements of the Primary World. It is easier to produce this kind of "reality" with more "sober" material. Fantasy thus, too often, remains undeveloped; it is and has been used frivolously, or only half-seriously, or merely for decoration: it remains merely "fanciful." Anyone inheriting the fantastic device of human language can say *the green sun*. Many can then imagine or picture it. But that is not enough—though it may already be a more potent thing than many a "thumbnail sketch" or "transcript of life" that receives literary praise.

To make a Secondary World inside which the green sun will be credible, commanding Secondary Belief, will probably require labour and thought, and will certainly demand a special skill, a kind of elvish craft. Few attempt such difficult tasks. But when they are attempted and in any degree accomplished then we have a rare achievement of Art: indeed narrative art, story-making in its primary and most potent mode.

In human art Fantasy is a thing best left to words, to true literature. In painting, for instance, the visible presentation of the fantastic image is technically too easy; the hand tends to outrun the mind, even to overthrow it.[30] Silliness or morbidity are frequent results. It is a misfortune that Drama, an art fundamentally distinct from Literature, should so commonly be considered together with it, or as a branch of it. Among these misfortunes we may reckon the depreciation of Fantasy. For in part at least this depreciation is due to the natural desire of critics to cry up the forms of literature or "imagination" that they themselves, innately or by training, prefer. And criticism in a country that has produced so great a Drama, and possesses the works of William Shakespeare, tends to be far too dramatic. But Drama is naturally hostile to Fantasy. Fantasy, even of the simplest kind, hardly ever succeeds in Drama, when that is presented as it should be, visibly and audibly acted. Fantastic forms are not to be counterfeited. Men dressed up as talking animals may achieve buffoonery or mimicry, but they do not achieve Fantasy. This is, I think, well illustrated by the failure of the bastard form, pantomime. The nearer it is to "dramatized fairy-story" the worse

[30] See Note E at end (p. 144).

it is. It is only tolerable when the plot and its fantasy are reduced to a mere vestigiary framework for farce, and no "belief" of any kind in any part of the performance is required or expected of anybody. This is, of course, partly due to the fact that the producers of drama have to, or try to, work with mechanism to represent either Fantasy or Magic. I once saw a so-called "children's pantomime," the straight story of *Puss-in-Boots*, with even the metamorphosis of the ogre into a mouse. Had this been mechanically successful it would either have terrified the spectators or else have been just a turn of high-class conjuring. As it was, though done with some ingenuity of lighting, disbelief had not so much to be suspended as hanged, drawn, and quartered.

In *Macbeth*, when it is read, I find the witches tolerable: they have a narrative function and some hint of dark significance; though they are vulgarized, poor things of their kind. They are almost intolerable in the play. They would be quite intolerable, if I were not fortified by some memory of them as they are in the story as read. I am told that I should feel differently if I had the mind of the period, with its witch-hunts and witch-trials. But that is to say: if I regarded the witches as possible, indeed likely, in the Primary World; in other words, if they ceased to be "Fantasy." That argument concedes the point. To be dissolved, or to be degraded, is the likely fate of Fantasy when a dramatist tries to use it, even such a dramatist as Shakespeare. *Macbeth* is indeed a work by a playwright who ought, at least on this occasion, to have written a story, if he had the skill or patience for that art.

A reason, more important, I think, than the inadequacy of stage-effects, is this: Drama has, of its very nature, already attempted a kind of bogus, or shall I say at least substitute, magic: *the visible and audible presentation of imaginary men in a story*. That is in itself an attempt to counterfeit the magician's wand. To introduce, even with mechanical success, into this quasi-magical secondary world a further fantasy or magic is to demand, as it were, an inner or tertiary world. It is a world too much. To make such a thing may not be impossible. I have never seen it done with success. But at least it cannot be claimed as the proper mode of Drama, in which walking and talking people have been found to be the natural instruments of Art and illusion.[31]

For this precise reason—that thc characters, and even the scenes, are in Drama not imagined but actually beheld—Drama is, even though it uses a similar material (words, verse, plot), an art fundamentally different from narrative art. Thus, if you prefer Drama to Literature (as many literary critics plainly do), or form your critical theories primarily from

[31]See Note F at end (p. 144–145).

dramatic critics, or even from Drama, you are apt to misunderstand pure story-making, and to constrain it to the limitations of stage-plays. You are, for instance, likely to prefer characters, even the basest and dullest, to things. Very little about trees as trees can be got into a play.

Now "Faërian Drama"—those plays which according to abundant records the elves have often presented to men—can produce Fantasy with a realism and immediacy beyond the compass of any human mechanism. As a result their usual effect (upon a man) is to go beyond Secondary Belief. If you are present at a Faërian drama you yourself are, or think that you are, bodily inside its Secondary World. The experience may be very similar to Dreaming and has (it would seem) sometimes (by men) been confounded with it. But in Faërian drama you are in a dream that some other mind is weaving, and the knowledge of that alarming fact may slip from your grasp. To experience *directly* a Secondary World: the potion is too strong, and you give to it Primary Belief, however marvellous the events. You are deluded—whether that is the intention of the elves (always or at any time) is another question. They at any rate are not themselves deluded. This is for them a form of Art, and distinct from Wizardry or Magic, properly so called. They do not live in it, though they can, perhaps, afford to spend more time at it than human artists can. The Primary World, Reality, of elves and men is the same, if differently valued and perceived.

We need a word for this elvish craft, but all the words that have been applied to it have been blurred and confused with other things. Magic is ready to hand, and I have used it above (p. 103), but I should not have done so: Magic should be reserved for the operations of the Magician. Art is the human process that produces by the way (it is not its only or ultimate object) Secondary Belief. Art of the same sort, if more skilled and effortless, the elves can also use, or so the reports seem to show; but the more potent and specially elvish craft I will, for lack of a less debatable word, call Enchantment. Enchantment produces a Secondary World into which both designer and spectator can enter, to the satisfaction of their senses while they are inside; but in its purity it is artistic in desire and purpose. Magic produces, or pretends to produce, an alteration in the Primary World. It does not matter by whom it is said to be practised, fay or mortal, it remains distinct from the other two; it is not an art but a technique; its desire is *power* in this world, domination of things and wills.

To the elvish craft, Enchantment, Fantasy aspires, and when it is successful of all forms of human art most nearly approaches. At the heart of many man-made stories of the elves lies, open or concealed, pure or alloyed, the desire for a living, realized sub-creative art, which (however much it may outwardly resemble it) is inwardly wholly different from the greed for self-centred power which is the mark of the mere Magician. Of this desire the elves, in their better (but still perilous) part, are largely made; and it is from them that we may learn what is the central desire and aspiration of human Fantasy—even if the elves are, all the more in so far as they are, only a product of Fantasy itself. That creative desire is only cheated by counterfeits, whether the innocent but clumsy devices of the human dramatist, or the malevolent frauds of the magicians. In this world it is for men unsatisfiable, and so imperishable. Uncorrupted, it does not seek delusion nor bewitchment and domination; it seeks shared enrichment, partners in making and delight, not slaves.

To many, Fantasy, this sub-creative art which plays strange tricks with the world and all that is in it, combining nouns and redistributing adjectives, has seemed suspect, if not illegitimate. To some it has seemed at least a childish folly, a thing only for peoples or for persons in their youth. As for its legitimacy I will say no more than to quote a brief passage from a letter I once wrote to a man who described myth and fairy-story as "lies"; though to do him justice he was kind enough and confused enough to call fairy-story-making "Breathing a lie through Silver."

> *"Dear Sir,"* I said—*"Although now long estranged,*
> *Man is not wholly lost nor wholly changed.*
> *Dis-graced he may be, yet is not de-throned,*
> *and keeps the rags of lordship once he owned:*
> *Man, Sub-creator, the refracted Light*
> *through whom is splintered from a single White*
> *to many hues, and endlessly combined*
> *in living shapes that move from mind to mind.*
> *Though all the crannies of the world we filled*
> *with Elves and Goblins, though we dared to build*
> *Gods and their houses out of dark and light,*
> *and sowed the seed of dragons—'twas our right*
> *(used or misused). That right has not decayed:*
> *we make still by the law in which we're made."*

Fantasy is a natural human activity. It certainly does not destroy or even insult Reason; and it does not either blunt the appetite for, nor obscure the perception of, scientific verity. On the contrary. The keener and the clearer is the reason, the better fantasy will it make. If men were ever in a state in which they did not want to know or could not perceive truth (facts or evidence), then Fantasy would languish until they were cured. If they ever get into that state (it would not seem at all impossible), Fantasy will perish, and become Morbid Delusion.

For creative Fantasy is founded upon the hard recognition that things are so in the world as it appears under the sun; on a recognition of fact, but not a slavery to it. So upon logic was founded the nonsense that displays itself in the tales and rhymes of Lewis Carroll. If men really could not distinguish between frogs and men, fairy-stories about frog-kings would not have arisen.

Fantasy can, of course, be carried to excess. It can be ill done. It can be put to evil uses. It may even delude the minds out of which it came. But of what human thing in this fallen world is that not true? Men have conceived not only of elves, but they have imagined gods, and worshipped them, even worshipped those most deformed by their authors' own evil. But they have made false gods out of other materials: their notions, their banners, their monies; even their sciences and their social and economic theories have demanded human sacrifice. *Abusus non tollit usum.* Fantasy remains a human right: we make in our measure and in our derivative mode, because we are made: and not only made, but made in the image and likeness of a Maker.

RECOVERY, ESCAPE, CONSOLATION

As for old age, whether personal or belonging to the times in which we live, it may be true, as is often supposed, that this imposes disabilities (cf. p. 118). But it is in the main an idea produced by the mere *study* of fairy-stories. The analytic study of fairy-stories is as bad a preparation for the enjoying or the writing of them as would be the historical study of the drama of all lands and times for the enjoyment or writing of stage-plays. The study may indeed become depressing. It is easy for the student to feel that with all his labour he is collecting only a few leaves, many of them now torn or decayed, from the countless foliage of the Tree of Tales, with which the Forest of Days is carpeted. It seems vain to add to the litter. Who can design a new leaf? The patterns from bud to unfolding, and the colours from spring to autumn were all discovered by men long ago. But that is not true. The seed of the tree can be replanted in almost any soil, even in one so smoke-ridden (as Lang said) as that of England. Spring is, of course, not really less beautiful because we have seen or heard of other like events: like events, never from world's beginning to world's end the same event. Each leaf, of oak and ash and thorn, is a unique embodiment of the pattern, and for some this very year may be *the* embodiment, the first ever seen and recognized, though oaks have put forth leaves for countless generations of men.

We do not, or need not, despair of drawing because all lines must be either curved or straight, nor of painting because there are only three "primary" colours. We may indeed be older now, in so far as we are heirs in enjoyment or in practice of many generations of ancestors in the arts. In this inheritance of wealth there may be a danger of boredom or of anxiety to be original, and that may lead to a distaste for fine drawing, delicate pattern, and "pretty" colours, or else to mere manipulation and over-elaboration of old material, clever and heartless. But the true road of escape from such weariness is not to be found in the wilfully awkward, clumsy, or misshapen, not in making all things dark or unremittingly violent; nor in the mixing of colours on through subtlety to drabness, and the fantastical complication of shapes to the point of silliness and on towards delirium. Before we reach such states we need recovery. We should look at green again, and be startled anew (but not blinded) by blue and yellow and red. We should meet the centaur and the dragon, and then perhaps suddenly behold, like the ancient shepherds, sheep, and dogs, and horses—and wolves. This recovery fairy-stories help us to make. In that sense only a taste for them may make us, or keep us, childish.

Recovery (which includes return and renewal of health) is a regaining—regaining of a clear view. I do not say "seeing things as they are" and involve myself with the philosophers, though I might venture to say "seeing things as we are (or were) meant to see them"—as things apart from ourselves. We need, in any case, to clean our windows; so that the things seen clearly may be freed from the drab blur of triteness or familiarity—from possessiveness. Of all faces those of our *familiares* are the ones both most difficult to play fantastic tricks with, and most difficult really to see with fresh attention, perceiving their likeness and unlikeness: that they are faces, and yet unique faces. This triteness is really the penalty of "appropriation": the things that are trite, or (in a bad sense) familiar, are the things that we have appropriated, legally or mentally. We say we know them. They have become like the things which once attracted us by their glitter, or their colour, or their shape, and we laid hands on them, and then locked them in our hoard, acquired them, and acquiring ceased to look at them.

Of course, fairy-stories are not the only means of recovery, or prophylactic against loss. Humility is enough. And there is (especially for the humble) *Mooreeffoc*, or Chestertonian Fantasy. *Mooreeffoc* is a fantastic word, but it could be seen written up in every town in this land. It is Coffee-room, viewed from the inside through a glass door, as it was seen by Dickens on a dark London day; and it was used by Chesterton to denote the queerness of things that have become trite, when they are seen suddenly from a new angle. That kind of "fantasy" most people would allow to be wholesome enough; and it can never lack for material. But it has, I think, only a limited power; for the reason that recovery of freshness of vision is its only virtue. The word *Mooreeffoc* may cause you suddenly to realize that England is an utterly alien land, lost either in some remote past age glimpsed by history, or in some strange dim future to be reached only by a time-machine; to see the amazing oddity and interest of its inhabitants and their customs and feeding-habits; but it cannot do more than that: act as a time-telescope focused on one spot. Creative fantasy, because it is mainly trying to do something else (make something new), may open your hoard and let all the locked things fly away like cage-birds. The gems all turn into flowers or flames, and you will be warned that all you had (or knew) was dangerous and potent, not really effectively chained, free and wild; no more yours than they were you.

The "fantastic" elements in verse and prose of other kinds, even when only decorative or occasional, help in this release. But not so thoroughly as a fairy-story, a thing built on or about Fantasy, of which Fantasy is the core. Fantasy is made out of the Primary World, but a good craftsman loves his material, and has a knowledge and feeling for clay, stone and wood which only the art of making can give. By the forging of Gram cold iron was revealed; by the making of Pegasus horses were ennobled; in the Trees of the Sun and Moon root and stock, flower and fruit are manifested in glory.

And actually fairy-stories deal largely, or (the better ones) mainly, with simple or fundamental things, untouched by Fantasy, but these simplicities are made all the more luminous by their setting. For the story-maker who allows himself to be "free with" Nature can be her lover not her slave. It was in fairy-stories that I first divined the potency of the words, and the wonder of the things, such as stone, and wood, and iron; tree and grass; house and fire; bread and wine.

I will now conclude by considering Escape and Consolation, which are naturally closely connected. Though fairy-stories are of course by no means the only medium of Escape, they are today one of the most obvious and (to some) outrageous forms of "escapist" literature; and it is thus reasonable to attach to a consideration of them some considerations of this term "escape" in criticism generally.

I have claimed that Escape is one of the main functions of fairy-stories, and since I do not disapprove of them, it is plain that I do not accept the tone of scorn or pity with which "Escape" is now so often used: a tone for which the uses of the word outside literary criticism give no warrant at all. In what the misusers are fond of calling Real Life, Escape is evidently as a rule very practical, and may even be heroic. In real life it is difficult to blame it, unless it fails; in criticism it would seem to be the worse the better it succeeds. Evidently we are faced by a misuse of words, and also by a confusion of thought. Why should a man be scorned if, finding himself in prison, he tries to get out and go home? Or if, when he cannot do so, he thinks and talks about other topics than jailers and prison-walls? The world outside has not become less real because the prisoner cannot see it. In using Escape in this way the critics have chosen the wrong word, and, what is more, they are confusing, not always by sincere error, the Escape of the Prisoner with the Flight of the Deserter. Just so a Party-spokesman might have labelled departure from the misery of the Führer's or any other Reich and even criticism of it as treachery. In the same way these critics, to make confusion worse, and so to bring into contempt their opponents, stick their label of scorn not only on to Desertion, but on to real Escape, and what are often its companions, Disgust, Anger, Condemnation, and Revolt. Not only do they confound the escape of the prisoner with the flight of the deserter; but they would seem to prefer the acquiescence of the "quisling" to the resistance of the patriot. To such thinking you have only to say "the land you loved is doomed" to excuse any treachery, indeed to glorify it.

For a trifling instance: not to mention (indeed not to parade) electric street-lamps of mass-produced pattern in your tale is Escape (in that sense). But it may, almost certainly does, proceed from a considered disgust for so typical a product of the Robot Age, that combines elaboration and ingenuity of means with ugliness, and (often) with inferiority of result. These lamps may be excluded from the tale simply because they are bad lamps; and it is possible that one of the lessons to be learnt from the story is the realization of this fact. But out comes the big stick: "Electric lamps have come to stay," they say. Long ago Chesterton truly remarked that, as soon as he heard that anything "had come to stay," he knew that it would be very soon replaced—indeed regarded as pitiably obsolete and shabby. "The march of Science, its tempo quickened by the needs of war, goes inexorably on . . . making some things obsolete, and foreshadowing new developments in the utilization of electricity": an advertisement. This says the same thing only more menacingly. The electric street-lamp may indeed be ignored, simply because it is so insignificant and transient. Fairy-stories, at any rate, have many more permanent and fundamental things to talk about. Lightning, for example. The escapist is not so subservient to the whims of evanescent fashion as these opponents. He does not make things (which it may be quite rational to regard as bad) his masters or his gods by worshipping them as inevitable, even "inexorable." And his opponents, so easily contemptuous, have no guarantee that he will stop there: he might rouse men to pull down the streetlamps. Escapism has another and even wickeder face: Reaction.

Not long ago—incredible though it may seem—I heard a clerk of Oxenford declare that he "welcomed" the proximity of mass-production robot factories, and the roar of self-obstructive mechanical traffic, because it brought his university into "contact with real life." He may have meant that the way men were living and working in the twentieth century was increasing in barbarity at an alarming rate, and that the loud demonstration of this in the streets of Oxford might serve as a warning that it is not possible to preserve for long an oasis of sanity in a desert of unreason by mere fences, without actual offensive action (practical and intellectual). I fear he did not. In any case the expression "real life" in this context seems to fall short of academic standards. The notion that motor-cars are more "alive" than, say, centaurs or dragons is curious; that they are more "real" than, say, horses is pathetically absurd. How real, how startlingly alive is a factory chimney compared with an elm-tree: poor obsolete thing, insubstantial dream of an escapist!

For my part, I cannot convince myself that the roof of Bletchley station is more "real" than the clouds. And as an artefact I find it less inspiring than the legendary dome of heaven. The bridge to platform 4 is to me less interesting than Bifröst guarded by Heimdall with the Gjallarhorn. From the wildness of my heart I cannot exclude the question whether railway-engineers, if they had been brought up on more fantasy, might not have done better with all their abundant means than they commonly do. Fairy-stories might be, I guess, better Masters of Arts than the academic person I have referred to.

Much that he (I must suppose) and others (certainly) would call "serious" literature is no more than play under a glass roof by the side of a municipal swimming-bath. Fairy-stories may invent monsters that fly the air or dwell in the deep, but at least they do not try to escape from heaven or the sea.

And if we leave aside for a moment "fantasy," I do not think that the reader or the maker of fairy-stories need even be ashamed of the "escape" of archaism: of preferring not dragons but horses, castles, sailing-ships, bows and arrows; not only elves, but knights and kings and priests. For it is after all possible for a rational man, after reflection (quite unconnected with fairy-story or romance), to arrive at the condemnation, implicit at least in the mere silence of "escapist" literature, of progressive things like factories, or the machine-guns and bombs that appear to be their most natural and inevitable, dare we say "inexorable," products.

"The rawness and ugliness of modern European life"—that real life whose contact we should welcome—"is the sign of a biological inferiority, of an insufficient or false reaction to environment."[32] The maddest castle that ever came out of a giant's bag in a wild Gaelic story is not only much less ugly than a robot-factory, it is also (to use a very modern phrase) "in a very real sense" a great deal more real. Why should we not escape from or condemn the "grim Assyrian" absurdity of top-hats, or the Morlockian horror of factories? They are condemned even by the writers of that most escapist form of all literature, stories of Science fiction. These prophets often foretell (and many seem to yearn for) a world like one big glass-roofed railway-station. But from them it is as a rule very hard to gather what men in such a world-town will *do*. They may abandon the "full Victorian panoply" for loose garments (with zip-fasteners), but will use this freedom mainly, it would appear, in order to play with mechanical toys in the soon-cloying game of moving at high speed. To judge by some of these tales they will still be as lustful, vengeful, and greedy as ever; and the ideals of their idealists hardly reach farther than the splendid notion of building more towns of the same sort on other planets. It is indeed an age of "improved means to deteriorated ends." It is part of the essential malady of such days—producing the desire to escape, not indeed from life, but from our present time and self-made misery—that we are acutely conscious both of the ugliness of our works, and of their evil. So that to us evil and ugliness seem indissolubly allied. We find it difficult to conceive of evil and beauty together. The fear of the beautiful fay that ran through the elder ages almost eludes our grasp. Even more alarming: goodness is itself bereft of its proper beauty. In Faërie one can indeed conceive of an ogre who possesses a castle hideous as a nightmare (for the evil of the ogre wills it so), but one cannot conceive of a house built with a good purpose—an inn, a hostel for travellers, the hall of a virtuous and noble king—that is yet sickeningly ugly. At the present day it would

[32]Christopher Dawson, *Progress and Religion*, pp. 58, 59. Later he adds: "The full Victorian panoply of top-hat and frock-coat undoubtedly expressed something essential in the nineteenth-century culture, and hence it has with that culture spread all over the world, as no fashion of clothing has ever done before. It is possible that our descendants will recognize in it a kind of grim Assyrian beauty, fit emblem of the ruthless and great age that created it; but however that may be, it misses the direct and inevitable beauty that all clothing should have, because like its parent culture, it was out of touch with the life of nature and of human nature as well."

be rash to hope to see one that was not—unless it was built before our time.

This, however, is the modern and special (or accidental) "escapist" aspect of fairy-stories, which they share with romances, and other stories out of or about the past. Many stories out of the past have only become "escapist" in their appeal through surviving from a time when men were as a rule delighted with the work of their hands into our time, when many men feel disgust with man-made things.

But there are also other and more profound "escapisms" that have always appeared in fairy-tale and legend. There are other things more grim and terrible to fly from than the noise, stench, ruthlessness, and extravagance of the internal-combustion engine. There are hunger, thirst, poverty, pain, sorrow, injustice, death. And even when men are not facing hard things such as these, there are ancient limitations from which fairy-stories offer a sort of escape, and old ambitions and desires (touching the very roots of fantasy) to which they offer a kind of satisfaction and consolation. Some are pardonable weaknesses or curiosities: such as the desire to visit, free as a fish, the deep sea; or the longing for the noiseless, gracious, economical flight of a bird, that longing which the aeroplane cheats, except in rare moments, seen high and by wind and distance noiseless, turning in the sun: that is, precisely when imagined and not used. There are profounder wishes: such as the desire to converse with other living things. On this desire, as ancient as the Fall, is largely founded the talking of beasts and creatures in fairy-tales, and especially the magical understanding of their proper speech. This is the root, and not the "confusion" attributed to the minds of men of the unrecorded past, an alleged "absence of the sense of separation of ourselves from beasts."[33] A vivid sense of that separation is very ancient; but also a sense that it was a severance: a strange fate and a guilt lies on us. Other creatures are like other realms with which Man has broken off relations, and sees now only from the outside at a distance, being at war with them, or on the terms of an uneasy armistice. There are a few men who are privileged to travel abroad a little; others must be content with travellers' tales. Even about frogs. In speaking of that rather odd but widespread fairy-story *The Frog-King* Max Müller asked in his prim way: "How came such a story ever to be invented? Human beings were, we may hope, at all times sufficiently enlightened to know that a marriage between a frog and the daughter of a queen was absurd." Indeed we may hope so! For if not, there would be no point in this story at all, depending as it does essentially on the sense of the absur-

[33]See Note G at end (p. 145–146).

dity. Folk-lore origins (or guesses about them) are here quite beside the point. It is of little avail to consider totemism. For certainly, whatever customs or beliefs about frogs and wells lie behind this story, the frog-shape was and is preserved in the fairy-story[34] precisely because it was so queer and the marriage absurd, indeed abominable. Though, of course, in the versions which concern us, Gaelic, German, English,[35] there is in fact no wedding between a princess and a frog: the frog was an enchanted prince. And the point of the story lies not in thinking frogs possible mates, but in the necessity of keeping promises (even those with intolerable consequences) that, together with observing prohibitions, runs through all Fairyland. This is one of the notes of the horns of Elfland, and not a dim note.

And lastly there is the oldest and deepest desire, the Great Escape: the Escape from Death. Fairy-stories provide many examples and modes of this—which might be called the genuine *escapist*, or (I would say) *fugitive* spirit. But so do other stories (notably those of scientific inspiration), and so do other studies. Fairy-stories are made by men not by fairies. The Human-stories of the elves are doubtless full of the Escape from Deathlessness. But our stories cannot be expected always to rise above our common level. They often do. Few lessons are taught more clearly in them than the burden of that kind of immortality, or rather endless serial living, to which the "fugitive" would fly. For the fairy-story is specially apt to teach such things, of old and still today. Death is the theme that most inspired George MacDonald.

But the "consolation" of fairy-tales has another aspect than the imaginative satisfaction of ancient desires. Far more important is the Consolation of the Happy Ending. Almost I would venture to assert that all complete fairy-stories must have it. At least I would say that Tragedy is the true form of Drama, its highest function; but the opposite is true of Fairy-story. Since we do not appear to possess a word that expresses this opposite—I will call it *Eucatastrophe*. The *eucatastrophic* tale is the true form of fairy-tale, and its highest function.

The consolation of fairy-stories, the joy of the happy ending: or more correctly of the good catastrophe, the sudden joyous "turn" (for there is no true end to any fairy-tale):[36] this joy, which is one of the things which fairy-stories can produce supremely well, is not essentially "escapist," nor "fugitive." In its fairy-tale—or otherworld—setting, it is a

[34]Or group of similar stories.

[35]*The Queen who sought drink from a certain Well and the Lorgann* (Campbell, xxiii); *Der Froschkönig; The Maid and the Frog.*

[36]See Note H at end (p. 146–147).

sudden and miraculous grace: never to be counted on to recur. It does not deny the existence of *dyscatastrophe*, of sorrow and failure: the possibility of these is necessary to the joy of deliverance; it denies (in the face of much evidence, if you will) universal final defeat and in so far is *evangelium*, giving a fleeting glimpse of Joy, Joy beyond the walls of the world, poignant as grief.

It is the mark of a good fairy-story, of the higher or more complete kind, that however wild its events, however fantastic or terrible the adventures, it can give to child or man that hears it, when the "turn" comes, a catch of the breath, a beat and lifting of the heart, near to (or indeed accompanied by) tears, as keen as that given by any form of literary art, and having a peculiar quality.

Even modern fairy-stories can produce this effect sometimes. It is not an easy thing to do; it depends on the whole story which is the setting of the turn, and yet it reflects a glory backwards. A tale that in any measure succeeds in this point has not wholly failed, whatever flaws it may possess, and whatever mixture or confusion of purpose. It happens even in Andrew Lang's own fairy-story, *Prince Prigio*, unsatisfactory in many ways as that is. When "each knight came alive and lifted his sword and shouted 'long live Prince Prigio,' " the joy has a little of that strange mythical fairy-story quality, greater than the event described. It would have none in Lang's tale, if the event described were not a piece of more serious fairy-story "fantasy" than the main bulk of the story, which is in general more frivolous, having the half-mocking smile of the courtly, sophisticated *Conte*.[37] Far more powerful and poignant is the effect in a serious tale of Faërie.[38] In such stories when the sudden "turn" comes we get a piercing glimpse of joy, and heart's desire, that for a moment passes outside the frame, rends indeed the very web of story, and lets a gleam come through.

> *"Seven long years I served for thee,*
> *The glassy hill I clamb for thee,*
> *The bluidy shirt I wrang for thee,*
> *And wilt thou not wauken and turn to me?"*

He heard and turned to her.[39]

[37]This is characteristic of Lang's wavering balance. On the surface the story is a follower of the "courtly" French *conte* with a satirical twist, and of Thackeray's *Rose and the Ring* in particular—a kind which being superficial, even frivolous, by nature, does not produce or aim at producing anything so profound; but underneath lies the deeper spirit of the romantic Lang.

[38]Of the kind which Lang called "traditional," and really preferred.

[39]*The Black Bull of Norroway.*

EPILOGUE

This "joy" which I have selected as the mark of the true fairy-story (or romance), or as the seal upon it, merits more consideration.

Probably every writer making a secondary world, a fantasy, every sub-creator, wishes in some measure to be a real maker, or hopes that he is drawing on reality: hopes that the peculiar quality of this secondary world (if not all the details)[40] are derived from Reality, or are flowing into it. If he indeed achieves a quality that can fairly be described by the dictionary definition: "inner consistency of reality," it is difficult to conceive how this can be, if the work does not in some way partake of reality. The peculiar quality of the "joy" in successful Fantasy can thus be explained as a sudden glimpse of the underlying reality or truth. It is not only a "consolation" for the sorrow of this world, but a satisfaction, and an answer to that question, "Is it true?" The answer to this question that I gave at first was (quite rightly): "If you have built your little world well, yes: it is true in that world." That is enough for the artist (or the artist part of the artist). But in the "eucatastrophe" we see in a brief vision that the answer may be greater—it may be a far-off gleam or echo of *evangelium* in the real world. The use of this word gives a hint of my epilogue. It is a serious and dangerous matter. It is presumptuous of me to touch upon such a theme; but if by grace what I say has in any respect any validity, it is, of course, only one facet of a truth incalculably rich: finite only because the capacity of Man for whom this was done is finite.

I would venture to say that approaching the Christian Story from this direction, it has long been my feeling (a joyous feeling) that God redeemed the corrupt making-creatures, men, in a way fitting to this aspect, as to others, of their strange nature. The Gospels contain a fairy-story, or a story of a larger kind which embraces all the essence of fairy-stories. They contain many marvels—peculiarly artistic,[41] beautiful, and moving: "mythical" in their perfect, self-contained significance; and among the marvels is the greatest and most complete conceivable eucatastrophe. But this story has entered History and the primary world; the desire and aspiration of sub-creation has been raised to the fulfilment of Creation. The Birth of Christ is the eucatastrophe of Man's history. The Resurrection is the eucatastrophe of the story of

[40]For all the details may not be "true": it is seldom that the "inspiration" is so strong and lasting that it leavens all the lump, and does not leave much that is mere uninspired "invention."

[41]The Art is here in the story itself rather than in the telling; for the Author of the story was not the evangelists.

the Incarnation. This story begins and ends in joy. It has pre-eminently the "inner consistency of reality." There is no tale ever told that men would rather find was true, and none which so many sceptical men have accepted as true on its own merits. For the Art of it has the supremely convincing tone of Primary Art, that is, of Creation. To reject it leads either to sadness or to wrath.

It is not difficult to imagine the peculiar excitement and joy that one would feel, if any specially beautiful fairy-story were found to be "primarily" true, its narrative to be history, without thereby necessarily losing the mythical or allegorical significance that it had possessed. It is not difficult, for one is not called upon to try and conceive anything of a quality unknown. The joy would have exactly the same quality, if not the same degree, as the joy which the "turn" in a fairy-story gives: such joy has the very taste of primary truth. (Otherwise its name would not be joy.) It looks forward (or backward: the direction in this regard is unimportant) to the Great Eucatastrophe. The Christian joy, the *Gloria*, is of the same kind; but it is pre-eminently (infinitely, if our capacity were not finite) high and joyous. But this story is supreme; and it is true. Art has been verified. God is the Lord, of angels, and of men—and of elves. Legend and History have met and fused.

But in God's kingdom the presence of the greatest does not depress the small. Redeemed Man is still man. Story, fantasy, still go on, and should go on. The Evangelium has not abrogated legends; it has hallowed them, especially the "happy ending." The Christian has still to work, with mind as well as body, to suffer, hope, and die; but he may now perceive that all his bents and faculties have a purpose, which can be redeemed. So great is the bounty with which he has been treated that he may now, perhaps, fairly dare to guess that in Fantasy he may actually assist in the effoliation and multiple enrichment of creation. All tales may come true; and yet, at the last, redeemed, they may be as like and as unlike the forms that we give them as Man, finally redeemed, will be like and unlike the fallen that we know.

NOTES

A (page 106)

THE VERY ROOT (not only the use) of their "marvels" is satiric, a mockery of unreason; and the "dream" element is not a mere machinery of introduction and ending, but inherent in the action and transitions. These things children can perceive and appreciate, if left to themselves. But to many, as it was to me, *Alice* is presented as a fairy-story and while this misunderstanding lasts, the distaste for the dream-machinery is felt. There is no suggestion of dream in *The Wind in the Willows*. "The Mole had been working very hard all the morning, spring-cleaning his little house." So it begins, and that correct tone is maintained. It is all the more remarkable that A. A. Milne, so great an admirer of this excellent book, should have prefaced to his dramatized version a "whimsical" opening in which a child is seen telephoning with a daffodil. Or perhaps it is not very remarkable, for a perceptive admirer (as distinct from a great admirer) of the book would never have attempted to dramatize it. Naturally only the simpler ingredients, the pantomime, and the satiric beast-fable elements, are capable of presentation in this form. The play is, on the lower level of drama, tolerably good fun, especially for those who have not read the book; but some children that I took to see *Toad of Toad Hall*, brought away as their chief memory nausea at the opening. For the rest they preferred their recollections of the book.

B (page 116)

OF COURSE, these details, as a rule, got into the tales, *even in the days when they were real practices*, because they had a story-making value. If I were to write a story in which it happened that a man was hanged, that *might* show in later ages, if the story survived—in itself a sign that the story possessed some permanent, and more than local or temporary, value—that it was written at a period when men were really hanged, as a legal practice. *Might*: the inference would not, of course, in that future time be certain. For certainty on that point the future inquirer would have to know definitely when hanging was practised and when I lived. I could have borrowed the incident from other times and places, from other stories; I could simply have invented it. But even if this inference happened to be correct, the hanging-scene would only occur in the story, (*a*) because I was aware of the dramatic, tragic, or macabre force of this incident in my tale, and (*b*) because those who handed it down felt this force enough to make them keep the incident in. Distance of time, sheer antiquity and alienness, might later sharpen the edge of the tragedy or the horror; but the edge must be there even for the elvish hone of antiquity to whet it. The least useful question, therefore, for literary critics at any rate, to ask or to answer about Iphigeneia, daughter of Agamemnon, is: Does the legend of her sacrifice at Aulis come down from a time when human-sacrifice was commonly practised?

I say only "as a rule," because it is conccivablc that what is now regarded as a "story" was once something different in intent: e.g. a record of fact or ritual. I mean "record" strictly. A story invented to explain a ritual (a process that is sometimes supposed to have frequently occurred) remains primarily a story. It takes form as such, and will survive (long after the ritual evidently) only because of its story-values. In some cases details that now are notable merely because they are strange may have once been so everyday and unregarded that they were slipped in casually: like mentioning that a man "raised his hat," or "caught a train." But such casual details will not long survive change in everyday habits. Not in a period of oral transmission. In a period of writing (and of rapid changes in habits) a story may remain unchanged long enough for even its casual details to acquire the value of quaintness or queerness. Much of Dickens now has this air. One can open today an edition of a novel of his that was bought and first read when things were so in everyday life as they are in the story, though these everyday details are now already as remote from our daily habits as the Elizabethan period. But that is a special modern situation. The anthropologists and folk-lorists do not imagine any conditions of that kind. But if they are dealing with unlettered oral transmission, then they should all the more reflect that in that case they are dealing with items whose primary object was story-building, and whose primary reason for survival was the same. The Frog-King (see p. 136) is not a *Credo*, nor a manual of totem-law: it is a queer tale with a plain moral.

C (page 118)

AS FAR AS my knowledge goes, children who have an early bent for writing have no special inclination to attempt the writing of fairy-stories, unless that has been almost the sole form of literature presented to them; and they fail most markedly when they try. It is not an easy form. If children have any special leaning it is to Beast-fable, which adults often confuse with Fairy-story. The best stories by children that I have seen have been either "realistic" (in intent), or have had as their characters animals and birds, who were in the main the zoomorphic human beings usual in Beast-fable. I imagine that this form is so often adopted principally because it allows a large measure of realism: the representation of domestic events and talk that children really know. The form itself is, however, as a rule, suggested or imposed by adults. It has a curious preponderance in the literature, good and bad, that is nowadays commonly presented to young children: I suppose it is felt to go with "Natural History," semi-scientific books about beasts and birds that are also considered to be proper pabulum for the young. And it is reinforced by the bears and rabbits that seem in recent times almost to have ousted human dolls from the playrooms even of little girls. Children make up sagas, often long and elaborate, about their dolls. If these are shaped like bears, bears will be the characters of the sagas; but they will talk like people.

D (page 121)

I WAS INTRODUCED to zoology and palaeontology ("for children") quite as early as to Faërie. I saw pictures of living beasts and of true (so I was told) prehistoric animals. I liked the "prehistoric" animals best: they had at least lived long ago, and hypothesis (based on somewhat slender evidence) cannot avoid a gleam of fantasy. But I did not like being told that these creatures were "dragons." I can still re-feel the irritation that I felt in childhood at assertions of instructive relatives (or their gift-books) such as these: "snowflakes are fairy jewels," or "are more beautiful than fairy jewels"; "the marvels of the ocean depths are more wonderful than fairyland." Children expect the differences they feel but cannot analyse to be explained by their elders, or at least recognized, not to be ignored or denied. I was keenly alive to the beauty of "Real things," but it seemed to me quibbling to confuse this with the wonder of "Other things." I was eager to study Nature, actually more eager than I was to read most fairy-stories; but I did not want to be quibbled into Science and cheated out of Faërie by people who seemed to assume that by some kind of original sin I should prefer fairy-tales, but according to some kind of new religion I ought to be induced to like science. Nature is no doubt a life-study, or a study for eternity (for those so gifted); but there is a part of man which is not "Nature," and which therefore is not obliged to study it, and is, in fact, wholly unsatisfied by it.

E (page 126)

THERE IS, for example, in surrealism commonly present a morbidity or un-ease very rarely found in literary fantasy. The mind that produced the depicted images may often be suspected to have been in fact already morbid; yet this is not a necessary explanation in all cases. A curious disturbance of the mind is often set up by the very act of drawing things of this kind, a state similar in quality and consciousness of morbidity to the sensations in a high fever, when the mind develops a distressing fecundity and facility in figure-making, seeing forms sinister or grotesque in all visible objects about it.

I am speaking here, of course, of the primary expression of Fantasy in "pictorial" arts, not of "illustrations"; nor of the cinematograph. However good in themselves, illustrations do little good to fairy-stories. The radical distinction between all art (including drama) that offers a *visible* presentation and true literature is that it imposes one visible form. Literature works from mind to mind and is thus more progenitive. It is at once more universal and more poignantly particular. If it speaks of *bread* or *wine* or *stone* or *tree*, it appeals to the whole of these things, to their ideas; yet each hearer will give to them a peculiar personal embodiment in his imagination. Should the story say "he ate bread," the dramatic producer or painter can only show "a piece of bread" according to his taste or fancy, but the hearer of the story will think of bread in general and picture it in some form of his own. If a story says "he climbed a hill and saw a river in the valley below," the illustrator may catch, or nearly catch, his own vision of such a scene; but every hearer of the words will have his own picture, and it will be made out of all the hills and rivers and dales he has ever seen, but specially out of The Hill, The River, The Valley which were for him the first embodiment of the word.

F (page 127)

I AM REFERRING, of course, primarily to fantasy of forms and visible shapes. Drama can be made out of the impact upon human characters of some event of Fantasy, or Faërie, that requires no machinery, or that can be assumed or reported to have happened. But that is not fantasy in dramatic result; the human characters hold the stage and upon them attention is concentrated. Drama of this sort (exemplified by some of Barrie's plays) can be used frivolously, or it can be used for satire, or for conveying such "messages" as the playwright may have in his mind—for men. Drama is anthropocentric. Fairy-story and Fantasy need not be. There are, for instance, many stories telling how men and women have disappeared and spent years among the fairies, without noticing the passage of time, or appearing to grow older. In *Mary Rose* Barrie wrote a play on this theme. No fairy is seen. The cruelly tormented human beings are there all the time. In spite of the sentimental star and the angelic voices at the end (in the printed version) it is a painful play, and can easily be made diabolic: by substituting (as I have seen it done) the elvish call for "angel voices" at the end. The non-dramatic fairy-stories, in so far as they are concerned with the human victims, can also be pathetic or horrible. But they need not be. In most of them the fairies are also there, on equal terms. In some stories they are the real interest. Many of the short folk-lore accounts of such incidents purport to be just pieces of "evidence" about fairies, items in an agelong accumulation of "lore" concerning them and the modes of their existence. The sufferings of human beings who come into contact with them (often enough, wilfully) are thus seen in quite a different perspective. A drama could be made about the sufferings of a victim of research in radiology, but hardly about radium itself. But it is possible to be primarily interested in radium (not radiologists)—or primarily interested in Faërie, not tortured mortals. One interest will produce a scientific book, the other a fairy-story. Drama cannot well cope with either.

G (page 136)

THE ABSENCE OF this sense is a mere hypothesis concerning men of the lost past, whatever wild confusions men of today, degraded or deluded, may suffer. It is just as legitimate an hypothesis, and one more in agreement with what little is recorded concerning the thoughts of men of old on this subject, that this sense was once stronger. That fantasies which blended the human form with animal and vegetable forms, or gave human faculties to beasts, are ancient is, of course, no evidence for confusion at all. It is, if anything, evidence to the contrary. Fantasy does not blur the sharp outlines of the real world; for it depends on them. As far as our western, European, world is concerned, this "sense of separation" has in fact been attacked and weakened in modern times not by fantasy but by scientific theory. Not by stories of centaurs or werewolves or enchanted bears, but by the hypotheses (or dogmatic guesses) of scientific writers who classed Man not only as "an animal"—that correct classification is ancient—but as "only an animal." There has been a consequent distortion of sentiment. The natural love of men not wholly corrupt for beasts, and the human desire to "get inside the skin" of living things, has run riot. We now get men who love animals more than men;

who pity sheep so much that they curse shepherds as wolves; who weep over a slain war-horse and vilify dead soldiers. It is now, not in the days when fairy-stories were begotten, that we get "an absence of the sense of separation."

H (page 137)

THE VERBAL ENDING—usually held to be as typical of the end of fairy-stories as "once upon a time" is of the beginning—"and they lived happily ever after" is an artificial device. It does not deceive anybody. End-phrases of this kind are to be compared to the margins and frames of pictures, and are no more to be thought of as the real end of any particular fragment of the seamless Web of Story than the frame is of the visionary scene, or the casement of the Outer World. These phrases may be plain or elaborate, simple or extravagant, as artificial and as necessary as frames plain, or carved, or gilded. "And if they have not gone away they are there still." "My story is done—see there is a little mouse; anyone who catches it may make himself a fine fur cap of it." "And they lived happily ever after." "And when the wedding was over, they sent me home with little paper shoes on a causeway of pieces of glass."

Endings of this sort suit fairy-stories, because such tales have a greater sense and grasp of the endlessness of the World of Story than most modern "realistic" stories, already hemmed within the narrow confines of their own small time. A sharp cut in the endless tapestry is not unfittingly marked by a formula, even a grotesque or comic one. It was an irresistible development of modern illustration (so largely photographic) that borders should be abandoned and the "picture" end only with the paper. This method may be suitable for photographs; but it is altogether inappropriate for the pictures that illustrate or are inspired by fairy-stories. An enchanted forest requires a margin, even an elaborate border. To print it conterminous with the page, like a "shot" of the Rockies in *Picture Post*, as if it were indeed a "snap" of fairyland or a "sketch by our artist on the spot," is a folly and an abuse.

As for the beginnings of fairy-stories: one can scarcely improve on the formula *Once upon a time*. It has an immediate effect. This effect can be appreciated by reading, for instance, the fairy-story *The Terrible Head* in the *Blue Fairy Book*. It is Andrew Lang's own adaptation of the story of Perseus and the Gorgon. It begins "once upon a time," and it does not name any year or land or person. Now this treatment does something which could be called "turning mythology into fairy-story." I should prefer to say that it turns high fairy-story (for such is the Greek tale) into a particular form that is at present familiar in our land: a nursery or "old wives" form. Namelessness is not a virtue but an accident, and should not have been imitated; for vagueness in this regard is a debasement, a corruption due to forgetfulness and lack of skill. But not so, I think, the timelessness. That beginning is not poverty-stricken but significant. It produces at a stroke the sense of a great uncharted world of time.

LEAF BY NIGGLE

THERE was once a little man called Niggle, who had a long journey to make. He did not want to go, indeed the whole idea was distasteful to him; but he could not get out of it. He knew he would have to start some time, but he did not hurry with his preparations.

Niggle was a painter. Not a very successful one, partly because he had many other things to do. Most of these things he thought were a nuisance; but he did them fairly well, when he could not get out of them: which (in his opinion) was far too often. The laws in his country were rather strict. There were other hindrances, too. For one thing, he was sometimes just idle, and did nothing at all. For another, he was kindhearted, in a way. You know the sort of kind heart: it made him uncomfortable more often than it made him do anything; and even when he did anything, it did not prevent him from grumbling, losing his temper, and swearing (mostly to himself). All the same, it did land him in a good many odd jobs for his neighbour, Mr. Parish, a man with a lame leg. Occasionally he even helped other people from further off, if they came and asked him to. Also, now and again, he remembered his journey, and began to pack a few things in an ineffectual way: at such times he did not paint very much.

He had a number of pictures on hand; most of them were too large and ambitious for his skill. He was the sort of painter who can paint leaves better than trees. He used to spend a long time on a single leaf, trying to catch its shape, and its sheen, and the glistening of dewdrops on its edges. Yet he wanted to paint a whole tree, with all of its leaves in the same style, and all of them different.

There was one picture in particular which bothered him. It had begun with a leaf caught in the wind, and it became a tree; and the tree grew, sending out innumerable branches, and thrusting out the most fantastic roots. Strange birds came and settled on the twigs and had to be attended to. Then all round the Tree, and behind it, through the gaps in the leaves and boughs, a country began to open out; and there were glimpses of a forest marching over the land, and of mountains tipped with snow. Niggle lost interest in his other pictures; or else he took them and tacked them on to the edges of his great picture. Soon the canvas became so large that he had to get a ladder; and he ran up and down it, putting in a touch here, and rubbing out a patch there. When people came to call, he seemed polite enough, though he fiddled a little with the pencils on his desk. He listened to what they said, but underneath he was thinking all the time about his big canvas, in the tall shed that had been built for it out in his garden (on a plot where once he had grown potatoes).

He could not get rid of his kind heart. "I wish I was more strong-minded!" he sometimes said to himself, meaning that he wished other people's troubles did not make him feel uncomfortable. But for a long time he was not seriously perturbed. "At any rate, I shall get this one picture done, my real picture, before I have to go on that wretched journey," he used to say. Yet he was beginning to see that he could not put off his start indefinitely. The picture would have to stop just growing and get finished.

One day, Niggle stood a little way off from his picture and considered it with unusual attention and detachment. He could not make up his mind what he thought about it, and wished he had some friend who would tell him what to think. Actually it seemed to him wholly unsatisfactory, and yet very lovely, the only really beautiful picture in the world. What he would have liked at that moment would have been to see himself walk in, and slap him on the back, and say (with obvious sincerity): "Absolutely magnificent! I see exactly what you are getting at. Do get on with it, and don't bother about anything else! We will arrange for a public pension, so that you need not."

However, there was no public pension. And one thing he could see: it would need some concentration, some *work*, hard uninterrupted work, to finish the picture, even at its present size. He rolled up his sleeves, and began to concentrate. He tried for several days not to bother about other things. But there came a tremendous crop of interruptions. Things went wrong in his house; he had to go and serve on a jury in the town; a distant friend fell ill; Mr. Parish was laid up with lumbago; and visitors kept on coming. It was springtime, and they wanted a free tea in the country: Niggle lived in a pleasant little house, miles away from the town. He cursed them in his heart, but he could not deny that he had invited them himself, away back in the winter, when he had not thought it an "interruption" to visit the shops and have tea with acquaintances in the town. He tried to harden his heart; but it was not a success. There were many things that he had not the face to say *no* to, whether he thought them duties or not; and there were some things he was compelled to do, whatever he thought. Some of his visitors hinted that his garden was rather neglected, and that he might get a visit from an Inspector. Very few of them knew about his picture, of course; but if they had known, it would not have made much difference. I doubt if they would have thought that it mattered much. I dare say it was not really a very good picture, though it may have had some good passages. The Tree, at any rate, was curious. Quite unique in its way. So was Niggle; though he was also a very ordinary and rather silly little man.

At length Niggle's time became really precious. His acquaintances in the distant town began to remember that the little man had got to make a troublesome journey, and some began to calculate how long at the latest he could put off starting. They wondered who would take his house, and if the garden would be better kept.

The autumn came, very wet and windy. The little painter was in his shed. He was up on the ladder, trying to catch the gleam of the westering sun on the peak of a snow-mountain, which he had glimpsed just to the left of the leafy tip of one of the Tree's branches. He knew that he would have to be leaving soon: perhaps early next year. He could only just get the picture finished, and only so so, at that: there were some corners where he would not have time now to do more than hint at what he wanted.

There was a knock on the door. "Come in!" he said sharply, and climbed down the ladder. He stood on the floor twiddling his brush. It was his neighbour, Parish: his only real neighbour, all other folk lived a long way off. Still, he did not like the man very much: partly because he was so often in trouble and in need of help; and also because he did not care about painting, but was very critical about gardening. When Parish looked at Niggle's garden (which was often) he saw mostly weeds; and when he looked at Niggle's pictures (which was seldom) he saw only green and grey patches and black lines, which seemed to him nonsensical. He did not mind mentioning the weeds (a neighbourly duty), but he refrained from giving any opinion of the pictures. He thought this was very kind, and he did not realize that, even if it was kind, it was not kind enough. Help with the weeds (and perhaps praise for the pictures) would have been better.

"Well, Parish, what is it?" said Niggle.

"I oughtn't to interrupt you, I know," said Parish (without a glance at the picture). "You are very busy, I'm sure."

Niggle had meant to say something like that himself, but he had missed his chance. All he said was: "Yes."

"But I have no one else to turn to," said Parish.

"Quite so," said Niggle with a sigh: one of those sighs that are a private comment, but which are not made quite inaudible. "What can I do for you?"

"My wife has been ill for some days, and I am getting worried," said Parish. "And the wind has blown half the tiles off my roof, and water is pouring into the bedroom. I think I ought to get the doctor. And the builders, too, only they take so long to come. I was wondering if you had any wood and canvas you could spare, just to patch me up and see me through for a day or two." Now he did look at the picture.

"Dear, dear!" said Niggle. "You *are* unlucky. I hope it is no more than a cold that your wife has got. I'll come round presently, and help you move the patient downstairs."

"Thank you very much," said Parish, rather coolly. "But it is not a cold, it is a fever. I should not have bothered you for a cold. And my wife is in bed downstairs already. I can't get up and down with trays, not with my leg. But I see you are busy. Sorry to have troubled you. I had rather hoped you might have been able to spare the time to go for the doctor, seeing how I'm placed; and the builder too, if you really have no canvas you can spare."

"Of course," said Niggle; though other words were in his heart, which at the moment was merely soft without feeling at all kind. "I could go. I'll go, if you are really worried."

"I am worried, very worried. I wish I was not lame," said Parish.

So Niggle went. You see, it was awkward. Parish was his neighbour, and everyone else a long way off. Niggle had a bicycle, and Parish had not, and could not ride one. Parish had a lame leg, a genuine lame leg which gave him a good deal of pain: that had to be remembered, as well as his sour expression and whining voice. Of course, Niggle had a picture and barely time to finish it. But it seemed that this was a thing that Parish had to reckon with and not Niggle. Parish, however, did not reckon with pictures; and Niggle could not alter that. "Curse it!" he said to himself, as he got out his bicycle.

It was wet and windy, and daylight was waning. "No more work for me today!" thought Niggle, and all the time that he was riding, he was either swearing to himself, or imagining the strokes of his brush on the mountain, and on the spray of leaves beside it, that he had first imagined in the spring. His fingers twitched on the handlebars. Now he was out of the shed, he saw exactly the way in which to treat that shining spray which framed the distant vision of the mountain. But he had a sinking feeling in his heart, a sort of fear that he would never now get a chance to try it out.

Niggle found the doctor, and he left a note at the builder's. The office was shut, and the builder had gone home to his fireside. Niggle got soaked to the skin, and caught a chill himself. The doctor did not set out as promptly as Niggle had done. He arrived next day, which was quite convenient for him, as by that time there were two patients to deal with, in neighbouring houses. Niggle was in bed, with a high temperature, and marvellous patterns of leaves and involved branches forming in his head and on the ceiling. It did not comfort him to learn that Mrs. Parish had only had a cold, and was getting up. He turned his face to the wall and buried himself in leaves.

He remained in bed some time. The wind went on blowing. It took away a good many more of Parish's tiles, and some of Niggle's as well: his own roof began to leak. The builder did not come. Niggle did not care; not for a day or two. Then he crawled out to look for some food (Niggle had no wife). Parish did not come round: the rain had got into his leg and made it ache; and his wife was busy mopping up water, and wondering if "that Mr. Niggle" had forgotten to call at the builder's. Had she seen any chance of borrowing anything useful, she would have sent Parish round, leg or no leg; but she did not, so Niggle was left to himself.

At the end of a week or so Niggle tottered out to his shed again. He tried to climb the ladder, but it made his head giddy. He sat and looked at the picture, but there were no patterns of leaves or visions of mountains in his mind that day. He could have painted a far-off view of a sandy desert, but he had not the energy.

Next day he felt a good deal better. He climbed the ladder, and began to paint. He had just begun to get into it again, when there came a knock on the door.

"Damn!" said Niggle. But he might just as well have said "Come in!" politely, for the door opened all the same. This time a very tall man came in, a total stranger.

"This is a private studio," said Niggle. "I am busy. Go away!"

"I am an Inspector of Houses," said the man, holding up his appointment-card, so that Niggle on his ladder could see it.

"Oh!" he said.

"Your neighbour's house is not satisfactory at all," said the Inspector.

"I know," said Niggle. "I took a note to the builders a long time ago, but they have never come. Then I have been ill."

"I see," said the Inspector. "But you are not ill now."

"But I'm not a builder. Parish ought to make a complaint to the Town Council, and get help from the Emergency Service."

"They are busy with worse damage than any up here," said the Inspector. "There has been a flood in the valley, and many families are homeless. You should have helped your neighbour to make temporary repairs and prevent the damage from getting more costly to mend than necessary. That is the law. There is plenty of material here: canvas, wood, waterproof paint."

"Where?" asked Niggle indignantly.

"There!" said the Inspector, pointing to the picture.

"My picture!" exclaimed Niggle.

"I dare say it is," said the Inspector. "But houses come first. That is the law."

"But I can't . . ." Niggle said no more, for at that moment another man came in. Very much like the Inspector he was, almost his double: tall, dressed all in black.

"Come along!" he said. "I am the Driver."

Niggle stumbled down from the ladder. His fever seemed to have come on again, and his head was swimming; he felt cold all over.

"Driver? Driver?" he chattered. "Driver of what?"

"You, and your carriage," said the man. "The carriage was ordered long ago. It has come at last. It's waiting. You start today on your journey, you know."

"There now!" said the Inspector. "You'll have to go; but it's a bad way to start on your journey, leaving your jobs undone. Still, we can at least make some use of this canvas now."

"Oh, dear!" said poor Niggle, beginning to weep. "And it's not, not even finished!"

"Not finished?" said the Driver. "Well, it's finished with, as far as you're concerned, at any rate. Come along!"

Niggle went, quite quietly. The Driver gave him no time to pack, saying that he ought to have done that before, and they would miss the train; so all Niggle could do was to grab a little bag in the hall. He found that it contained only a paint-box and a small book of his own sketches: neither food nor clothes. They caught the train all right. Niggle was feeling very tired and sleepy; he was hardly aware of what was going on when they bundled him into his compartment. He did not care much: he had forgotten where he was supposed to be going, or what he was going for. The train ran almost at once into a dark tunnel.

Niggle woke up in a very large, dim railway station. A Porter went along the platform shouting, but he was not shouting the name of the place; he was shouting *Niggle!*

Niggle got out in a hurry, and found that he had left his little bag behind. He turned back, but the train had gone away.

"Ah, there you are!" said the Porter. "This way! What! No luggage? You will have to go to the Workhouse."

Niggle felt very ill, and fainted on the platform. They put him in an ambulance and took him to the Workhouse Infirmary.

He did not like the treatment at all. The medicine they gave him was bitter. The officials and attendants were unfriendly, silent, and strict; and he never saw anyone else, except a very severe doctor, who visited him occasionally. It was more like being in a prison than in a hospital. He had to work hard, at stated hours: at digging, carpentry, and painting bare boards all one plain colour. He was never allowed outside, and the windows all looked inwards. They kept him in the dark for hours at a stretch, "to do some thinking," they said. He lost count of time. He did not even begin to feel better, not if that could be judged by whether he felt any pleasure in doing anything. He did not, not even in getting into bed.

At first, during the first century or so (I am merely giving his impressions), he used to worry aimlessly about the past. One thing he kept on repeating to himself, as he lay in the dark: "I wish I had called on Parish the first morning after the high winds began. I meant to. The first loose tiles would have been easy to fix. Then Mrs. Parish might never have caught cold. Then I should not have caught cold either. Then I should have had a week longer." But in time he forgot what it was that he had wanted a week longer for. If he worried at all after that, it was about his jobs in the hospital. He planned them out, thinking how quickly he could stop that board creaking, or rehang that door, or mend that table-leg. Probably he really became rather useful, though no one ever told him so. But that, of course, cannot have been the reason why they kept the poor little man so long. They may have been waiting for him to get better, and judging "better" by some odd medical standard of their own.

At any rate, poor Niggle got no pleasure out of life, not what he had been used to call pleasure. He was certainly not amused. But it could not be denied that he began to have a feeling of—well, satisfaction: bread rather than jam. He could take up a task the moment one bell rang, and lay it aside promptly the moment the next one went, all tidy and ready to be continued at the right time. He got through quite a lot in a day, now; he finished small things off neatly. He had no "time of his own" (except alone in his bed-cell), and yet he was becoming master of his time; he began to know just what he could do with it. There was no sense of rush. He was quieter inside now, and at resting-time he could really rest.

Then suddenly they changed all his hours; they hardly let him go to bed at all; they took him off carpentry altogether and kept him at plain digging, day after day. He took it fairly well. It was a long while before he even began to grope in the back of his mind for the curses that he had practically forgotten. He went on digging, till his back seemed broken, his hands were raw, and he felt that he could not manage another spadeful. Nobody thanked him. But the doctor came and looked at him.

"Knock off!" he said. "Complete rest—in the dark."

Niggle was lying in the dark, resting completely; so that, as he had not been either feeling or thinking at all, he might have been lying there for hours or for years, as far as he could tell. But now he heard Voices: not voices that he had ever heard before. There seemed to be a Medical Board, or perhaps a Court of Inquiry, going on close at hand, in an adjoining room with the door open, possibly, though he could not see any light.

"Now the Niggle case," said a Voice, a severe voice, more severe than the doctor's.

"What was the matter with him?" said a Second Voice, a voice that you might have called gentle, though it was not soft—it was a voice of authority, and sounded at once hopeful and sad. "What was the matter with Niggle? His heart was in the right place."

"Yes, but it did not function properly," said the First Voice. "And his head was not screwed on tight enough: he hardly ever thought at all. Look at the time he wasted, not even amusing himself! He never got ready for his journey. He was moderately well-off, and yet he arrived here almost destitute, and had to be put in the paupers' wing. A bad case, I am afraid. I think he should stay some time yet."

"It would not do him any harm, perhaps," said the Second Voice. "But, of course, he is only a little man. He was never meant to be anything very much; and he was never very strong. Let us look at the Records. Yes. There are some favourable points, you know."

"Perhaps," said the First Voice; "but very few that will really bear examination."

"Well," said the Second Voice, "there are these. He was a painter by nature. In a minor way, of course; still, a Leaf by Niggle has a charm of its own. He took a great deal of pains with leaves, just for their own sake. But he never thought that that made him important. There is no note in the Records of his pretending, even to himself, that it excused his neglect of things ordered by the law."

"Then he should not have neglected so many," said the First Voice.

"All the same, he did answer a good many Calls."

"A small percentage, mostly of the easier sort, and he called those Interruptions. The Records are full of the word, together with a lot of complaints and silly imprecations."

"True; but they looked like interruptions to him, of course, poor little man. And there is this: he never expected any Return, as so many of his sort call it. There is the Parish case, the one that came in later. He was Niggle's neighbour, never did a stroke for him, and seldom showed any gratitude at all. But there is no note in the Records that Niggle expected Parish's gratitude; he does not seem to have thought about it."

"Yes, that is a point," said the First Voice; "but rather small. I think you will find Niggle often merely forgot. Things he had to do for Parish he put out of his mind as a nuisance he had done with."

"Still, there is this last report," said the Second Voice, "that wet bicycle-ride. I rather lay stress on that. It seems plain that this was a genuine sacrifice: Niggle guessed that he was throwing away his last chance with his picture, and he guessed, too, that Parish was worrying unnecessarily."

"I think you put it too strongly," said the First Voice. "But you have the last word. It is your task, of course, to put the best interpretation on the facts. Sometimes they will bear it. What do you propose?"

"I think it is a case for a little gentle treatment now," said the Second Voice.

Niggle thought that he had never heard anything so generous as that Voice. It made Gentle Treatment sound like a load of rich gifts, and the summons to a King's feast. Then suddenly Niggle felt ashamed. To hear that he was considered a case for Gentle Treatment overwhelmed him, and made him blush in the dark. It was like being publicly praised, when you and all the audience knew that the praise was not deserved. Niggle hid his blushes in the rough blanket.

There was a silence. Then the First Voice spoke to Niggle, quite close. "You have been listening," it said.

"Yes," said Niggle.

"Well, what have you to say?"

"Could you tell me about Parish?" said Niggle. "I should like to see him again. I hope he is not very ill? Can you cure his leg? It used to give him a wretched time. And please don't worry about him and me. He was a very good neighbour, and let me have excellent potatoes very cheap, which saved me a lot of time."

"Did he?" said the First Voice. "I am glad to hear it."

There was another silence. Niggle heard the Voices receding. "Well, I agree," he heard the First Voice say in the distance. "Let him go on to the next stage. Tomorrow, if you like."

Niggle woke up to find that his blinds were drawn, and his little cell was full of sunshine. He got up, and found that some comfortable clothes had been put out for him, not hospital uniform. After breakfast the doctor treated his sore hands, putting some salve on them that healed them at once. He gave Niggle some good advice, and a bottle of tonic (in case he needed it). In the middle of the morning they gave Niggle a biscuit and a glass of wine; and then they gave him a ticket.

"You can go to the railway station now," said the doctor. "The Porter will look after you. Good-bye."

Niggle slipped out of the main door, and blinked a little. The sun was very bright. Also he had expected to walk out into a large town, to match the size of the station; but he did not. He was on the top of a hill, green, bare, swept by a keen invigorating wind. Nobody else was about. Away down under the hill he could see the roof of the station shining.

He walked downhill to the station briskly, but without hurry. The Porter spotted him at once.

"This way!" he said, and led Niggle to a bay, in which there was a very pleasant little local train standing: one coach, and a small engine, both very bright, clean, and newly painted. It looked as if this was their first run. Even the track that lay in front of the engine looked new: the rails shone, the chairs were painted green, and the sleepers gave off a delicious smell of fresh tar in the warm sunshine. The coach was empty.

"Where does this train go, Porter?" asked Niggle.

"I don't think they have fixed its name yet," said the Porter. "But you'll find it all right." He shut the door.

The train moved off at once. Niggle lay back in his seat. The little engine puffed along in a deep cutting with high green banks, roofed with blue sky. It did not seem very long before the engine gave a whistle, the brakes were put on, and the train stopped. There was no station, and no signboard, only a flight of steps up the green embankment. At the top of the steps there was a wicket-gate in a trim hedge. By the gate stood his bicycle; at least, it looked like his, and there was a yellow label tied to the bars with NIGGLE written on it in large black letters.

Niggle pushed open the gate, jumped on the bicycle, and went bowling downhill in the spring sunshine. Before long he found that the path on which he had started had disappeared, and the bicycle was rolling along over a marvellous turf. It was green and close; and yet he could see every blade distinctly. He seemed to remember having seen or dreamed of that sweep of grass somewhere or other. The curves of the land were familiar somehow. Yes: the ground was becoming level, as it should, and now, of course, it was beginning to rise again. A great green shadow came between him and the sun. Niggle looked up, and fell off his bicycle.

Before him stood the Tree, his Tree, finished. If you could say that of a Tree that was alive, its leaves opening, its branches growing and bending in the wind that Niggle had so often felt or guessed, and had so often failed to catch. He gazed at the Tree, and slowly he lifted his arms and opened them wide.

"It's a gift!" he said. He was referring to his art, and also to the result; but he was using the word quite literally.

He went on looking at the Tree. All the leaves he had ever laboured at were there, as he had imagined them rather than as he had made them; and there were others that had only budded in his mind, and many that might have budded, if only he had had time. Nothing was written on them, they were just exquisite leaves, yet they were dated as clear as a calendar. Some of the most beautiful—and the most characteristic, the most perfect examples of the Niggle style—were seen to have been produced in collaboration with Mr. Parish: there was no other way of putting it.

The birds were building in the Tree. Astonishing birds: how they sang! They were mating, hatching, growing wings, and flying away singing into the Forest, even while he looked at them. For now he saw that the Forest was there too, opening out on either side, and marching away into the distance. The Mountains were glimmering far away.

After a time Niggle turned towards the Forest. Not because he was tired of the Tree, but he seemed to have got it all clear in his mind now, and was aware of it, and of its growth, even when he was not looking at it. As he walked away, he discovered an odd thing: the Forest, of course, was a distant Forest, yet he could approach it, even enter it, without its losing that particular charm. He had never before been able to walk into the distance without turning it into mere surroundings. It really added a considerable attraction to walking in the country, because, as you walked, new distances opened out; so that you now had doubled, treble, and quadruple distances, doubly, trebly, and quadruply enchanting. You could go on and on, and have a whole country in a garden, or in a picture (if you preferred to call it that). You could go on and on, but not perhaps for ever. There were the Mountains in the background. They did get nearer, very slowly. They did not seem to belong to the picture, or only as a link to something else, a glimpse through the trees of something different, a further stage: another picture.

Niggle walked about, but he was not merely pottering. He was looking round carefully. The Tree was finished, though not finished with—"Just the other way about to what it used to be," he thought—but in the Forest there were a number of inconclusive regions, that still needed work and thought. Nothing needed altering any longer, nothing was wrong, as far as it had gone, but it needed continuing up to a definite point. Niggle saw the point precisely, in each case.

He sat down under a very beautiful distant tree—a variation of the Great Tree, but quite individual, or it would be with a little more attention—and he considered where to begin work, and where to end it, and how much time was required. He could not quite work out his scheme.

"Of course!" he said. "What I need is Parish. There are lots of things about earth, plants, and trees that he knows and I don't. This place cannot be left just as my private park. I need help and advice: I ought to have got it sooner."

He got up and walked to the place where he had decided to begin work. He took off his coat. Then, down in a little sheltered hollow hidden from a further view, he saw a man looking round rather bewildered. He was leaning on a spade, but plainly did not know what to do. Niggle hailed him. "Parish!" he called.

Parish shouldered his spade and came up to him. He still limped a little. They did not speak, just nodded as they used to do, passing in the lane; but now they walked about together, arm in arm. Without talking, Niggle and Parish agreed exactly where to make the small house and garden, which seemed to be required.

As they worked together, it became plain that Niggle was now the better of the two at ordering his time and getting things done. Oddly enough, it was Niggle who became most absorbed in building and gardening, while Parish often wandered about looking at trees, and especially at the Tree.

One day Niggle was busy planting a quickset hedge, and Parish was lying on the grass near by, looking attentively at a beautiful and shapely little yellow flower growing in the green turf. Niggle had put a lot of them among the roots of his Tree long ago. Suddenly Parish looked up: his face was glistening in the sun, and he was smiling.

"This is grand!" he said. "I oughtn't to be here, really. Thank you for putting in a word for me."

"Nonsense," said Niggle. "I don't remember what I said, but anyway it was not nearly enough."

"Oh yes, it was," said Parish. "It got me out a lot sooner. That Second Voice, you know: he had me sent here; he said you had asked to see me. I owe it to you."

"No. You owe it to the Second Voice," said Niggle. "We both do."

They went on living and working together: I do not know how long. It is no use denying that at first they occasionally disagreed, especially when they got tired. For at first they did sometimes get tired. They found that they had both been provided with tonics. Each bottle had the same label: *A few drops to be taken in water from the Spring, before resting*.

They found the Spring in the heart of the Forest; only once long ago had Niggle imagined it, but he had never drawn it. Now he perceived that it was the source of the lake that glimmered, far away and the nourishment of all that grew in the country. The few drops made the water astringent, rather bitter, but invigorating; and it cleared the head. After drinking they rested alone; and then they got up again and things went on merrily. At such times Niggle would think of wonderful new flowers and plants, and Parish always knew exactly how to set them and where they would do best. Long before the tonics were finished they had ceased to need them. Parish lost his limp.

As their work drew to an end they allowed themselves more and more time for walking about, looking at the trees, and the flowers, and the lights and shapes, and the lie of the land. Sometimes they sang together; but Niggle found that he was now beginning to turn his eyes, more and more often, towards the Mountains.

The time came when the house in the hollow, the garden, the grass, the forest, the lake, and all the country was nearly complete, in its own proper fashion. The Great Tree was in full blossom.

"We shall finish this evening," said Parish one day. "After that we will go for a really long walk."

They set out next day, and they walked until they came right through the distances to the Edge. It was not visible, of course: there was no line, or fence, or wall; but they knew that they had come to the margin of that country. They saw a man, he looked like a shepherd; he was walking towards them, down the grass-slopes that led up into the Mountains.

"Do you want a guide?" he asked. "Do you want to go on?"

For a moment a shadow fell between Niggle and Parish, for Niggle knew that he did now want to go on, and (in a sense) ought to go on; but Parish did not want to go on, and was not yet ready to go.

"I must wait for my wife," said Parish to Niggle. "She'd be lonely. I rather gathered that they would send her after me, some time or other, when she was ready, and when I had got things ready for her. The house is finished now, as well as we could make it; but I should like to show it to her. She'll be able to make it better, I expect: more homely. I hope she'll like this country, too." He turned to the shepherd. "Are you a guide?" he asked. "Could you tell me the name of this country?"

"Don't you know?" said the man. "It is Niggle's Country. It is Niggle's Picture, or most of it: a little of it is now Parish's Garden."

"Niggle's Picture!" said Parish in astonishment. "Did *you* think of all this, Niggle? I never knew you were so clever. Why didn't you tell me?"

"He tried to tell you long ago," said the man; "but you would not look. He had only got canvas and paint in those days, and you wanted to mend your roof with them. This is what you and your wife used to call Niggle's Nonsense, or That Daubing."

"But it did not look like this then, not *real*," said Parish.

"No, it was only a glimpse then," said the man; "but you might have caught the glimpse, if you had ever thought it worth while to try."

"I did not give you much chance," said Niggle. "I never tried to explain. I used to call you Old Earth-grubber. But what does it matter? We have lived and worked together now. Things might have been different, but they could not have been better. All the same, I am afraid I shall have to be going on. We shall meet again, I expect: there must be many more things we can do together. Good-bye!" He shook Parish's hand warmly: a good, firm, honest hand it seemed. He turned and looked back for a moment. The blossom on the Great Tree was shining like flame. All the birds were flying in the air and singing. Then he smiled, and nodded to Parish, and went off with the shepherd.

He was going to learn about sheep, and the high pasturages, and look at a wider sky, and walk ever further and further towards the Mountains, always uphill. Beyond that I cannot guess what became of him. Even little Niggle in his old home could glimpse the Mountains far away, and they got into the borders of his picture; but what they are really like, and what lies beyond them, only those can say who have climbed them.

* * *

"I think he was a silly little man," said Councillor Tompkins. "Worthless, in fact; no use to Society at all."

"Oh, I don't know," said Atkins, who was nobody of importance, just a schoolmaster. "I am not so sure: it depends on what you mean by *use*."

"No practical or economic use," said Tompkins. "I dare say he could have been made into a serviceable cog of some sort, if you schoolmasters knew your business. But you don't, and so we get useless people of his sort. If I ran this country I should put him and his like to some job that they're fit for, washing dishes in a communal kitchen or something, and I should see that they did it properly. Or I would put them away. I should have put *him* away long ago."

"Put him away? You mean you'd have made him start on the journey before his time?"

"Yes, if you must use that meaningless old expression. Push him through the tunnel into the great Rubbish Heap: that's what I mean."

"Then you don't think painting is worth anything, not worth preserving, or improving, or even making use of?"

"Of course, painting has uses," said Tompkins. "But you couldn't make use of his painting. There is plenty of scope for bold young men not afraid of new ideas and new methods. None for this old-fashioned stuff. Private day-dreaming. He could not have designed a telling poster to save his life. Always fiddling with leaves and flowers. I asked him why, once. He said he thought they were pretty! Can you believe it? He said *pretty!* "What, digestive and genital organs of plants?" I said to him; and he had nothing to answer. Silly footler."

"Footler," sighed Atkins. "Yes, poor little man, he never finished anything. Ah well, his canvases have been put to 'better uses,' since he went. But I am not sure, Tompkins. You remember that large one, the one they used to patch the damaged house next door to his, after the gales and floods? I found a corner of it torn off, lying in a field. It was damaged, but legible: a mountain-peak and a spray of leaves. I can't get it out of my mind."

"Out of your what?" said Tompkins.

"Who are you two talking about?" said Perkins, intervening in the cause of peace: Atkins had flushed rather red.

"The name's not worth repeating," said Tompkins. "I don't know why we are talking about him at all. He did not live in town."

"No," said Atkins; "but you had your eye on his house, all the same. That is why you used to go and call, and sneer at him while drinking his tea. Well, you've got his house now, as well as the one in town, so you need not grudge him his name. We were talking about Niggle, if you want to know, Perkins."

"Oh, poor little Niggle!" said Perkins. "Never knew he painted."

That was probably the last time Niggle's name ever came up in conversation. However, Atkins preserved the odd corner. Most of it crumbled; but one beautiful leaf remained intact. Atkins had it framed. Later he left it to the Town Museum, and for a long while "Leaf: by Niggle" hung there in a recess, and was noticed by a few eyes. But eventually the Museum was burnt down, and the leaf, and Niggle, were entirely forgotten in his old country.

"It is proving very useful indeed," said the Second Voice. "As a holiday, and a refreshment. It is splendid for convalescence; and not only for that, for many it is the best introduction to the Mountains. It works wonders in some cases. I am sending more and more there. They seldom have to come back."

"No, that is so," said the First Voice. "I think we shall have to give the region a name. What do you propose?"

"The Porter settled that some time ago," said the Second Voice. "*Train for Niggle's Parish in the bay:* he has shouted that for a long while now. Niggle's Parish. I sent a message to both of them to tell them."

"What did they say?"

"They both laughed. Laughed—the Mountains rang with it!"

THE ADVENTURES OF TOM BOMBADIL

and other verses
from The Red Book

WITH ILLUSTRATIONS BY

PAULINE BAYNES

PREFACE

The Red Book contains a large number of verses. A few are included in the narrative of the *Downfall of the Lord of the Rings*, or in the attached stories and chronicles; many more are found on loose leaves, while some are written carelessly in margins and blank spaces. Of the last sort most are nonsense, now often unintelligible even when legible, or half-remembered fragments. From these marginalia are drawn Nos. 4, 11, 13; though a better example of their general character would be the scribble, on the page recording Bilbo's *When winter first begins to bite:*

The wind so whirled a weathercock
He could not hold his tail up;
The frost so nipped a throstlecock
He could not snap a snail up.
'My case is hard' the throstle cried,
And 'All is vane' the cock replied;
And so they set their wail up.

The present selection is taken from the older pieces, mainly concerned with legends and jests of the Shire at the end of the Third Age, that appear to have been made by Hobbits, especially by Bilbo and his friends, or their immediate descendants. Their authorship is, however, seldom indicated. Those outside the narratives are in various hands, and were probably written down from oral tradition.

In the Red Book it is said that No. 5 was made by Bilbo, and No. 7 by Sam Gamgee. No. 8 is marked SG, and the ascription may be accepted. No. 12 is also marked SG, though at most Sam can only have touched up an older piece of the comic bestiary lore of which Hobbits appear to have been fond. In *The Lord of the Rings* Sam stated that No. 10 was traditional in the Shire.

No. 3 is an example of another kind which seems to have amused Hobbits: a rhyme or story which returns to its own beginning, and so may be recited until the hearers revolt. Several specimens are found in the Red Book, but the others are simple and crude. No. 3 is much the longest and most elaborate. It was evidently made by Bilbo. This is indicated by its obvious relationship to the long poem recited by Bilbo, as his own composition, in the house of Elrond. In origin a 'nonsense rhyme', it is in the Rivendell version found transformed and applied, somewhat incongruously, to the High-elvish and Númenorean legends of Eärendil. Probably because Bilbo invented its metrical devices and was proud of them. They do not appear in other pieces in the Red Book. The older form, here given, must belong to the early days after Bilbo's return from his journey. Though the influence of Elvish traditions is seen, they are not seriously treated, and the names used (*Derrilyn, Thellamie, Belmarie, Aerie*) are mere inventions in the Elvish style, and are not in fact Elvish at all.

The influence of the events at the end of the Third Age, and the widening of the horizons of the Shire by contact with Rivendell and Gondor, is to be seen in other pieces. No. 6, though here placed next to Bilbo's Man-in-the-Moon rhyme, and the last item, No. 16, must be derived ultimately from Gondor. They are evidently based on the traditions of Men, living in shorelands and familiar with rivers running into the Sea. No. 6 actually mentions *Belfalas* (the windy bay of Bel), and the Sea-ward Tower, *Tirith Aear*, of Dol Amroth. No. 16 mentions the Seven Rivers[1] that flowed into the Sea in the South Kingdom, and uses the Gondorian name, of High-elvish form, *Fíriel*, mortal woman.[2] In the Langstrand and Dol Amroth there were many traditions of the ancient Elvish dwellings, and of the haven at the mouth of the Morthond from which 'westward ships' had sailed as far back as the fall of Eregion in the Second Age. These two pieces, therefore, are only re-handlings of Southern matter, though this may have reached Bilbo by way of Rivendell. No. 14 also depends on the lore of Rivendell, Elvish and Númenorean, concerning the heroic days at the end of the First Age; it seems to contain echoes of the Númenorean tale of Túrin and Mim the Dwarf.

[1]*Lefnui, Morthond-Kiril-Ringló, Gilrain-Sernui*, and *Anduin*.

[2]The name was borne by a princess of Gondor, through whom Aragorn claimed descent from the Southern line. It was also the name of a daughter of Elanor, daughter of Sam, but her name, if connected with the rhyme, must be derived from it; it could not have arisen in Westmarch.

Nos. 1 and 2 evidently come from the Buckland. They show more knowledge of that country, and of the Dingle, the wooded valley of the Withywindle,[1] than any Hobbits west of the Marish were likely to possess. They also show that the Bucklanders knew Bombadil,[2] though, no doubt, they had as little understanding of his powers as the Shire-folk had of Gandalf's: both were regarded as benevolent persons, mysterious maybe and unpredictable but nonetheless comic. No. 1 is the earlier piece, and is made up of various hobbit-versions of legends concerning Bombadil. No. 2 uses similar traditions, though Tom's raillery is here turned in jest upon his friends, who treat it with amusement (tinged with fear); but it was probably composed much later and after the visit of Frodo and his companions to the house of Bombadil.

The verses, of hobbit origin, here presented have generally two features in common. They are fond of strange words, and of rhyming and metrical tricks—in their simplicity Hobbits evidently regarded such things as virtues or graces, though they were, no doubt, mere imitations of Elvish practices. They are also, at least on the surface, lighthearted or frivolous, though sometimes one may uneasily suspect that more is meant than meets the ear. No. 15, certainly of hobbit origin, is an exception. It is the latest piece and belongs to the Fourth Age; but it is included here, because a hand has scrawled at its head *Frodos Dreme*. That is remarkable, and though the piece is most unlikely to have been written by Frodo himself, the title shows that it was associated with the dark and despairing dreams which visited him in March and October during his last three years. But there were certainly other traditions concerning Hobbits that were taken by the 'wandering-madness', and if they ever returned, were afterwards queer and uncommunicable. The thought of the Sea was ever-present in the background of hobbit imagination; but fear of it and distrust of all Elvish lore, was the prevailing mood in the Shire at the end of the Third Age, and that mood was certainly not entirely dispelled by the events and changes with which that Age ended.

[1]*Grindwall* was a small hythe on the north bank of the Withywindle; it was outside the Hay, and so was well watched and protected by a *grind* or fence extended into the water. *Breredon* (Briar Hill) was a little village on rising ground behind the hythe, in the narrow tongue between the end of the High Hay and the Brandywine. At the *Mithe*, the outflow of the Shirebourn, was a landing-stage, from which a lane ran to Deephallow and so on to the Causeway road that went through Rushey and Stock.

[2]Indeed they probably gave him this name (it is Bucklandish in form) to add to his many older ones.

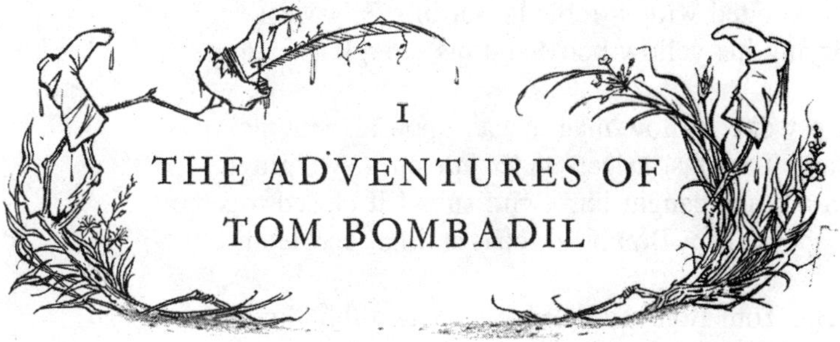

I
THE ADVENTURES OF TOM BOMBADIL

Old Tom Bombadil was a merry fellow;
bright blue his jacket was and his boots were yellow,
green were his girdle and his breeches all of leather;
he wore in his tall hat a swan-wing feather.
He lived up under Hill, where the Withywindle
ran from a grassy well down into the dingle.

Old Tom in summertime walked about the meadows
gathering the buttercups, running after shadows,
tickling the bumblebees that buzzed among the flowers,
sitting by the waterside for hours upon hours.

There his beard dangled long down into the water:
up came Goldberry, the River-woman's daughter;
pulled Tom's hanging hair. In he went a-wallowing
under the water-lilies, bubbling and a-swallowing.

'Hey, Tom Bombadil! Whither are you going?'
said fair Goldberry. 'Bubbles you are blowing,
frightening the finny fish and the brown water-rat,
startling the dabchicks, and drowning your feather-hat!'

'You bring it back again, there's a pretty maiden!'
said Tom Bombadil. 'I do not care for wading.
Go down! Sleep again where the pools are shady
far below willow-roots, little water-lady!'

Back to her mother's house in the deepest hollow
swam young Goldberry. But Tom, he would not follow;

on knotted willow-roots he sat in sunny weather,
drying his yellow boots and his draggled feather.

Up woke Willow-man, began upon his singing,
sang Tom fast asleep under branches swinging;
in a crack caught him tight: snick! it closed together,
trapped Tom Bombadil, coat and hat and feather.

'Ha, Tom Bombadil! What be you a-thinking,
peeping inside my tree, watching me a-drinking
deep in my wooden house, tickling me with feather,
dripping wet down my face like a rainy weather?'

'You let me out again, Old Man Willow!
I am stiff lying here; they're no sort of pillow,
your hard crooked roots. Drink your river-water!
Go back to sleep again like the River-daughter!'

Willow-man let him loose when he heard him speaking;
locked fast his wooden house, muttering and creaking,
whispering inside the tree. Out from willow-dingle
Tom went walking on up the Withywindle.
Under the forest-eaves he sat a while a-listening:
on the boughs piping birds were chirruping and whistling.
Butterflies about his head went quivering and winking,
until grey clouds came up, as the sun was sinking.

Then Tom hurried on. Rain began to shiver,
round rings spattering in the running river;
a wind blew, shaken leaves chilly drops were dripping;
into a sheltering hole Old Tom went skipping.

Out came Badger-brock with his snowy forehead
and his dark blinking eyes. In the hill he quarried
with his wife and many sons. By the coat they caught him,
pulled him inside their earth, down their tunnels brought him.

Inside their secret house, there they sat a-mumbling:
'Ho, Tom Bombadil! Where have you come tumbling,
bursting in the front-door? Badger-folk have caught you.
You'll never find it out, the way that we have brought you!'

'Now, old Badger-brock, do you hear me talking?
You show me out at once! I must be a-walking.
Show me to your backdoor under briar-roses;
then clean grimy paws, wipe your earthy noses!
Go back to sleep again on your straw pillow,
like fair Goldberry and Old Man Willow!'

Then all the Badger-folk said: 'We beg your pardon!'
They showed Tom out again to their thorny garden,
went back and hid themselves, a-shivering and a-shaking,
blocked up all their doors, earth together raking.

Rain had passed. The sky was clear, and in the summer-gloaming
Old Tom Bombadil laughed as he came homing,
unlocked his door again, and opened up a shutter.
In the kitchen round the lamp moths began to flutter;
Tom through the window saw waking stars come winking,
and the new slender moon early westward sinking.

Dark came under Hill. Tom, he lit a candle;
upstairs creaking went, turned the door-handle.
'Hoo, Tom Bombadil! Look what night has brought you!
I'm here behind the door. Now at last I've caught you!
You'd forgotten Barrow-wight dwelling in the old mound
up there on hill-top with the ring of stones round.
He's got loose again. Under earth he'll take you.
Poor Tom Bombadil, pale and cold he'll make you!'

'Go out! Shut the door, and never come back after!
Take away gleaming eyes, take your hollow laughter!
Go back to grassy mound, on your stony pillow
lay down your bony head, like Old Man Willow,
like young Goldberry, and Badger-folk in burrow!
Go back to buried gold and forgotten sorrow!'

Out fled Barrow-wight through the window leaping,
through the yard, over wall like a shadow sweeping,
up hill wailing went back to leaning stone-rings,
back under lonely mound, rattling his bone-rings.

Old Tom Bombadil lay upon his pillow
sweeter than Goldberry, quieter than the Willow,

snugger than the Badger-folk or the Barrow-dwellers;
slept like a humming-top, snored like a bellows.

He woke in morning-light, whistled like a starling,
sang, 'Come, derry-dol, merry-dol, my darling!'
He clapped on his battered hat, boots, and coat and feather;
opened the window wide to the sunny weather.

Wise old Bombadil, he was a wary fellow;
bright blue his jacket was, and his boots were yellow.
None ever caught old Tom in upland or in dingle,
walking the forest-paths, or by the Withywindle,
or out on the lily-pools in boat upon the water.
But one day Tom, he went and caught the River-daughter,
in green gown, flowing hair, sitting in the rushes,
singing old water-songs to birds upon the bushes.

He caught her, held her fast! Water-rats went scuttering
reeds hissed, herons cried, and her heart was fluttering.
Said Tom Bombadil: 'Here's my pretty maiden!
You shall come home with me! The table is all laden:
yellow cream, honeycomb, white bread and butter;
roses at the window-sill and peeping round the shutter.
You shall come under Hill! Never mind your mother
in her deep weedy pool: there you'll find no lover!'

Old Tom Bombadil had a merry wedding,
crowned all with buttercups, hat and feather shedding;
his bride with forgetmenots and flag-lilies for garland
was robed all in silver-green. He sang like a starling,
hummed like a honey-bee, lilted to the fiddle,
clasping his river-maid round her slender middle.

Lamps gleamed within his house, and white was the bedding;
in the bright honey-moon Badger-folk came treading,
danced down under Hill, and Old Man Willow
tapped, tapped at window-pane, as they slept on the pillow,
on the bank in the reeds River-woman sighing
heard old Barrow-wight in his mound crying.

Old Tom Bombadil heeded not the voices,
taps, knocks, dancing feet, all the nightly noises;

slept till the sun arose, then sang like a starling:
'Hey! Come derry-dol, merry-dol, my darling!'
sitting on the door-step chopping sticks of willow,
while fair Goldberry combed her tresses yellow.

2
BOMBADIL GOES BOATING

The old year was turning brown; the West Wind was calling;
Tom caught a beechen leaf in the Forest falling.
'I've caught a happy day blown me by the breezes!
Why wait till morrow-year? I'll take it when me pleases.
This day I'll mend my boat and journey as it chances
west down the withy-stream, following my fancies!'

Little Bird sat on twig. 'Whillo, Tom! I heed you.
I've a guess, I've a guess where your fancies lead you.
Shall I go, shall I go, bring him word to meet you?'

'No names, you tell-tale, or I'll skin and eat you,
babbling in every ear things that don't concern you!
If you tell Willow-man where I've gone, I'll burn you,
roast you on a willow-spit. That'll end your prying!'

Willow-wren cocked her tail, piped as she went flying:
'Catch me first, catch me first! No names are needed.
I'll perch on his hither ear: the message will be heeded.
"Down by Mithe", I'll say, "just as sun is sinking".
Hurry up, hurry up! That's the time for drinking!'

Tom laughed to himself: 'Maybe then I'll go there.
I might go by other ways, but today I'll row there.'
He shaved oars, patched his boat; from hidden creek he hauled her

through reed and sallow-brake, under leaning alder,
then down the river went, singing: 'Silly-sallow,
Flow withy-willow-stream over deep and shallow!'
'Whee! Tom Bombadil! Whither be you going,
bobbing in a cockle-boat, down the river rowing?'

'Maybe to Brandywine along the Withywindle;
maybe friends of mine fire for me will kindle
down by the Hays-end. Little folk I know there,
kind at the day's end. Now and then I go there'.

'Take word to my kin, bring me back their tidings!
Tell me of diving pools and the fishes' hidings!'

'Nay then', said Bombadil, 'I am only rowing
just to smell the water like, not on errands going'.

'Tee hee! Cocky Tom! Mind your tub don't founder!
Look out for willow-snags! I'd laugh to see you flounder'.

'Talk less, Fisher Blue! Keep your kindly wishes!
Fly off and preen yourself with the bones of fishes!
Gay lord on your bough, at home a dirty varlet
living in a sloven house, though your breast be scarlet.
I've heard of fisher-birds beak in air a-dangling
to show how the wind is set: that's an end of angling!'

The King's fisher shut his beak, winked his eye, as singing
Tom passed under bough. Flash! then he went winging;
dropped down jewel-blue a feather, and Tom caught it
gleaming in a sun-ray: a pretty gift he thought it.
He stuck it in his tall hat, the old feather casting:
'Blue now for Tom', he said, 'a merry hue and lasting!'

Rings swirled round his boat, he saw the bubbles quiver.
Tom slapped his oar, smack! at a shadow in the river.
'Hoosh! Tom Bombadil! 'Tis long since last I met you.
Turned water-boatman, eh? What if I upset you?'

'What? Why, Whisker-lad, I'd ride you down the river.
My fingers on your back would set your hide a-shiver.'
'Pish, Tom Bombadil! I'll go and tell my mother;

"Call all our kin to come, father, sister, brother!
Tom's gone mad as a coot with wooden legs: he's paddling
down Withywindle stream, an old tub a-straddling!" '

'I'll give your otter-fell to Barrow-wights. They'll taw you!
Then smother you in gold-rings! Your mother if she saw you,
she'd never know her son, unless 'twas by a whisker.
Nay, don't tease old Tom, until you be far brisker!'

'Whoosh! said otter-lad, river-water spraying
over Tom's hat and all; set the boat a-swaying,
dived down under it, and by the bank lay peering,
till Tom's merry song faded out of hearing.

Old Swan of Elvet-isle sailed past him proudly,
gave Tom a black look, snorted at him loudly.
Tom laughed: 'You old cob, do you miss your feather?
Give me a new one then! The old was worn by weather.
Could you speak a fair word, I would love you dearer:
long neck and dumb throat, but still a haughty sneerer!
If one day the King returns, in upping he may take you,
brand your yellow bill, and less lordly make you!'
Old Swan huffed his wings, hissed, and paddled faster;
in his wake bobbing on Tom went rowing after.

Tom came to Withy-weir. Down the river rushing
foamed into Windle-reach, a-bubbling and a-splashing;
bore Tom over stone spinning like a windfall,
bobbing like a bottle-cork, to the hythe at Grindwall.

'Hoy! Here's Woodman Tom with his billy-beard on!'
laughed all the little folk of Hays-end and Breredon.
'Ware, Tom! We'll shoot you dead with our bows and arrows!
We don't let Forest-folk nor bogies from the Barrows
cross over Brandywine by cockle-boat nor ferry'.
'Fie, little fatbellies! Don't ye make so merry!

I've seen hobbit-folk digging holes to hide 'em,
frightened if a horny goat or a badger eyed 'em,
afeared of the moony-beams, their own shadows shunning.
I'll call the orks on you: that'll send you running!'

'You may call, Woodman Tom. And you can talk your beard off.
Three arrows in your hat! You we're not afeared of!
Where would you go to now? If for beer you're making,
the barrels aint deep enough in Breredon for your slaking!'

'Away over Brandywine by Shirebourn I'd be going,
but too swift for cockle-boat the river now is flowing.
I'd bless little folk that took me in their wherry,
wish them evenings fair and many mornings merry'.

Red flowed the Brandywine; with flame the river kindled,
as sun sank beyond the Shire, and then to grey it dwindled.
Mithe Steps empty stood. None was there to greet him.
Silent the Causeway lay. Said Tom: 'A merry meeting!'

Tom stumped along the road, as the light was failing.
Rushey lamps gleamed ahead. He heard a voice him hailing.
'Whoa there!' Ponies stopped, wheels halted sliding.
Tom went plodding past, never looked beside him.

'Ho there! beggarman tramping in the Marish!
What's your business here? Hat all stuck with arrows!
Someone's warned you off, caught you at your sneaking?
Come here! Tell me now what it is you're seeking!
Shire-ale, I'll be bound, though you've not a penny.
I'll bid them lock their doors, and then you won't get any!'

'Well, well, Muddy-feet! From one that's late for meeting
away back by the Mithe that's a surly greeting!
You old farmer fat that cannot walk for wheezing,
cart-drawn like a sack, ought to be more pleasing.

Penny-wise tub-on-legs! A beggar can't be chooser,
or else I'd bid you go, and you would be the loser.
Come, Maggot! Help me up! A tankard now you owe me.
Even in cockshut light an old friend should know me!'

Laughing they drove away, in Rushey never halting,
though the inn open stood and they could smell the malting.
They turned down Maggot's Lane, rattling and bumping,
Tom in the farmer's cart dancing round and jumping.

Stars shone on Bamfurlong, and Maggot's house was lighted;
fire in the kitchen burned to welcome the benighted.

Maggot's sons bowed at door, his daughters did their curtsy,
his wife brought tankards out for those that might be thirsty.
Songs they had and merry tales, the supping and the dancing;
Goodman Maggot there for all his belt was prancing,
Tom did a hornpipe when he was not quaffing,
daughters did the Springle-ring, goodwife did the laughing.

When others went to bed in hay, fern, or feather,
close in the inglenook they laid their heads together,
old Tom and Muddy-feet, swapping all the tidings
from Barrow-downs to Tower Hills: of walkings and of ridings;
of wheat-ear and barley-corn, of sowing and of reaping;
queer tales from Bree, and talk at smithy, mill, and cheaping;
rumours in whispering trees, south-wind in the larches,
tall Watchers by the Ford, Shadows on the marches.

Old Maggot slept at last in chair beside the embers.
Ere dawn Tom was gone: as dreams one half remembers,
some merry, some sad, and some of hidden warning.
None heard the door unlocked; a shower of rain at morning
his footprints washed away, at Mithe he left no traces,
at Hays-end they heard no song nor sound of heavy paces.

Three days his boat lay by the hythe at Grindwall,
and then one morn was gone back up Withywindle.
Otter-folk, hobbits said, came by night and loosed her,
dragged her over weir, and up stream they pushed her.

Out from Elvet-isle Old Swan came sailing,
in beak took her painter up in the water trailing,
drew her proudly on; otters swam beside her
round old Willow-man's crooked roots to guide her;
the King's fisher perched on bow, on thwart the wren was singing,
merrily the cockle-boat homeward they were bringing.
To Tom's creek they came at last. Otter-lad said: 'Whish now!
What's a coot without his legs, or a finless fish now?'
O! silly-sallow-willow-stream! The oars they'd left behind them!
Long they lay at Grindwall hythe for Tom to come and find them.

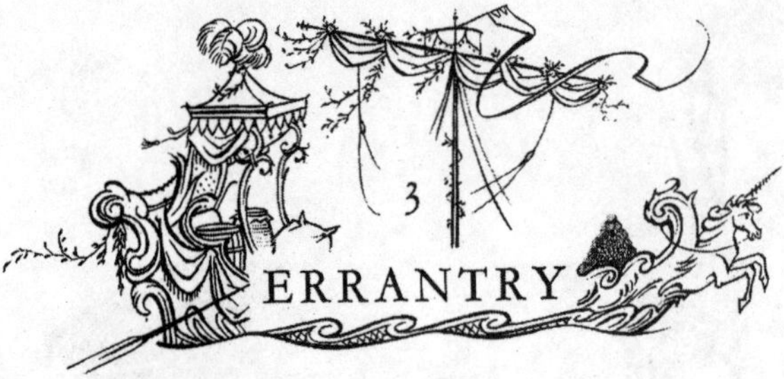

3

ERRANTRY

There was a merry passenger,
a messenger, a mariner:
he built a gilded gondola
to wander in, and had in her
a load of yellow oranges
and porridge for his provender;
he perfumed her with marjoram
and cardamom and lavender.

He called the winds of argosies
with cargoes in to carry him
across the rivers seventeen
that lay between to tarry him.
He landed all in loneliness
where stonily the pebbles on
the running river Derrilyn
goes merrily for ever on
He journeyed then through meadow-lands
to Shadow-land that dreary lay,
and under hill and over hill
went roving still a weary way.

He sat and sang a melody,
his errantry a-tarrying;
he begged a pretty butterfly
that fluttered by to marry him.
She scorned him and she scoffed at him,
she laughed at him unpitying;
so long he studied wizardry
and sigaldry and smithying.

He wove a tissue airy-thin
to snare her in; to follow her
he made him beetle-leather wing
and feather wing of swallow-hair
He caught her in bewilderment
with filament of spider-thread;
he made her soft pavilions
of lilies, and a bridal bed
of flowers and of thistle-down
to nestle down and rest her in;
and silken webs of filmy white
and silver light he dressed her in.

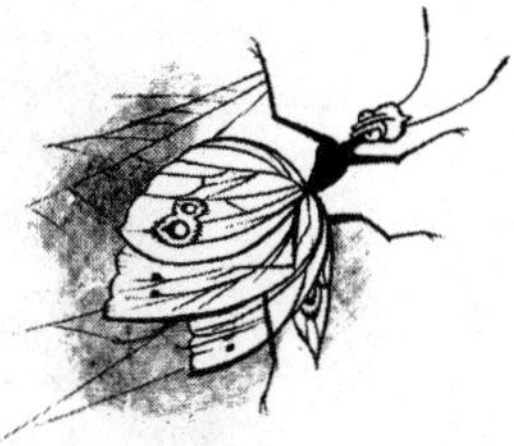

He threaded gems in necklaces,
but recklessly she squandered them
and fell to bitter quarrelling;
then sorrowing he wandered on,
and there he left her withering,
as shivering he fled away;
with windy weather following
on swallow-wing he sped away.

He passed the archipelagoes
where yellow grows the marigold,
where countless silver fountains are,
and mountains are of fairy-gold.
He took to war and foraying,
a-harrying beyond the sea,
and roaming over Belmarie
and Thellamie and Fantasie.

He made a shield and morion
of coral and of ivory,
a sword he made of emerald,
and terrible his rivalry
with elven-knights of Aerie
and Faerie, with paladins
that golden-haired and shining-eyed
came riding by and challenged him.

Of crystal was his habergeon,
his scabbard of chalcedony;

with silver tipped at plenilune
his spear was hewn of ebony.
His javelins were of malachite
and stalactite—he brandished them,
and went and fought the dragon-flies
of Paradise, and vanquished them.

He battled with the Dumbledors,
the Hummerhorns, and Honeybees,
and won the Golden Honeycomb;
and running home on sunny seas
in ship of leaves and gossamer
with blossom for a canopy,
he sat and sang, and furbished up
and burnished up his panoply.

He tarried for a little while
in little isles that lonely lay,
and found there naught but blowing grass;
and so at last the only way
he took, and turned, and coming home
with honeycomb, to memory
his message came, and errand too!
In derring-do and glamoury
he had forgot them, journeying
and tourneying, a wanderer.
So now he must depart again
and start again his gondola,
for ever still a messenger,
a passenger, a tarrier,
a-roving as a feather does,
a weather-driven mariner.

4
PRINCESS MEE

Little Princess Mee
Lovely was she
As in elven-song is told:
She had pearls in hair
All threaded fair;
Of gossamer shot with gold
Was her kerchief made,
And a silver braid
Of stars about her throat.
Of moth-web light
All moonlit-white
She wore a woven coat,
And round her kirtle
Was bound a girdle
Sewn with diamond dew.

She walked by day
Under mantle grey
And hood of clouded blue;
But she went by night
All glittering bright
Under the starlit sky,
And her slippers frail
Of fishes' mail
Flashed as she went by
To her dancing-pool,
And on mirror cool
Of windless water played.
As a mist of light
In whirling flight
A glint like glass she made
Wherever her feet

Of silver fleet
Flicked the dancing-floor.

She looked on high
To the roofless sky,
And she looked to the shadowy shore;
Then round she went,
And her eyes she bent
And saw beneath her go
A Princess Shee
As fair as Mee:
They were dancing toe to toe!

Shee was as light
As Mee, and as bright;
But Shee was, strange to tell,
Hanging down
With starry crown
Into a bottomless well!
Her gleaming eyes
In great surprise
Looked up to the eyes of Mee:
A marvellous thing,
Head-down to swing
Above a starry sea!

Only their feet
Could ever meet;
For where the ways might lie
To find a land
Where they do not stand
But hang down in the sky
No one could tell
Nor learn in spell
In all the elven-lore.

So still on her own
An elf alone
Dancing as before
With pearls in hair
And kirtle fair
And slippers frail

Of fishes' mail went Mee:
Of fishes' mail
And slippers frail
And kirtle fair
With pearls in hair went Shee!

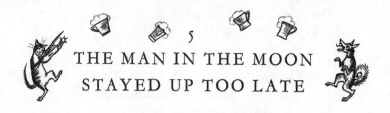

5
THE MAN IN THE MOON STAYED UP TOO LATE

There is an inn, a merry old inn
   beneath an old grey hill,
And there they brew a beer so brown
That the Man in the Moon himself came down
   one night to drink his fill.

The ostler has a tipsy cat
   that plays a five-stringed fiddle;
And up and down he runs his bow,
Now squeaking high, now purring low,
   now sawing in the middle.

The landlord keeps a little dog
   that is mighty fond of jokes;
When there's good cheer among the guests,
He cocks an ear at all the jests
   and laughs until he chokes.

They also keep a hornéd cow
   as proud as any queen;
But music turns her head like ale,
And makes her wave her tufted tail
   and dance upon the green.

And O! the row of silver dishes
   and the store of silver spoons!
For Sunday there's a special pair,
And these they polish up with care
   on Saturday afternoons.

The Man in the Moon was drinking deep,
   and the cat began to wail;
A dish and a spoon on the table danced,

The cow in the garden madly pranced,
  and the little dog chased his tail.

The Man in the Moon took another mug,
  and then rolled beneath his chair;
And there he dozed and dreamed of ale,
Till in the sky the stars were pale,
  and dawn was in the air.

The ostler said to his tipsy cat:
  'The white horses of the Moon,
They neigh and champ their silver bits;
But their master's been and drowned his wits,
  and the Sun'll be rising soon!'

So the cat on his fiddle played hey-diddle-diddle,
  a jig that would wake the dead:
He squeaked and sawed and quickened the tune,
While the landlord shook the Man in the Moon:
  'It's after three!' he said.

They rolled the Man slowly up the hill
  and bundled him into the Moon,
While his horses galloped up in rear,
And the cow came capering like a deer,
  and a dish ran up with a spoon.

Now quicker the fiddle went deedle-dum-diddle;
  the dog began to roar,
The cow and the horses stood on their heads;
The guests all bounded from their beds
  and danced upon the floor.

With a ping and a pong the fiddle-strings broke!
  the cow jumped over the Moon,
And the little dog laughed to see such fun,
And the Saturday dish went off at a run
  with the silver Sunday spoon.

The round Moon rolled behind the hill,
  as the Sun raised up her head.

She hardly believed her fiery eyes;
For though it was day, to her surprise
  they all went back to bed!

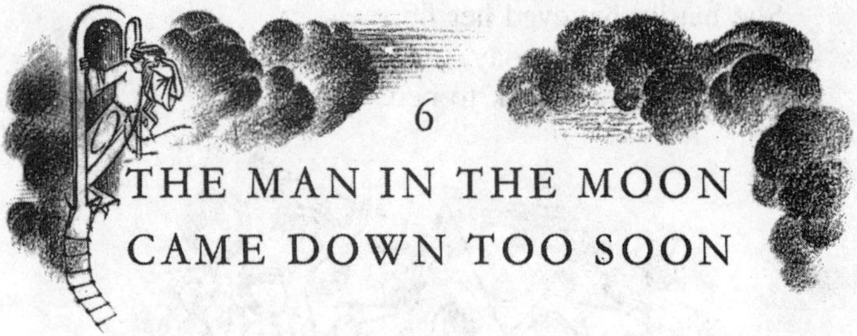

6

THE MAN IN THE MOON CAME DOWN TOO SOON

The Man in the Moon had silver shoon,
  and his beard was of silver thread;
With opals crowned and pearls all bound
  about his girdlestead,
In his mantle grey he walked one day
  across a shining floor,
And with crystal key in secrecy
  he opened an ivory door.

On a filigree stair of glimmering hair
  then lightly down he went,
And merry was he at last to be free
  on a mad adventure bent.
In diamonds white he had lost delight;
  he was tired of his minaret
Of tall moonstone that towered alone
  on a lunar mountain set.

He would dare any peril for ruby and beryl
  to broider his pale attire,
For new diadems of lustrous gems,
  emerald and sapphire.
He was lonely too with nothing to do
  but stare at the world of gold
And heark to the hum that would distantly come
  as gaily round it rolled.

At plenilune in his argent moon
  in his heart he longed for Fire:
Not the limpid lights of wan selenites;
  for red was his desire,
For crimson and rose and ember-glows,

for flame with burning tongue,
For the scarlet skies in a swift sunrise
when a stormy day is young.

He'd have seas of blues, and the living hues
of forest green and fen;
And he yearned for the mirth of the populous earth
and the sanguine blood of men.
He coveted song, and laughter long,
and viands hot, and wine,
Eating pearly cakes of light snowflakes
and drinking thin moonshine.

He twinkled his feet, as he thought of the meat,
of pepper, and punch galore;
And he tripped unaware on his slanting stair,
and like a meteor,
A star in flight, ere Yule one night
flickering down he fell
From his laddery path to a foaming bath
in the windy Bay of Bel.

He began to think, lest he melt and sink,
what in the moon to do,
When a fisherman's boat found him far afloat
to the amazement of the crew,
Caught in their net all shimmering wet
in a phosphorescent sheen
Of bluey whites and opal lights
and delicate liquid green.

Against his wish with the morning fish
they packed him back to land:
'You had best get a bed in an inn', they said;
'the town is near at hand'.
Only the knell of one slow bell
high in the Seaward Tower
Announced the news of his moonsick cruise
at that unseemly hour.

Not a hearth was laid, not a breakfast made,
and dawn was cold and damp.

There were ashes for fire, and for grass the mire,
 for the sun a smoking lamp
In a dim back-street. Not a man did he meet,
 no voice was raised in song;
There were snores instead, for all folk were abed
 and still would slumber long.

He knocked as he passed on doors locked fast,
 and called and cried in vain,
Till he came to an inn that had light within,
 and tapped at a window-pane.
A drowsy cook gave a surly look,
 and 'What do you want?' said he.
'I want fire and gold and songs of old
 and red wine flowing free!'

'You won't get them here', said the cook with a leer,
 'but you may come inside.
Silver I lack and silk to my back—
 maybe I'll let you bide'.
A silver gift the latch to lift,
 a pearl to pass the door;
For a seat by the cook in the ingle-nook
 it cost him twenty more.

For hunger or drouth naught passed his mouth
 till he gave both crown and cloak;
And all that he got, in an earthen pot
 broken and black with smoke,
Was porridge cold and two days old
 to eat with a wooden spoon.
For puddings of Yule with plums, poor fool,
 he arrived so much too soon:
An unwary guest on a lunatic quest
 from the Mountains of the Moon.

7
THE STONE TROLL

Troll sat alone on his seat of stone,
And munched and mumbled a bare old bone;
   For many a year he had gnawed it near,
      For meat was hard to come by.
         Done by! Gum by!
   In a cave in the hills he dwelt alone,
      And meat was hard to come by.

Up came Tom with his big boots on.
Said he to Troll: 'Pray, what is yon?
   For it looks like the shin o' my nuncle Tim,
      As should be a-lyin' in graveyard.
         Caveyard! Paveyard!
   This many a year has Tim been gone,
      And I thought he were lyin' in graveyard'.

'My lad', said Troll, 'this bone I stole.
But what be bones that lie in a hole?
   Thy nuncle was dead as a lump o' lead,
      Afore I found his shinbone.
      Tinbone! Thinbone!
   He can spare a share for a poor old troll;
      For he don't need his shinbone'.

Said Tom: 'I don't see why the likes o' thee
Without axin' leave should go makin' free
   With the shank or the shin o' my father's kin;
      So hand the old bone over!
         Rover! Trover!
   Though dead he be, it belongs to he;
      So hand the old bone over!'

'For a couple o' pins', says Troll, and grins,
"I'll eat thee too, and gnaw thy shins.
  A bit o' fresh meat will go down sweet!
    I'll try my teeth on thee now.
      Hee now! See now!
  I'm tired o' gnawing old bones and skins;
    I've a mind to dine on thee now'.

But just as he thought his dinner was caught,
He found his hands had hold of naught.
  Before he could mind, Tom slipped behind
    And gave him the boot to larn him.
      Warn him! Darn him!
  A bump o' the boot on the seat, Tom thought,
    Would be the way to larn him.

But harder than stone is the flesh and bone
Of a troll that sits in the hills alone.
  As well set your boot to the mountain's root,
    For the seat of a troll don't feel it.
      Peel it! Heal it!
  Old Troll laughed, when he heard Tom groan,
    And he knew his toes could feel it.

Tom's leg is game, since home he came,
And his bootless foot is lasting lame;
  But Troll don't care, and he's still there
    With the bone he boned from its owner.
      Doner! Boner!
  Troll's old seat is still the same,
    And the bone he boned from its owner!

8
PERRY-THE-WINKLE

The Lonely Troll he sat on a stone
   and sang a mournful lay:
'O why, O why must I live on my own
   in the hills of Faraway?
My folk are gone beyond recall
   and take no thought of me;
alone I'm left, the last of all
   from Weathertop to the Sea'.

'I steal no gold, I drink no beer,
   I eat no kind of meat;
but People slam their doors in fear,
   whenever they hear my feet.
O how I wish that they were neat,
   and my hands were not so rough!
Yet my heart is soft, my smile is sweet,
   and my cooking good enough.'

'Come, come!' he thought, 'this will not do!
   I must go and find a friend;
a-walking soft I'll wander through
   the Shire from end to end'.
Down he went, and he walked all night
   with his feet in boots of fur;
to Delving he came in the morning light,
   when folk were just astir.

He looked around, and who did he meet
   but old Mrs. Bunce and all
with umbrella and basket walking the street;
   and he smiled and stopped to call:
'Good morning, ma'am! Good day to you!
   I hope I find you well?'

But she dropped umbrella and basket too,
and yelled a frightful yell.

Old Pott the Mayor was strolling near;
when he heard that awful sound,
he turned all purple and pink with fear,
and dived down underground.

The Lonely Troll was hurt and sad:
'Don't go!' he gently said,
but old Mrs. Bunce ran home like mad
and hid beneath her bed.

The Troll went on to the market-place
and peeped above the stalls;
the sheep went wild when they saw his face,
and the geese flew over the walls.

Old Farmer Hogg he spilled his ale,
Bill Butcher threw a knife,
and Grip his dog, he turned his tail
and ran to save his life.

The old Troll sadly sat and wept
outside the Lockholes gate,
and Perry-the-Winkle up he crept
and patted him on the pate.

'O why do you weep, you great big lump?
You're better outside than in!'
He gave the Troll a friendly thump,
and laughed to see him grin.

'O Perry-the-Winkle boy', he cried,
'come, you're the lad for me!

Now if you're willing to take a ride,
I'll carry you home to tea'.

He jumped on his back and held on tight,
and 'Off you go!' said he;
and the Winkle had a feast that night,
and sat on the old Troll's knee.

There were pikelets, there was buttered toast,
and jam, and cream, and cake,

and the Winkle strove to eat the most,
  though his buttons all should break.
The kettle sang, the fire was hot,
  the pot was large and brown,
and the Winkle tried to drink the lot,
  in tea though he should drown.

When full and tight were coat and skin,
  they rested without speech,
till the old Troll said: 'I'll now begin
  the baker's art to teach,
the making of beautiful cramsome bread,
  of bannocks light and brown;
and then you can sleep on a heather-bed
  with pillows of owlets' down'.

'Young Winkle, where've you been?' they said.
  'I've been to a fulsome tea,
and I feel so fat, for I have fed
  on cramsome bread', said he.
'But where, my lad, in the Shire was that?
  Or out in Bree?' said they.
But Winkle he up and answered flat:
  'I aint a-going to say'.

'But I know where', said Peeping Jack,
  'I watched him ride away:
he went upon the old Troll's back
  to the hills of Faraway'.
Then all the People went with a will,
  by pony, cart, or moke,
until they came to a house in a hill
  and saw a chimney smoke.

They hammered upon the old Troll's door.
  'A beautiful cramsome cake
O bake for us, please, or two, or more;
  O bake!' they cried, 'O bake!'
'Go home, go home!' the old Troll said.
  'I never invited you.
Only on Thursdays I bake my bread,
  and only for a few'.

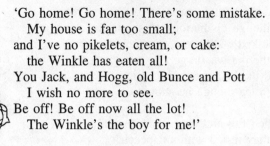

'Go home! Go home! There's some mistake.
My house is far too small;
and I've no pikelets, cream, or cake:
the Winkle has eaten all!
You Jack, and Hogg, old Bunce and Pott
I wish no more to see.
Be off! Be off now all the lot!
The Winkle's the boy for me!'

Now Perry-the-Winkle grew so fat
through eating of cramsome bread,
his weskit bust, and never a hat
would sit upon his head;
for Every Thursday he went to tea,
and sat on the kitchen floor,
and smaller the old Troll seemed to be,
as he grew more and more.

The Winkle a Baker great became,
as still is said in song;
from the Sea to Bree there went the fame
of his bread both short and long.
But it weren't so good as the cramsome bread:
no butter so rich and free,
as Every Thursday the old Troll spread
for Perry-the-Winkle's tea.

9
THE MEWLIPS

The shadows where the Mewlips dwell
   Are dark and wet as ink,
And slow and softly rings their bell,
   As in the slime you sink.

You sink into the slime, who dare
   To knock upon their door,
While down the grinning gargoyles stare
   And noisome waters pour.

Beside the rotting river-strand
   The drooping willows weep,
And gloomily the gorcrows stand
   Croaking in their sleep.

Over the Merlock Mountains a long and weary way,
   In a mouldy valley where the trees are grey,
By a dark pool's borders without wind or tide,
   Moonless and sunless, the Mewlips hide.

The cellars where the Mewlips sit
   Are deep and dank and cold
With single sickly candle lit;
   And there they count their gold.

Their walls are wet, their ceilings drip;
   Their feet upon the floor
Go softly with a squish-flap-flip,
   As they sidle to the door.

They peep out slyly; through a crack
   Their feeling fingers creep,
And when they've finished, in a sack
   Your bones they take to keep.

Beyond the Merlock Mountains, a long and lonely road,
Through the spider-shadows and the marsh of Tode,
And through the wood of hanging trees and the gallows-weed,
You go to find the Mewlips—and the Mewlips feed.

10

OLIPHAUNT

Grey as a mouse,
Big as a house,
Nose like a snake,
I make the earth shake,
As I tramp through the grass;
Trees crack as I pass.
With horns in my mouth
I walk in the South,
Flapping big ears.
Beyond count of years
I stump round and round,
Never lie on the ground,
Not even to die.
Oliphaunt am I,
Biggest of all,
Huge, old, and tall.
If ever you'd met me,
You wouldn't forget me.
If you never do,
You won't think I'm true;
But old Oliphaunt am I,
And I never lie.

II
FASTITOCALON

Look, there is Fastitocalon!
An island good to land upon,
Although 'tis rather bare.
Come, leave the sea! And let us run,
Or dance, or lie down in the sun!
See, gulls are sitting there!
Beware!
Gulls do not sink.
There they may sit, or strut and prink:
Their part it is to tip the wink,
If anyone should dare
Upon that isle to settle,
Or only for a while to get
Relief from sickness or the wet,
Or maybe boil a kettle.

Ah! foolish folk, who land on HIM,
And little fires proceed to trim
And hope perhaps for tea!
It may be that His shell is thick,
He seems to sleep; but He is quick,
And floats now in the sea
With guile;
And when He hears their tapping feet,
Or faintly feels the sudden heat,
With smile
HE dives,
And promptly turning upside-down
He tips them off, and deep they drown,
And lose their silly lives
To their surprise.
Be wise!
There are many monsters in the Sea,
But none so perilous as HE,

Old horny Fastitocalon,
Whose mighty kindred all have gone,
The last of the old Turtle-fish.
So if to save your life you wish
Then I advise:
Pay heed to sailors' ancient lore,
Set foot on no uncharted shore!
Or better still,
Your days at peace on Middle-earth
In mirth
Fulfill!

12

CAT

The fat cat on the mat
may seem to dream
of nice mice that suffice
for him, or cream;
but he free, maybe,
walks in thought
unbowed, proud, where loud
roared and fought
his kin, lean and slim,
or deep in den
in the East feasted on beasts
and tender men.

The giant lion with iron
claw in paw,
and huge ruthless tooth
in gory jaw;
the pard dark-starred,
fleet upon feet,
that oft soft from aloft
leaps on his meat
where woods loom in gloom—
far now they be,
fierce and free,
and tamed is he;
but fat cat on the mat
kept as a pet,
he does not forget.

13

SHADOW-BRIDE

There was a man who dwelt alone,
as day and night went past
he sat as still as carven stone,
and yet no shadow cast.
The white owls perched upon his head
beneath the winter moon;
they wiped their beaks and thought him dead
under the stars of June.

There came a lady clad in grey
in the twilight shining:
one moment she would stand and stay,
her hair with flowers entwining.
He woke, as had he sprung of stone,
and broke the spell that bound him;
he clasped her fast, both flesh and bone,
and wrapped her shadow round him.

There never more she walks her ways
by sun or moon or star;
she dwells below where neither days
nor any nights there are.
But once a year when caverns yawn
and hidden things awake,
they dance together then till dawn
and a single shadow make.

14 THE HOARD

When the moon was new and the sun young
of silver and gold the gods sung:
in the green grass they silver spilled,
and the white waters they with gold filled.
Ere the pit was dug or Hell yawned,
ere dwarf was bred or dragon spawned,
there were Elves of old, and strong spells
under green hills in hollow dells
they sang as they wrought many fair things,
and the bright crowns of the Elf-kings.
But their doom fell, and their song waned,
by iron hewn and by steel chained.
Greed that sang not, nor with mouth smiled,
in dark holes their wealth piled,
graven silver and carven gold:
over Elvenhome the shadow rolled.

There was an old dwarf in a dark cave,
to silver and gold his fingers clave;
with hammer and tongs and anvil-stone
he worked his hands to the hard bone,
and coins he made, and strings of rings,
and thought to buy the power of kings.
But his eyes grew dim and his ears dull
and the skin yellow on his old skull;
through his bony claw with a pale sheen
the stony jewels slipped unseen.
No feet he heard, though the earth quaked,
when the young dragon his thirst slaked,
and the stream smoked at his dark door.
The flames hissed on the dank floor.
and he died alone in the red fire;
his bones were ashes in the hot mire.

There was an old dragon under grey stone;
his red eyes blinked as he lay alone.
His joy was dead and his youth spent,
he was knobbed and wrinkled, and his limbs bent
in the long years to his gold chained;
in his heart's furnace the fire waned.
To his belly's slime gems stuck thick,
silver and gold he would snuff and lick:
he knew the place of the least ring
beneath the shadow of his black wing.
Of thieves he thought on his hard bed,
and dreamed that on their flesh he fed,
their bones crushed, and their blood drank:
his ears drooped and his breath sank.
Mail-rings rang. He heard them not.
A voice echoed in his deep grot:
a young warrior with a bright sword
called him forth to defend his hoard.
His teeth were knives, and of horn his hide,
but iron tore him, and his flame died.

There was an old king on a high throne:
his white beard lay on knees of bone;
his mouth savoured neither meat nor drink,
nor his ears song; he could only think
of his huge chest with carven lid
where pale gems and gold lay hid
in secret treasury in the dark ground;
its strong doors were iron-bound.
The swords of his thanes were dull with rust,
his glory fallen, his rule unjust,
his halls hollow, and his bowers cold,
but king he was of elvish gold.
He heard not the horns in the mountain-pass,
he smelt not the blood on the trodden grass,
but his halls were burned, his kingdom lost;
in a cold pit his bones were tossed.

There is an old hoard in a dark rock,
forgotten behind doors none can unlock;
that grim gate no man can pass.
On the mound grows the green grass;

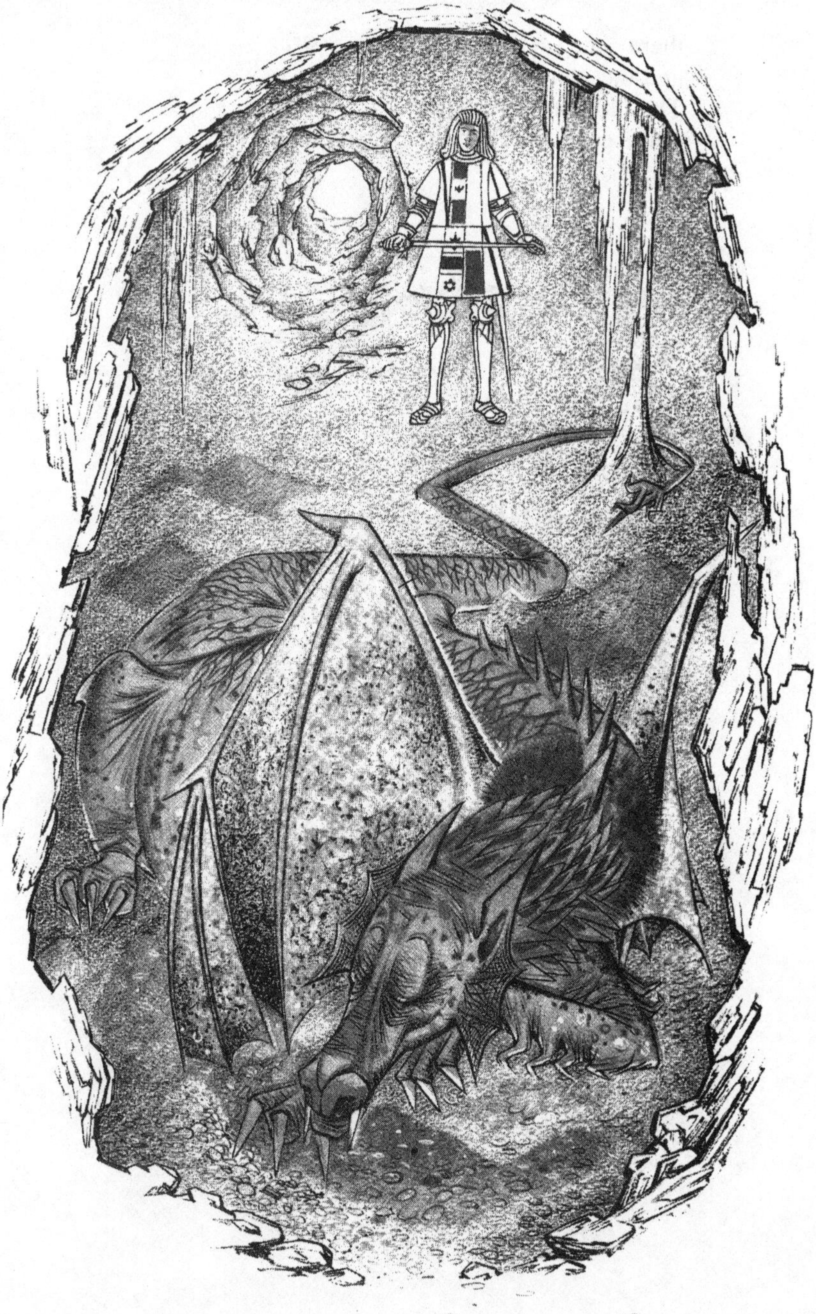

there sheep feed and the larks soar,
and the wind blows from the sea-shore.
The old hoard the Night shall keep,
while earth waits and the Elves sleep.

15
THE SEA-BELL

I walked by the sea, and there came to me,
  as a star-beam on the wet sand,
a white shell like a sea-bell;
  trembling it lay in my wet hand.
In my fingers shaken I heard waken
  a ding within, by a harbour bar
a buoy swinging, a call ringing
  over endless seas, faint now and far.

Then I saw a boat silently float
  on the night-tide, empty and grey.
'It is later than late! Why do we wait?'
  I leapt in and cried: 'Bear me away!'

It bore me away, wetted with spray,
  wrapped in a mist, wound in a sleep,
to a forgotten strand in a strange land.
  In the twilight beyond the deep
I heard a sea-bell swing in the swell,
  dinging, dinging, and the breakers roar
on the hidden teeth of a perilous reef;
  and at last I came to a long shore.
White it glimmered, and the sea simmered
  with star-mirrors in a silver net;
cliffs of stone pale as ruel-bone
  in the moon-foam were gleaming wet.
Glittering sand slid through my hand,
  dust of pearl and jewel-grist,
trumpets of opal, roses of coral,
  flutes of green and amethyst.

But under cliff-eaves there were glooming caves,
  weed-curtained, dark and grey;

a cold air stirred in my hair,
  and the light waned, as I hurried away.

Down from a hill ran a green rill;
  its water I drank to my heart's ease.
Up its fountain-stair to a country fair
  of ever-eve I came, far from the seas,
climbing into meadows of fluttering shadows:
  flowers lay there like fallen stars,
and on a blue pool, glassy and cool,
  like floating moons the nenuphars.
Alders were sleeping, and willows weeping
  by a slow river of rippling weeds;
gladdon-swords guarded the fords,
  and green spears, and arrow-reeds.

There was echo of song all the evening long
  down in the valley; many a thing
running to and fro: hares white as snow,
  voles out of holes; moths on the wing
with lantern-eyes; in quiet surprise
  brocks were staring out of dark doors.
I heard dancing there, music in the air,
  feet going quick on the green floors.
But wherever I came it was ever the same:
  the feet fled, and all was still;
never a greeting, only the fleeting
  pipes, voices, horns on the hill.

Of river-leaves and the rush-sheaves
  I made me a mantle of jewel-green,
a tall wand to hold, and a flag of gold;
  my eyes shone like the star-sheen.
With flowers crowned I stood on a mound,
  and shrill as a call at cock-crow
proudly I cried: 'Why do you hide?
  Why do none speak, wherever I go?
Here now I stand, king of this land,
  with gladdon-sword and reed-mace.
Answer my call! Come forth all!
  Speak to me words! Show me a face!'

Black came a cloud as a night-shroud.
  Like a dark mole groping I went,
to the ground falling, on my hands crawling
  with eyes blind and my back bent.
I crept to a wood: silent it stood
  in its dead leaves; bare were its boughs.
There must I sit, wandering in wit,
  while owls snored in their hollow house.
For a year and a day there must I stay:
  beetles were tapping in the rotten trees,
spiders were weaving, in the mould heaving
  puffballs loomed about my knees.

At last there came light in my long night,
  and I saw my hair hanging grey.
'Bent though I be, I must find the sea!
  I have lost myself, and I know not the way,
but let me be gone!' Then I stumbled on;
  like a hunting bat shadow was over me;
in my ears dinned a withering wind,
  and with ragged briars I tried to cover me.
My hands were torn and my knees worn,
  and years were heavy upon my back,
when the rain in my face took a salt taste,
  and I smelled the smell of sea-wrack.

Birds came sailing, mewing, wailing;
  I heard voices in cold caves,
seals barking, and rocks snarling,
  and in spout-holes the gulping of waves.
Winter came fast; into a mist I passed,
  to land's end my years I bore;
snow was in the air, ice in my hair,
  darkness was lying on the last shore.

There still afloat waited the boat,
  in the tide lifting, its prow tossing.
Weary I lay, as it bore me away,
  the waves climbing, the seas crossing,
passing old hulls clustered with gulls
  and great ships laden with light,

coming to haven, dark as a raven,
silent as snow, deep in the night.

Houses were shuttered, wind round them muttered,
roads were empty. I sat by a door,
and where drizzling rain poured down a drain
I cast away all that I bore:
in my clutching hand some grains of sand,
and a sea-shell silent and dead.
Never will my ear that bell hear,
never my feet that shore tread,
never again, as in sad lane,
in blind alley and in long street
ragged I walk. To myself I talk;
for still they speak not, men that I meet.

16
THE LAST SHIP

Fíriel looked out at three o'clock:
  the grey night was going;
far away a golden cock
  clear and shrill was crowing.
The trees were dark, and the dawn pale,
  waking birds were cheeping,
a wind moved cool and frail
  through dim leaves creeping.

She watched the gleam at window grow,
  till the long light was shimmering
on land and leaf; on grass below
  grey dew was glimmering.
Over the floor her white feet crept,
  down the stair they twinkled,
through the grass they dancing stepped
  all with dew besprinkled.

Her gown had jewels upon its hem,
  as she ran down to the river,
and leaned upon a willow-stem,
  and watched the water quiver.
A kingfisher plunged down like a stone
  in a blue flash falling,
bending reeds were softly blown,
  lily-leaves were sprawling.

A sudden music to her came,
  as she stood there gleaming
with free hair in the morning's flame
  on her shoulders streaming.

Flutes there were, and harps were wrung,
  and there was sound of singing,
like wind-voices keen and young
  and far bells ringing.

A ship with golden beak and oar
  and timbers white came gliding;
swans went sailing on before,
  her tall prow guiding.
Fair folk out of Elvenland
  in silver-grey were rowing,
and three with crowns she saw there stand
  with bright hair flowing.

With harp in hand they sang their song
  to the slow oars swinging:
'Green is the land, the leaves are long,
  and the birds are singing.
Many a day with dawn of gold
  this earth will lighten,
many a flower will yet unfold,
  ere the cornfields whiten.

'Then whither go ye, boatmen fair,
  down the river gliding?
To twilight and to secret lair
  in the great forest hiding?
To Northern isles and shores of stone
  on strong swans flying,
by cold waves to dwell alone
  with the white gulls crying?'

'Nay!' they answered. 'Far away
  on the last road faring,
leaving western havens grey,
  the seas of shadow daring,
we go back to Elvenhome,
  where the White Tree is growing,
and the Star shines upon the foam
  on the last shore flowing.

'To mortal fields say farewell,
   Middle-earth forsaking!
In Elvenhome a clear bell
   in the high tower is shaking.
Here grass fades and leaves fall,
   and sun and moon wither,
and we have heard the far call
   that bids us journey thither'.

The oars were stayed. They turned aside:
   'Do you hear the call, Earth-maiden?
Fíriel! Fíriel!' they cried.
   'Our ship is not full-laden.
One more only we may bear.
   Come! For your days are speeding.
Come! Earth-maiden elven-fair,
   our last call heeding.'

Fíriel looked from the river-bank,
   one step daring;
then deep in clay her feet sank,
   and she halted staring.
Slowly the elven-ship went by
   whispering through the water:
'I cannot come!' they heard her cry.
   'I was born Earth's daughter!'

No jewels bright her gown bore,
   as she walked back from the meadow
under roof and dark door,
   under the house-shadow.
She donned her smock of russet brown,
   her long hair braided,
and to her work came stepping down.
   Soon the sunlight faded.

Year still after year flows
   down the Seven Rivers;
cloud passes, sunlight glows,
   reed and willow quivers
at morn and eve, but never more

westward ships have waded
in mortal waters as before,
and their song has faded.

SIR GAWAIN
AND THE GREEN KNIGHT

PREFACE

When my father, Professor J. R. R. Tolkien, died in 1973 he left unpublished his translations of the medieval English poem *Sir Gawain and the Green Knight, Pearl,* and *Sir Orfeo*. A form of his *Pearl* translation was in existence more than thirty years ago, though it was much revised later; and that of *Sir Gawain* soon after 1950. The latter was broadcast on the BBC Third Programme in 1953. His version of *Sir Orfeo* was also made many years ago, and had been (I believe) for long laid aside; but he certainly wished to see it published.

He wished to provide both a general introduction and a commentary; and it was largely because he could not decide on the form that these should take that the translations remained unpublished. On the one hand, he undoubtedly sought an audience without any knowledge of the original poems; he wrote of his translation of *Pearl*: '*The Pearl* certainly deserves to be heard by lovers of English poetry who have not the opportunity or the desire to master its difficult idiom. To such readers I offer this translation.' But he also wrote: 'A translation may be a useful form of commentary; and this version may possibly be acceptable even to those who already know the original, and possess editions with all their apparatus.' He wished therefore to explain the basis of his version in debatable passages; and indeed a very great deal of unshown editorial labour lies behind his translations, which not only reflect his long study of the language and metre of the originals, but were also in some degree the inspiration of it. As he wrote: 'These translations were first made long ago for my own instruction, since a translator must first try to discover as precisely as he can what his original means, and may be led by ever closer attention to understand it better for its own sake. Since I first began I have given to the idiom of these texts very close study, and I have certainly learned more about them than I knew when I first presumed to translate them.'

But the commentary was never written, and the introduction did not get beyond the point of tentative beginnings. My concern in preparing this book has been that it should remain his own; and I have not provided any commentary. Those readers whom he most wished to reach will be content to know that in passages of doubt or difficulty these translations are the product of long scrutiny of the originals, and of great pains to embody his conclusions in a rendering at once precise and metrical; and for explanations and discussions of detail reference must be made to editions of the originals. But readers who are wholly unacquainted with these poems will wish to know something about them; and it seemed to me that if it were at all possible the translations should be introduced in the words of the translator himself, who gave so much time and thought to these works. I have therefore composed the introductory and explanatory parts of the book in the following way.

The first section of the Introduction, on the author of *Sir Gawain* and *Pearl*, is derived from my father's notes. The second section, on *Sir Gawain*, is (in slightly reduced form) a radio talk which he gave after the broadcasts of his translation. For the third section, the only writing of his on *Pearl* that I could find suitable to the purpose was the original draft for an essay that was subsequently published in revised form. After my father and Professor E. V. Gordon had collaborated in making an edition of *Sir Gawain*, which was published in 1925, they began work on an edition of *Pearl*. In the event, that book was almost entirely the work of Professor Gordon alone, but my father's contribution to it included a small part of the Introduction; and the essay is here reproduced in the form it finally took as the result of their collaboration.[1] Its appearance here has been made possible through the generosity of Mrs I. L. Gordon. I wish also to thank the Delegates of the Clarendon Press for their permission to use it.

I was not able to discover any writing by my father on the subject of *Sir Orfeo*. Here therefore, in keeping with my general intentions for the book, I have restricted myself to a very brief factual note on the text.

Since a primary object of these translations was the close preservation of the metres of the originals, I thought that the book should contain, for those who want it, an account of the verse-forms of *Sir Gawain* and *Pearl*. The section on *Sir Gawain* is composed from drafts made for, but not used in, the introductory talk to the broadcasts of the translation; and that on the verse-form of *Pearl* from other unpublished notes. There

[1] *Pearl*, edited by E. V. Gordon, Oxford 1953, pages xi–xix: 'Form and Purpose'.

is very little in these accounts (and nothing that is a matter of opinion) that is not in my father's own words.

It is inevitable that in thus using materials written at different times and for different purposes the result should not be entirely homogeneous; but it seemed to me better to accept this consequence than not to use them at all.

At his death my father had not finally decided on the form of every line in the translations. In choosing between competing versions I have tried throughout to determine his latest intention, and that has in most cases been discoverable with fair certainty.

At the end of the book I have provided a short glossary. On the last page will be found some verses translated by my father from a medieval English poem. He called them 'Gawain's Leave-taking', clearly with reference to the passage in *Sir Gawain* where Gawain leaves the castle of Sir Bertilak to go to the tryst at the Green Chapel. The original poem has no connection with Sir Gawain; the verses translated are in fact the first three stanzas, and the last, of a somewhat longer poem found among a group of fourteenth-century lyrics with refrains in the Vernon manuscript in the Bodleian Library at Oxford.

Christopher Tolkien

INTRODUCTION

I

Sir Gawain and the Green Knight and *Pearl* are both contained in the same unique manuscript, which is now in the British Museum. Neither poem is given a title. Together with them are two other poems, also title-less, which are now known as *Purity* (or *Cleanness*), and *Patience*. All four are in the same handwriting, which is dated in round figures about 1400; it is small, angular, irregular and often difficult to read, quite apart from the fading of the ink in the course of time. But this is the hand of the copyist, not the author. There is indeed nothing to say that the four poems are the works of the same poet; but from elaborate comparative study it has come to be very generally believed that they are.

Of this author, nothing is now known. But he was a major poet of his day; and it is a solemn thought that his name is now forgotten, a reminder of the great gaps of ignorance over which we now weave the thin webs of our literary history. But something to the purpose may still be learned of this writer from his works. He was a man of serious and devout mind, though not without humour; he had an interest in theology, and some knowledge of it, though an amateur knowledge, perhaps, rather than a professional; he had Latin and French and was well enough read in French books, both romantic and instructive; but his home was in the West Midlands of England: so much his language shows, and his metre, and his scenery.

His active life must have lain in the later half of the fourteenth century, and he was thus a contemporary of Chaucer's; but whereas Chaucer has never become a closed book, and has continued to be read with pleasure since the fifteenth century, *Sir Gawain and the Green Knight* and *Pearl* are practically unintelligible to modern readers. Indeed in their own time the adjectives 'dark' and 'hard' would probably have been applied to these poems by most people who enjoyed the works of Chaucer. For Chaucer was a native of London and the populous South-East of England, and the language which he naturally used has proved to be the foundation of a standard English and literary English of later times; the kind of verse which he composed was the kind which English poets mostly used for the next five hundred years. But the language of this unknown author from the far less populous, far more conservative West Midlands, his grammar, his style, his vocabulary, were in many respects remote from those of London, off the main track of inevitable development; and in *Sir Gawain and the Green Knight* he used the ancient English measure which had descended from antiquity, that kind of verse which is now called 'alliterative'. It aimed at quite different effects from those achieved by the rhymed and syllable-counting metres derived from France and Italy; it seemed harsh and stiff and rugged to those unaccustomed to it. And quite apart from the (from a London point of view) dialectal character of the language, this 'alliterative' verse included in its tradition a number of special verse words, never used in ordinary talk or prose, that were 'dark' to those outside the tradition.

In short, this poet adhered to what is now known as the Alliterative Revival of the fourteenth century, the attempt to use the old native metre and style long rusticated for high and serious writing; and he paid the penalty for its failure, for alliterative verse was not in the event revived. The tides of time, of taste, of language, not to mention political power, trade and wealth, were against it; and all that remains of the chief artist of the 'Revival' is the one manuscript, of which nothing is now known before it found a place in the library of Henry Savile of Bank in Yorkshire, who lived from 1568 to 1617.

And these, then, are the reasons for translation: it is necessary if these poems are not to remain the literary pleasure only of mediaeval specialists. And they are difficult to translate. The main object of the present translations is to preserve the metres, which are essential to the poems as wholes; and to present the language and style, nonetheless, not as they may appear at a superficial glance, archaic, queer, crabbed and rustic, but as they were for the people to whom they were addressed: if English and conservative, yet courtly, wise, and well-bred—educated, indeed learned.

II

Sir Gawain and the Green Knight

If the most certain thing known about the author is that he also wrote *Patience, Purity* and *Pearl*, then we have in *Sir Gawain* the work of a man capable of weaving elements taken from diverse sources into a texture of his own; and a man who would have in that labour a serious purpose. I would myself say that it is precisely that purpose that has with its hardness proved the shaping tool which has given form to the material, given it the quality of a good tale on the surface, because it is more than that, if we look closer.

The story is good enough in itself. It is a romance, a fairy-tale for adults, full of life and colour; and it has virtues that would be lost in a summary, though they can be perceived when it is read at length: good scenery, urbane or humorous dialogue, and a skilfully ordered narrative. Of this the most notable example is the long Third Part with its interlacing of the hunting-scenes and the temptations. By this device all three main characters are kept vividly in view during the three crucial days, while the scenes at home and in the field are linked by the Exchange of Winnings, and we watch the gains of the chase diminish as the gains of Sir Gawain increase and the peril of his testing mounts to a crisis.

But all this care in formal construction serves also to make the tale a better vehicle of the 'moral' which the author has imposed on his antique material. He has re-drawn according to his own faith his ideal of knighthood, making it Christian knighthood, showing that the grace and beauty of its courtesy (which he admires) derive from the Divine generosity and grace, Heavenly Courtesy, of which Mary is the supreme creation: the Queen of Courtesy, as he calls her in *Pearl*. This he exhibits symbolically in mathematical perfection in the Pentangle, which he sets on Gawain's shield instead of the heraldic lion or eagle found in other romances. But while in *Pearl* he enlarged his vision of his dead daughter among the blessed to an allegory of the Divine generosity, in *Sir Gawain* he has given life to his ideal by showing it incarnate in a living person, modified by his individual character, so that we can see a man trying to work the ideal out, see its weaknesses (or man's weaknesses).

But he has done more. His major point is the rejection of unchastity and adulterous love, and this was an essential part of the original tradition of *amour courtois* or 'courtly love'; but this he has complicated again, after the way of morals in real life, by involving it in several minor problems of conduct, of courtly behaviour to women and fidelity to men, of what we might call sportsmanship or playing the game. On these problems he has been less explicit, and has left his hearers more or less to form their own views of the scale of their values, and their relation to the governing value of sin and virtue.

So this poem is made to be, as it were, all about Gawain. The rest is a web of circumstance in which he is involved for the revelation of his character and code. The 'Faerie' may with its strangeness and peril enlarge the adventure, making the test more tense and more potent, but Gawain is presented as a credible, living, person; and all that he thinks, or says, or does, is to be seriously considered, as of the real world. His character is drawn so as to make him peculiarly fitted to suffer acutely in the adventure to which he is destined.

We see his almost exaggerated courtesy of speech, his modesty of bearing, which yet goes with a subtle form of pride: a deep sense of his own honour, not to mention, we might say, a pleasure in his own repute as 'this fine father of breeding' (stanza 38). We note also the warmth of his character, generous, even impetuous, which by a slight excess leads him ever to promise more than necessary, beyond the consequences that he can foresee. We are shown his delight in the company of women, his sensitiveness to their beauty, his pleasure in the 'polished play of converse' with them, and at the same time his fervent piety, his devotion to the Blessed Virgin. We see him at the crisis of the action forced to distinguish in scale of value the elements of his code, preserving his chastity, and his loyalty on the highest plane to his host; finally rejecting in fact (if not in empty words) absolute worldly 'courtesy', that is complete obedience to the will of the sovereign lady, rejecting it in favour of virtue.

Yet later we see him, in the last scene with the Green Knight, so overwhelmed by shame at being discovered in a breach of his laughing word, given in a Christmas game, that the honour he has gained in the great test is of small comfort to him. With characteristic excess he vows to wear a badge of disgrace for the rest of his life. In a fit of remorse, so violent that it would be appropriate only to grievous sin, he accuses himself of Greed, Cowardice, and Treachery. Of the first two he is guiltless, except by a casuistry of shame. But how true to life, to a picture of a perhaps not very reflective man of honour, is this shame at being found out (especially at being found out) in something considered rather shabby, whatever in solemn conscience we may think of its real importance. How true also is this equality in emotion aroused by all parts of a personal code of conduct, however various in importance or ultimate sanctions each element may be.

Of the last charge: disloyalty, troth-breach, treachery, all the hard things that he calls it, Gawain was guilty only in so far as he had broken the rules of an absurd game imposed on him by his host (after he had rashly promised to do anything his host asked); and even that was at the request of a lady, made (we may note) after he had accepted her gift, and so was in a cleft stick. Certainly this is an imperfection upon some plane; but on how high a plane, and of what importance? The laughter of the Court of Camelot—and to what higher court in matters of honour could one go?—is probably sufficient answer.

But in terms of literature, undoubtedly this break in the mathematical perfection of an ideal creature, inhuman in flawlessness, is a great improvement. The credibility of Gawain is enormously enhanced by it. He becomes a real man, and we can thus really admire his actual virtue. We can indeed give serious thought to the movements of the English mind in the fourteenth century, which he represents, from which much of our sentiment and ideals of conduct have been derived. We see the attempt to preserve the graces of 'chivalry' and the courtesies, while wedding them, or by wedding them, to Christian morals, to marital fidelity, and indeed married love. The noblest knight of the highest order of Chivalry refuses adultery, places hatred of sin in the last resort above all other motives, and escapes from a temptation that attacks him in the guise of courtesy through grace obtained by prayer. That is what the author of *Sir Gawain and the Green Knight* was mainly thinking about, and with that thought he shaped the poem as we have it.

It was a matter of contemporary concern, for the English. *Sir Gawain* presents in its own way, more explicitly moral and religious, one facet of this movement of thought out of which also grew Chaucer's greatest poem, *Troilus and Criseyde*. Those who read *Sir Gawain* are likely to read the last stanzas of Chaucer's work with a renewed interest.

But if Chaucer's poem is much altered in tone and import from its immediate source in Boccaccio's *Filostrato*, it is utterly removed from the sentiments or ideas in the Homeric Greek poems on the fall of Troy, and still further removed (we may guess) from those of the ancient Aegean world. Research into these things has very little to do with Chaucer. The same is certainly true of *Sir Gawain and the Green Knight*, for which no immediate source has been discovered. For that reason, since I am speaking of this poem and this author, and not of ancient rituals, nor of pagan divinities of the Sun, nor of Fertility, nor of the Dark and the Underworld, in the almost wholly lost antiquity of the North and of these Western Isles—as remote from Sir Gawain of Camelot as the gods of the Aegean are from Troilus and Pandarus in Chaucer—for that reason I have not said anything about the story, or stories, that the author used. Research has discovered a lot about them, especially about the two main themes, the Beheading Challenge and the

Test. These are in *Sir Gawain and the Green Knight* cleverly combined, but are elsewhere found separately in varied forms, in Irish or in Welsh or in French. Research of that sort interests men of today greatly; it interests me; but it interested educated men of the fourteenth century very little. They were apt to read poems for what they could get out of them of *sentence*, as they said, of instruction for themselves, and their times; and they were shockingly incurious about authors as persons, or we should have known much more about Geoffrey Chaucer, and the name at least of the author of *Sir Gawain*. But there is not time for everything. Let us be grateful for what we have got, preserved by chary chance: another window of many-coloured glass looking back into the Middle Ages, and giving us another view. Chaucer was a great poet, and by the power of his poetry he tends to dominate the view of his time taken by readers of literature. But his was not the only mood or temper of mind in those days. There were others, such as this author, who while he may have lacked Chaucer's subtlety and flexibility, had, what shall we say?—a nobility to which Chaucer scarcely reached.

III

Pearl

When *Pearl* was first read in modern times it was accepted as what it purports to be, an elegy on the death of a child, the poet's daughter. The personal interpretation was first questioned in 1904 by W. H. Schofield, who argued that the maiden of the poem was an allegorical figure of a kind usual in medieval vision-literature, an abstraction representing 'clean maidenhood'. His view was not generally accepted, but it proved the starting-point of a long debate between the defenders of the older view and the exponents of other theories: that the whole poem is an allegory, though each interpreter has given it a different meaning; or that it is no more than a theological treatise in verse. Much space would be required to rehearse this debate, even in brief summary, and the labour would be unprofitable; but it has not been entirely wasted, for much learning has gone into it, and study has deepened the appreciation of the poem and brought out more clearly the allegorical and symbolical elements that it certainly includes.

A clear distinction between 'allegory' and 'symbolism' may be difficult to maintain, but it is proper, or at least useful, to limit allegory to narrative, to an account (however short) of events; and symbolism to the use of visible signs or things to represent other things or ideas. Pearls were a symbol of purity that especially appealed to the imagination of the Middle Ages (and notably of the fourteenth century); but this does not make a person who wears pearls, or even one who is called Pearl, or Margaret, into an allegorical figure. To be an 'allegory' a poem must *as a whole*, and with fair consistency, describe in other terms some event or process; its entire narrative and all its significant details should cohere and work together to this end. There are minor allegories within *Pearl*; the parable of the workers in the vineyard (stanzas 42–49) is a self-contained allegory; and the opening stanzas of the poem, where the pearl slips from the poet's hand through the grass to the ground, is an allegory in little of the child's death and burial. But an allegorical description of an event does not make that event itself allegorical. And this initial use is only one of the many applications of the pearl symbol, intelligible if the reference of the poem is personal, incoherent if one seeks for total allegory. For there are a number of precise details in *Pearl* that cannot be subordinated to any general allegorical interpretation, and these details are of special importance since they relate to the central figure, the maiden of the vision, in whom, if anywhere, the allegory should be concentrated and without disturbance.

The basis of criticism, then, must be the references to the child or maiden, and to her relations with the dreamer; and no good reason has ever been found for regarding these as anything but statements of 'fact': the real experiences that lie at the foundation of the poem.

When the dreamer first sees the maiden in the paradisal garden, he says (stanza 21):

> Art þou my perle þat I haf playned,
> Regretted by myn one on nyȝte?
> Much longeyng haf I for þe layned
> Syþen into gresse þou my aglyȝte.

This explains for us the minor allegory of the opening stanzas and reveals that the pearl he lost was a maid-child who died. For the maiden of the vision accepts the identification, and herself refers to her death in stanza 64. In stanza 35 she says she was at that time very young, and the dreamer himself in stanza 41 tells us that she was not yet two years old and had not yet learned her creed or prayers. The whole theological argument that follows assumes the infancy of the child when she left this world.

The actual relationship of the child in the world to the dreamer is referred to in stanza 20: when he first espied her in his vision he recognized her; he knew her well, he had seen her before (stanza 14); and so now beholding her visible on the farther bank of the stream he was the happiest man 'from here to Greece', for

Ho watȝ me nerre þen aunte or nece.

'She was more near akin to me than aunt or niece.' *Nerre* can in the language of the time only mean here 'nearer in blood-relationship'. In this sense it was normal and very frequent. And although it is true that 'nearer than aunt or niece' might, even so, refer to a sister, the disparity in age makes the assumption of this relationship far less probable. The depth of sorrow portrayed for a child so young belongs rather to parenthood. And there seems to be a special significance in the situation where the doctrinal lesson given by the celestial maiden comes from one of no earthly wisdom to her proper teacher and instructor in the natural order.

A modern reader may be ready to accept the personal basis of the poem, and yet may feel that there is no need to assume any immediate or particular foundation in autobiography. It is admittedly not necessary for the vision, which is plainly presented in literary or scriptural terms; the bereavement and the sorrow may also be imaginative fictions, adopted precisely because they heighten the interest of the theological discussion between the maiden and the dreamer.

This raises a difficult and important question for general literary history: whether the purely fictitious 'I' had yet appeared in the fourteenth century, a first person feigned as narrator who had no existence outside the imagination of the real author. Probably not; at least not in the kind of literature that we are here dealing with: visions related by a dreamer. The fictitious traveller had already appeared in 'Sir John Mandeville', the writer of whose 'voyages' seems not to have borne that name, nor indeed, according to modern critics, ever to have journeyed far beyond his study; and it is difficult to decide whether this is a case of fraud intended to deceive (as it certainly did), or an example of prose fiction (in the literary sense) still wearing the guise of truth according to contemporary convention.

This convention was strong, and not so 'conventional' as it may appear to modern readers. Although by those of literary experience it might, of course, be used as nothing more than a device to secure literary credibility (as often by Chaucer), it represented a deep-rooted habit of mind, and was strongly associated with the moral and didactic spirit of the times. Tales of the past required their grave authorities, and tales of new things at least an eyewitness, the author. This was one of the reasons for the popularity of visions: they allowed marvels to be placed within the real world, linking them with a person, a place, a time, while providing them with an explanation in the phantasies of sleep, and a defence against critics in the notorious deception of dreams. So even explicit allegory was usually presented as a thing seen in sleep. How far any such narrated vision, of the more serious kind, was supposed to resemble an actual dream experience is another question. A modern poet would indeed be very unlikely to put forward for factual acceptance a dream that in any way resembled the vision of *Pearl*, even when all allowance is made for the arrangement and formalizing of conscious art. But we are dealing with a period when men, aware of the vagaries of dreams, still thought that amid their japes came visions of truth. And their waking imagination was strongly moved by symbols and the figures of allegory, and filled vividly with the pictures evoked by the scriptures, directly or through the wealth of medieval art. And they thought that on occasion, as God willed, to some that slept blessed faces appeared and prophetic voices spoke. To them it might not seem so incredible that the dream of a poet, one wounded with a great bereavement and troubled in spirit, might resemble the vision in *Pearl*.[1] However that may be, the narrated vision in the more serious medieval writing represented, if not an actual dream, at least a real process of thought culminating in some resolution or turning-point of the interior life—as with Dante, and in *Pearl*. And in all forms, lighter or more grave, the 'I' of the dreamer remained the eyewitness, the author, and facts that he referred to outside the dream (especially those concerning himself) were on a different plane, meant to be taken as literally true, and even by modern critics so taken. In the *Divina Commedia* the *Nel mezzo del cammin di nostra vita* of the opening line, or *la decenne sete* of *Purgatorio xxxii*, are held to refer to real dates and events, the thirty-fifth year of Dante's life in 1300, and the death of Beatrice Portinari in 1290. Similarly the references to Malvern in the Prologue and Passus VII of *Piers Plowman*, and the numerous allusions to London, are taken as facts in someone's life, whoever the critic may favour as the author (or authors) of the poem.

It is true that the 'dreamer' may become a shadowy figure of small biographical substance. There is little left of the actual Chaucer in the 'I' who is the narrator in *The Boke of the Duchesse*. Few will debate how much autobiography there is in the bout of insomnia that is made

[1] Ek oother seyn that thorugh impressiouns,
As if a wight hath faste a thyng in mynde,
That thereof comen swiche avysiouns.
(*Troilus and Criseyde*, v. 372–4)

the occasion of the poem. Yet this fictitious and conventional vision is founded on a real event: the death of Blanche, the wife of John of Gaunt, in 1369. That was her real name, White (as she is called in the poem). However heightened the picture may be that is drawn of her loveliness and goodness, her sudden death was a lamentable event. Certainly it can have touched Chaucer far less deeply than the death of one 'nearer than aunt or niece'; but even so, it is this living drop of reality, this echo of sudden death and loss in the world, that gives to Chaucer's early poem a tone and feeling that raises it above the literary devices out of which he made it. So with the much greater poem *Pearl*, it is overwhelmingly more probable that it too was founded on a real sorrow, and drew its sweetness from a real bitterness.

And yet to the particular criticism of the poem decision on this point is not of the first importance. A feigned elegy remains an elegy; and feigned or unfeigned, it must stand or fall by its art. The reality of the bereavement will not save the poetry if it is bad, nor lend it any interest save to those who are in fact interested, not in poetry, but in documents, whose hunger is for history or biography or even for mere names. It is on general grounds, and considering its period in particular, that a 'real' or directly autobiographical basis for *Pearl* seems likely, since that is the most probable explanation of its form and its poetic quality. And for this argument the discovery of biographical details would have little importance. Of all that has been done in this line the only suggestion of value was made by Sir Israel Gollancz:[1] that the child may have been actually called a pearl by baptismal name, *Margarita* in Latin, *Margery* in English. It was a common name at the time, because of the love of pearls and their symbolism, and it had already been borne by several saints. If the child was really baptized a pearl, then the many pearls threaded on the strands of the poem in multiple significance receive yet another lustre. It is on such accidents of life that poetry crystallizes:

> And goode faire White she het;
> That was my lady name ryght.
> She was bothe fair and bryght;
> She hadde not hir name wrong.
>
> (*Boke of the Duchesse*, 948–51)

> 'O perle', quod I, 'in perleȝ pyȝt,
> Art þou my perle þat I haf playned?'

[1]Edition of *Pearl*, p. xliii: 'He perhaps named the child "Margery" or "Marguerite".' The form Marguerite would not have been used; it is a modern French form.

It has been objected that the child as seen in Heaven is not like an infant of two in appearance, speech, or manners: she addresses her father formally as *sir*, and shows no filial affection for him. But this is an apparition of a spirit, a soul not yet reunited with its body after the resurrection, so that theories relevant to the form and age of the glorified and risen body do not concern us. And as an immortal spirit, the maiden's relations to the earthly man, the father of her body, are altered. She does not deny his fatherhood, and when she addresses him as *sir* she only uses the form of address that was customary for medieval children. Her part is in fact truly imagined. The sympathy of readers may now go out more readily to the bereaved father than to the daughter, and they may feel that he is treated with some hardness. But it is the hardness of truth. In the manner of the maiden is portrayed the effect upon a clear intelligence of the persistent earthliness of the father's mind; all is revealed to him, and he has eyes, yet he cannot see. The maiden is now filled with the spirit of celestial charity, desiring only his eternal good and the cure of his blindness. It is not her part to soften him with pity, or to indulge in childish joy at their reunion. The final consolation of the father was not to be found in the recovery of a beloved daughter, as if death had not after all occurred or had no significance, but in the knowledge that she was redeemed and saved and had become a queen in Heaven. Only by resignation to the will of God, and through death, could he rejoin her.

And this is the main *purpose* of the poem as distinct from its genesis or literary form: the doctrinal theme, in the form of an argument on salvation, by which the father is at last convinced that his Pearl, as a baptized infant and innocent, is undoubtedly saved, and, even more, admitted to the blessed company of the 144,000 that follow the Lamb. But the doctrinal theme is, in fact, inseparable from the literary form of the poem and its occasion; for it arises directly from the grief, which imparts deep feeling and urgency to the whole discussion. Without the elegiac basis and the sense of great personal loss which pervades it, *Pearl* would indeed be the mere theological treatise on a special point, which some critics have called it. But without the theological debate the grief would never have risen above the ground. Dramatically the debate represents a long process of thought and mental struggle, an experience as real as the first blind grief of bereavement. In his first mood, even if he had been granted a vision of the blessed in Heaven, the dreamer would have received it incredulously or rebelliously. And he would have awakened by the mound again, not in the gentle and serene resignation of the last stanza, but still as he is first seen, looking only backward, his mind filled with the horror of decay, wringing his hands, while his *wreched wylle in wo ay wraȝte*.

IV

Sir Orfeo

Sir Orfeo is found in three manuscripts, of which the earliest gives very much the best text; this is the Auchinleck manuscript, a large miscellany made about 1330, probably in London, and now in the Advocates' Library in Edinburgh. The other manuscripts, both of the fifteenth century, offer very decrepit versions of the poem; but the Auchinleck text has also suffered from the corruptions of error and forgetfulness, if much less so than the others. The translation follows the Auchinleck text (with some emendations), except at the beginning, where a leaf is lost from the manuscript. Auchinleck begins with *Orfeo was a king* (line 25 of the translation); but the manuscript Harley 3810 precedes this with the 24-line prologue which is here translated. This prologue appears also in a very corrupt state in the third manuscript, Ashmole 61; and, remarkably, also elsewhere in the Auchinleck manuscript, as the prologue of another poem, *Lay le Freyne*, which has been thought to be the work of the same author. In addition, lines 33–46 in the translation are introduced from the Harley manuscript; they are agreed to be genuine lines of the original. It is agreed that the references to England (line 26) and to Winchester (lines 49–50, and line 478), which are peculiar to the Auchinleck version, are not authentic.

It cannot be said where or when *Sir Orfeo* was composed with any more precision than probably in the south-east of England in the latter part of the thirteenth century, or early in the fourteenth; and it seems at any rate more probable than not that it was translated from a French original.

V

Editions

Sir Gawain and the Green Knight, edited by J. R. R. Tolkein and E. V. Gordon, Oxford 1925. This has been extensively revised in a second edition by Norman Davis, Oxford 1967.

Pearl, edited by E. V. Gordon, Oxford 1953.

Sir Orfeo, edited by A. J. Bliss, second edition Oxford 1966. This edition contains all three texts of the poem, and a discussion of the origins of this treatment of the legend of Orpheus and Eurydice.

The Auchinleck text, with the same insertions as are made in the translation, is given in *Fourteenth Century Verse and Prose*, edited by Kenneth Sisam, with a glossary by J. R. R. Tolkien (Oxford University Press).

VI

Note on the text of the translations

The details of presentation (most notably, the absence of line-numbers in *Sir Gawain* and *Pearl*, and the use of inverted commas in interior quotations in *Pearl*) are in accordance with my father's wishes.

Line 4 in stanza 42, and line 18 in stanza 98, of the translation of *Sir Gawain* are not in the original. They were introduced into the translation on the assumption that at these points lines had been lost from the original poem, and they are based on suggestions by Sir Israel Gollancz (edition of *Sir Gawain and the Green Knight*, Early English Text Society, 1940).

SIR GAWAIN AND THE GREEN KNIGHT

I

When the siege and the assault had ceased at Troy,
and the fortress fell in flame to firebrands and ashes,
the traitor who the contrivance of treason there fashioned
was tried for his treachery, the most true upon earth—
it was Æneas the noble and his renowned kindred
who then laid under them lands, and lords became
of well-nigh all the wealth in the Western Isles.
When royal Romulus to Rome his road had taken,
in great pomp and pride he peopled it first,
and named it with his own name that yet now it bears;
Tirius went to Tuscany and towns founded,
Langaberde in Lombardy uplifted halls,
and far over the French flood Felix Brutus
on many a broad bank and brae Britain established
full fair,
where strange things, strife and sadness,
at whiles in the land did fare,
and each other grief and gladness
oft fast have followed there.

2 And when fair Britain was founded by this famous lord,
bold men were bred there who in battle rejoiced,
and many a time that betid they troubles aroused.
In this domain more marvels have by men been seen
than in any other that I know of since that olden time;
but of all that here abode in Britain as kings
ever was Arthur most honoured, as I have heard men tell.
Wherefore a marvel among men I mean to recall,
a sight strange to see some men have held it,
one of the wildest adventures of the wonders of Arthur.
If you will listen to this lay but a little while now,
I will tell it at once as in town I have heard
it told,
as it is fixed and fettered

in story brave and bold,
thus linked and truly lettered,
as was loved in this land of old.

3 This king lay at Camelot at Christmas-tide
with many a lovely lord, lieges most noble,
indeed of the Table Round all those tried brethren,
amid merriment unmatched and mirth without care.
There tourneyed many a time the trusty knights,
and jousted full joyously these gentle lords;
then to the court they came at carols to play.
For there the feast was unfailing full fifteen days,
with all meats and all mirth that men could devise,
such gladness and gaiety as was glorious to hear,
din of voices by day, and dancing by night;
all happiness at the highest in halls and in bowers
had the lords and the ladies, such as they loved most dearly.
With all the bliss of this world they abode together,
the knights most renowned after the name of Christ,
and the ladies most lovely that ever life enjoyed,
and he, king most courteous, who that court possessed.
For all that folk so fair did in their first estate
abide,
Under heaven the first in fame,
their king most high in pride;
it would now be hard to name
a troop in war so tried.

4 While New Year was yet young that yestereve had arrived,
that day double dainties on the dais were served,
when the king was there come with his courtiers to the hall,
and the chanting of the choir in the chapel had ended.
With loud clamour and cries both clerks and laymen
Noel announced anew, and named it full often;
then nobles ran anon with New Year gifts,
Handsels, handsels they shouted, and handed them out,
Competed for those presents in playful debate;
ladies laughed loudly, though they lost the game,
and he that won was not woeful, as may well be believed.
All this merriment they made, till their meat was served;
then they washed, and mannerly went to their seats,
ever the highest for the worthiest, as was held to be best.

Queen Guinevere the gay was with grace in the midst
of the adorned dais set. Dearly was it arrayed:
finest sendal at her sides, a ceiling above her
of true tissue of Tolouse, and tapestries of Tharsia
that were embroidered and bound with the brightest gems
one might prove and appraise to purchase for coin
any day.
That loveliest lady there
on them glanced with eyes of grey;
that he found ever one more fair
in sooth might no man say.

5 But Arthur would not eat until all were served;
his youth made him so merry with the moods of a boy,
he liked lighthearted life, so loved he the less
either long to be lying or long to be seated:
so worked on him his young blood and wayward brain.
And another rule moreover was his reason besides
that in pride he had appointed: it pleased him not to eat
upon festival so fair, ere he first were apprised
of some strange story or stirring adventure,
or some moving marvel that he might believe in
of noble men, knighthood, or new adventures;
or a challenger should come a champion seeking
to join with him in jousting, in jeopardy to set
his life against life, each allowing the other
the favour of fortune, were she fairer to him.
This was the king's custom, wherever his court was holden,
at each famous feast among his fair company
in hall.
So his face doth proud appear,
and he stands up stout and tall,
all young in the New Year;
much mirth he makes with all.

6 Thus there stands up straight the stern king himself,
talking before the high table of trifles courtly.
There good Gawain was set at Guinevere's side,
with Agravain a la Dure Main on the other side seated,
both their lord's sister-sons, loyal-hearted knights.
Bishop Baldwin had the honour of the board's service,
and Iwain Urien's son ate beside him.

These dined on the dais and daintily fared,
and many a loyal lord below at the long tables.
Then forth came the first course with fanfare of trumpets,
on which many bright banners bravely were hanging;
noise of drums then anew and the noble pipes,
warbling wild and keen, wakened their music,
so that many hearts rose high hearing their playing.
Then forth was brought a feast, fare of the noblest,
multitude of fresh meats on so many dishes
that free places were few in front of the people
to set the silver things full of soups on cloth
so white.
Each lord of his liking there
without lack took with delight:
twelve plates to every pair,
good beer and wine all bright.

7 Now of their service I will say nothing more,
for you are all well aware that no want would there be.
Another noise that was new drew near on a sudden,
so that their lord might have leave at last to take food.
For hardly had the music but a moment ended,
and the first course in the court as was custom been served,
when there passed through the portals a perilous horseman,
the mightiest on middle-earth in measure of height,
from his gorge to his girdle so great and so square,
and his loins and his limbs so long and so huge,
that half a troll upon earth I trow that he was,
but the largest man alive at least I declare him;
and yet the seemliest for his size that could sit on a horse,
for though in back and in breast his body was grim,
both his paunch and his waist were properly slight,
and all his features followed his fashion so gay
in mode;
for at the hue men gaped aghast
in his face and form that showed;
as a fay-man fell he passed,
and green all over glowed.

8 All of green were they made, both garments and man:
a coat tight and close that clung to his sides;
a rich robe above it all arrayed within

with fur finely trimmed, shewing fair fringes
of handsome ermine gay, as his hood was also,
that was lifted from his locks and laid on his shoulders;
and trim hose tight-drawn of tincture alike
that clung to his calves; and clear spurs below
of bright gold on silk broideries banded most richly,
though unshod were his shanks, for shoeless he rode.
And verily all this vesture was of verdure clear,
both the bars on his belt, and bright stones besides
that were richly arranged in his array so fair,
set on himself and on his saddle upon silk fabrics:
it would be too hard to rehearse one half of the trifles
that were embroidered upon them, what with birds and with flies
in a gay glory of green, and ever gold in the midst.
The pendants of his poitrel, his proud crupper,
his molains, and all the metal to say more, were enamelled,
even the stirrups that he stood in were stained of the same;
and his saddlebows in suit, and their sumptuous skirts,
which ever glimmered and glinted all with green jewels;
even the horse that upheld him in hue was the same,
I tell:
a green horse great and thick,
a stallion stiff to quell,
in broidered bridle quick:
he matched his master well.

9 Very gay was this great man guised all in green,
and the hair of his head with his horse's accorded:
fair flapping locks enfolding his shoulders,
a big beard like a bush over his breast hanging
that with the handsome hair from his head falling
was sharp shorn to an edge just short of his elbows,
so that half his arms under it were hid, as it were
in a king's capadoce that encloses his neck.
The mane of that mighty horse was of much the same sort,
well curled and all combed, with many curious knots
woven in with gold wire about the wondrous green,
ever a strand of the hair and a string of the gold;
the tail and the top-lock were twined all to match
and both bound with a band of a brilliant green:
with dear jewels bedight to the dock's ending,

and twisted then on top was a tight-knitted knot
on which many burnished bells of bright gold jingled.
Such a mount on middle-earth, or man to ride him,
was never beheld in that hall with eyes ere that time;
for there
his glance was as lightning bright,
so did all that saw him swear;
no man would have the might,
they thought, his blows to bear.

10 And yet hc had not a helm, nor a hauberk either,
not a pisane, not a plate that was proper to arms;
not a shield, not a shaft, for shock or for blow,
but in his one hand he held a holly-bundle,
that is greatest in greenery when groves are leafless,
and an axe in the other, ugly and monstrous,
a ruthless weapon aright for one in rhyme to describe:
the head was as large and as long as an ellwand,
a branch of green steel and of beaten gold;
the bit, burnished bright and broad at the edge,
as well shaped for shearing as sharp razors;
the stem was a stout staff, by which sternly he gripped it,
all bound with iron about to the base of the handle,
and engraven in green in graceful patterns,
lapped round with a lanyard that was lashed to the head
and down the length of the haft was looped many times;
and tassels of price were tied there in plenty
to bosses of the bright green, braided most richly.
Such was he that now hastened in, the hall entering,
pressing forward to the dais—no peril he feared.
To none gave he greeting, gazing above them,
and the first word that he winged: 'Now where is', he said,
'the governor of this gathering? For gladly I would
on the same set my sight, and with himself now talk
in town.'
On the courtiers he cast his eye,
and rolled it up and down;
he stopped, and stared to espy
who there had most renown.

11 Then they looked for a long while, on that lord gazing;
for every man marvelled what it could mean indeed

that horseman and horse such a hue should come by
as to grow green as the grass, and greener it seemed,
than green enamel on gold glowing far brighter.
All stared that stood there and stole up nearer,
watching him and wondering what in the world he would do.
For many marvels they had seen, but to match this nothing;
wherefore a phantom and fay-magic folk there thought it,
and so to answer little eager was any of those knights,
and astounded at his stern voice stone-still they sat there
in a swooning silence through that solemn chamber,
as if all had dropped into a dream, so died their voices
away.
Not only, I deem, for dread;
but of some 'twas their courtly way
to allow their lord and head
to the guest his word to say.

12 Then Arthur before the high dais beheld this wonder,
and freely with fair words, for fearless was he ever,
saluted him, saying: 'Lord, to this lodging thou'rt welcome!
The head of this household Arthur my name is.
Alight, as thou lovest me, and linger, I pray thee;
and what may thy wish be in a while we shall learn.'
'Nay, so help me,' quoth the horseman, 'He that on high is throned,
to pass any time in this place was no part of my errand.
But since thy praises, prince, so proud are uplifted,
and thy castle and courtiers are accounted the best,
the stoutest in steel-gear that on steeds may ride,
most eager and honourable of the earth's people,
valiant to vie with in other virtuous sports,
and here is knighthood renowned, as is noised in my ears:
'tis that has fetched me hither, by my faith, at this time.
You may believe by this branch that I am bearing here
that I pass as one in peace, no peril seeking.
For had I set forth to fight in fashion of war,
I have a hauberk at home, and a helm also,
a shield, and a sharp spear shining brightly,
and other weapons to wield too, as well I believe;
but since I crave for no combat, my clothes are softer.
Yet if thou be so bold, as abroad is published,

thou wilt grant of thy goodness the game that I ask for
by right.'
Then Arthur answered there,
and said: 'Sir, noble knight,
if battle thou seek thus bare,
thou'lt fail not here to fight.'

13 'Nay, I wish for no warfare, on my word I tell thee!
Here about on these benches are but beardless children.
Were I hasped in armour on a high charger,
there is no man here to match me—their might is so feeble.
And so I crave in this court only a Christmas pastime,
since it is Yule and New Year, and you are young here and merry.
If any so hardy in this house here holds that he is,
if so bold be his blood or his brain be so wild,
that he stoutly dare strike one stroke for another,
then I will give him as my gift this guisarm costly,
this axe—'tis heavy enough—to handle as he pleases;
and I will abide the first brunt, here bare as I sit.
If any fellow be so fierce as my faith to test,
hither let him haste to me and lay hold of this weapon—
I hand it over for ever, he can have it as his own—
and I will stand a stroke from him, stock-still on this floor,
provided thou'lt lay down this law: that I may deliver him another.
Claim I!
And yet a respite I'll allow,
till a year and a day go by.
Come quick, and let's see now
if any here dare reply!'

14 If he astounded them at first, yet stiller were then
all the household in the hall, both high men and low.
The man on his mount moved in his saddle,
and rudely his red eyes he rolled then about,
bent his bristling brows all brilliantly green,
and swept round his beard to see who would rise.
When none in converse would accost him, he coughed then loudly,
stretched himself haughtily and straightway exclaimed:
'What! Is this Arthur's house,' said he thereupon,

'the rumour of which runs through realms unnumbered?
Where now is your haughtiness, and your high conquests,
your fierceness and fell mood, and your fine boasting?
Now are the revels and the royalty of the Round Table
overwhelmed by a word by one man spoken,
for all blench now abashed ere a blow is offered!'
With that he laughed so loud that their lord was angered,
the blood shot for shame into his shining cheeks
and face;
as wroth as wind he grew,
so all did in that place.
Then near to the stout man drew
the king of fearless race,

15 And said: 'Marry! Good man, 'tis madness thou askest,
and since folly thou hast sought, thou deservest to find it.
I know no lord that is alarmed by thy loud words here.
Give me now thy guisarm, in God's name, sir,
and I will bring thee the blessing thou hast begged to receive.'
Quick then he came to him and caught it from his hand.
Then the lordly man loftily alighted on foot.
Now Arthur holds his axe, and the haft grasping
sternly he stirs it about, his stroke considering.
The stout man before him there stood his full height,
higher than any in that house by a head and yet more.
With stern face as he stood he stroked at his beard,
and with expression impassive he pulled down his coat,
no more disturbed or distressed at the strength of his blows
than if someone as he sat had served him a drink
of wine.
From beside the queen Gawain
to the king did then incline:
'I implore with prayer plain
that this match should now be mine.'

16 'Would you, my worthy lord,' said Wawain to the king,
'bid me abandon this bench and stand by you there,
so that I without discourtesy might be excused from the table,
and my liege lady were not loth to permit me,
I would come to your counsel before your courtiers fair.
For I find it unfitting, as in fact it is held,
when a challenge in your chamber makes choice so exalted,

though you yourself be desirous to accept it in person,
while many bold men about you on bench are seated:
on earth there are, I hold, none more honest of purpose,
no figures fairer on field where fighting is waged.
I am the weakest, I am aware, and in wit feeblest,
and the least loss, if I live not, if one would learn the truth.
Only because you are my uncle is honour given me:
save your blood in my body I boast of no virtue;
and since this affair is so foolish that it nowise befits you,
and I have requested it first, accord it then to me!
If my claim is uncalled-for without cavil shall judge
this court.'
To consult the knights draw near,
and this plan they all support;
the king with crown to clear,
and give Gawain the sport.

17 The king then commanded that he quickly should rise,
and he readily uprose and directly approached,
kneeling humbly before his highness, and laying hand on the weapon;
and he lovingly relinquished it, and lifting his hand
gave him God's blessing, and graciously enjoined him
that his hand and his heart should be hardy alike.
'Take care, cousin,' quoth the king, 'one cut to address,
and if thou learnest him his lesson, I believe very well
that thou wilt bear any blow that he gives back later.'
Gawain goes to the great man with guisarm in hand,
and he boldly abides there—he blenched not at all.
Then next said to Gawain the knight all in green:
'Let's tell again our agreement, ere we go any further.
I'd know first, sir knight, thy name; I entreat thee
to tell it me truly, that I may trust in thy word.'
'In good faith,' quoth the good knight, 'I Gawain am called
who bring thee this buffet, let be what may follow;
and at this time a twelvemonth in thy turn have another
with whatever weapon thou wilt, and in the world with none else
but me.'
The other man answered again:
'I am passing pleased,' said he,
'upon my life, Sir Gawain,
that this stroke should be struck by thee.'

18 'Begad,' said the green knight, 'Sir Gawain, I am pleased
to find from thy fist the favour I asked for!
And thou hast promptly repeated and plainly hast stated
without abatement the bargain I begged of the king here;
save that thou must assure me, sir, on thy honour
that thou'lt seek me thyself, search where thou thinkest
I may be found near or far, and fetch thee such payment
as thou deliverest me today before these lordly people,'
'Where should I light on thee,' quoth Gawain, 'where look for thy place?
I have never learned where thou livest, by the Lord that made me,
and I know thee not, knight, thy name nor thy court.
But teach me the true way, and tell what men call thee,
and I will apply all my purpose the path to discover:
and that I swear thee for certain and solemnly promise.'
'That is enough in New Year, there is need of no more!'
said the great man in green to Gawain the courtly.
'If I tell thee the truth of it, when I have taken the knock,
and thou handily hast hit me, if in haste I announce then
my house and my home and mine own title,
then thou canst call and enquire and keep the agreement;
and if I waste not a word, thou'lt win better fortune,
for thou mayst linger in thy land and look no further—
but stay!
To thy grim tool now take heed, sir!
Let us try thy knocks today!'
'Gladly', said he, 'indeed, sir!'
and his axe he stroked in play.

19 The Green Knight on the ground now gets himself ready,
leaning a little with the head he lays bare the flesh,
and his locks long and lovely he lifts over his crown,
letting the naked neck as was needed appear.
His left foot on the floor before him placing,
Gawain gripped on his axe, gathered and raised it,
from aloft let it swiftly land where 'twas naked,
so that the sharp of his blade shivered the bones,
and sank clean through the clear fat and clove it asunder,
and the blade of the bright steel then bit into the ground.
The fair head to the floor fell from the shoulders,

and folk fended it with their feet as forth it went rolling;
the blood burst from the body, bright on the greenness,
and yet neither faltered nor fell the fierce man at all,
but stoutly he strode forth, still strong on his shanks,
and roughly he reached out among the rows that stood there,
caught up his comely head and quickly upraised it,
and then hastened to his horse, laid hold of the bridle,
stepped into stirrup-iron, and strode up aloft,
his head by the hair in his hand holding;
and he settled himself then in the saddle as firmly
as if unharmed by mishap, though in the hall he might wear
no head.
His trunk he twisted round,
that gruesome body that bled,
and many fear then found,
as soon as his speech was sped.

20 For the head in his hand he held it up straight,
towards the fairest at the table he twisted the face,
and it lifted up its eyelids and looked at them broadly,
and made such words with its mouth as may be recounted.
'See thou get ready, Gawain, to go as thou vowedst,
and as faithfully seek till thou find me, good sir,
as thou hast promised in this place in the presence of these
knights.
To the Green Chapel go thou, and get thee, I charge thee,
such a dint as thou hast dealt—indeed thou hast earned
a nimble knock in return on New Year's morning!
The Knight of the Green Chapel I am known to many,
so if to find me thou endeavour, thou'lt fail not to do so.
Therefore come! Or to be called a craven thou deservest.'
With a rude roar and rush his reins he turned then,
and hastened out through the hall-door with his head in his
hand,
and fire of the flint flew from the feet of his charger.
To what country he came in that court no man knew,
no more than they had learned from what land he had
journeyed.
Meanwhile,
the king and Sir Gawain
at the Green Man laugh and smile;
yet to men had appeared, 'twas plain,
a marvel beyond denial.

21 Though Arthur the high king in his heart marvelled,
he let no sign of it be seen, but said then aloud
to the queen so comely with courteous words:
'Dear Lady, today be not downcast at all!
Such cunning play well becomes the Christmas tide,
interludes, and the like, and laughter and singing,
amid these noble dances of knights and of dames.
Nonetheless to my food I may fairly betake me,
for a marvel I have met, and I may not deny it.'
He glanced at Sir Gawain and with good point he said:
'Come, hang up thine axe, sir! It has hewn now enough.'
And over the table they hung it on the tapestry behind,
where all men might remark it, a marvel to see,
and by its true token might tell of that adventure.
Then to a table they turned, those two lords together,
the king and his good kinsman, and courtly men served them
with all dainties double, the dearest there might be,
with all manner of meats and with minstrelsy too.
With delight that day they led, till to the land came the night
again.
Sir Gawain, now take heed
lest fear make thee refrain
from daring the dangerous deed
that thou in hand hast ta'en!

II

With this earnest of high deeds thus Arthur began
the young year, for brave vows he yearned to hear made.
Though such words were wanting when they went to
table,
now of fell work to full grasp filled were their hands.
Gawain was gay as he began those games in the hall,
but if the end be unhappy, hold it no wonder!
For though men be merry of mood when they have mightily
drunk,
a year slips by swiftly, never the same returning;
the outset to the ending is equal but seldom.
And so this Yule passed over and the year after,
and severally the seasons ensued in their turn:

after Christmas there came the crabbed Lenten
that with fish tries the flesh and with food more meagre;
but then the weather in the world makes war on the winter,
cold creeps into the earth, clouds are uplifted,
shining rain is shed in showers that all warm
fall on the fair turf, flowers there open,
of grounds and of groves green is the raiment,
birds are busy a-building and bravely are singing
for sweetness of the soft summer that will soon be on
the way;
and blossoms burgeon and blow
in hedgerows bright and gay;
then glorious musics go
through the woods in proud array.

23 After the season of summer with its soft breezes,
when Zephyr goes sighing through seeds and herbs,
right glad is the grass that grows in the open,
when the damp dewdrops are dripping from the leaves,
to greet a gay glance of the glistening sun.
But then Harvest hurries in, and hardens it quickly,
warns it before winter to wax to ripeness.
He drives with his drought the dust, till it rises
from the face of the land and flies up aloft;
wild wind in the welkin makes war on the sun,
the leaves loosed from the linden alight on the ground,
and all grey is the grass that green was before:
all things ripen and rot that rose up at first,
and so the year runs away in yesterdays many,
and here winter wends again, as by the way of the world
it ought,
until the Michaelmas moon
has winter's boding brought;
Sir Gawain then full soon
of his grievous journey thought.

24 And yet till All Hallows with Arthur he lingered,
who furnished on that festival a feast for the knight
with much royal revelry of the Round Table.
The knights of renown and noble ladies
all for the love of that lord had longing at heart,
but nevertheless the more lightly of laughter they spoke:

many were joyless who jested for his gentle sake.
For after their meal mournfully he reminded his uncle
that his departure was near, and plainly he said:
'Now liege-lord of my life, for leave I beg you.
You know the quest and the compact; I care not further
to trouble you with tale of it, save a trifling point:
I must set forth to my fate without fail in the morning,
as God will me guide, the Green Man to seek.'
Those most accounted in the castle came then together,
Iwain and Erric and others not a few,
Sir Doddinel le Savage, the Duke of Clarence,
Lancelot, and Lionel, and Lucan the Good,
Sir Bors and Sir Bedivere that were both men of might,
and many others of mark with Mador de la Porte.
All this company of the court the king now approached
to comfort the knight with care in their hearts.
Much mournful lament was made in the hall
that one so worthy as Wawain should wend on that errand,
to endure a deadly dint and deal no more
with blade.
The knight ever made good cheer,
saying, 'Why should I be dismayed?
Of doom the fair or drear
by a man must be assayed.'

25 He remained there that day, and in the morning got ready,
asked early for his arms, and they all were brought him.
First a carpet of red silk was arrayed on the floor,
and the gilded gear in plenty there glittered upon it.
The stern man stepped thereon and the steel things handled,
dressed in a doublet of damask of Tharsia,
and over it a cunning capadoce that was closed at the throat
and with fair ermine was furred all within.
Then sabatons first they set on his feet,
his legs lapped in steel in his lordly greaves,
on which the polains they placed, polished and shining
and knit upon his knees with knots all of gold;
then the comely cuisses that cunningly clasped
the thick thews of his thighs they with thongs on him tied;
and next the byrnie, woven of bright steel rings
upon costly quilting, enclosed him about;
and armlets well burnished upon both of his arms,

with gay elbow-pieces and gloves of plate,
and all the goodly gear to guard him whatever
betide;
coat-armour richly made,
gold spurs on heel in pride;
girt with a trusty blade,
silk belt about his side.

26 When he was hasped in his armour his harness was splendid:
the least latchet or loop was all lit with gold.
Thus harnessed as he was he heard now his Mass,
that was offered and honoured at the high altar;
and then he came to the king and his court-companions,
and with love he took leave of lords and of ladies;
and they kissed him and escorted him, and to Christ him
commended.
And now Gringolet stood groomed, and girt with a saddle
gleaming right gaily with many gold fringes,
and all newly for the nonce nailed at all points;
adorned with bars was the bridle, with bright gold banded;
the apparelling proud of poitrel and of skirts,
and the crupper and caparison accorded with the saddlebows:
all was arrayed in red with rich gold studded,
so that it glittered and glinted as a gleam of the sun.
Then he in hand took the helm and in haste kissed it:
strongly was it stapled and stuffed within;
it sat high upon his head and was hasped at the back,
and a light kerchief was laid o'er the beaver,
all braided and bound with the brightest gems
upon broad silken broidery, with birds on the seams
like popinjays depainted, here preening and there,
turtles and true-loves, entwined as thickly
as if many sempstresses had the sewing full seven winters
in hand.
A circlet of greater price
his crown about did band;
The diamonds point-device
there blazing bright did stand.

27 Then they brought him his blazon that was of brilliant gules
with the pentangle depicted in pure hue of gold.
By the baldric he caught it and about his neck cast it:

right well and worthily it went with the knight.
And why the pentangle is proper to that prince so noble
I intend now to tell you, though it may tarry my story.
It is a sign that Solomon once set on a time
to betoken Troth, as it is entitled to do;
for it is a figure that in it five points holdeth,
and each line overlaps and is linked with another,
and every way it is endless; and the English, I hear,
everywhere name it the Endless Knot.
So it suits well this knight and his unsullied arms;
for ever faithful in five points, and five times under each,
Gawain as good was acknowledged and as gold refinéd,
devoid of every vice and with virtues adorned.
So there
the pentangle painted new
he on shield and coat did wear,
as one of word most true
and knight of bearing fair.

28 First faultless was he found in his five senses,
and next in his five fingers he failed at no time,
and firmly on the Five Wounds all his faith was set
that Christ received on the cross, as the Creed tells us;
and wherever the brave man into battle was come,
on this beyond all things was his earnest thought:
that ever from the Five Joys all his valour he gained
that to Heaven's courteous Queen once came from her Child.
For which cause the knight had in comely wise
on the inner side of his shield her image depainted,
that when he cast his eyes thither his courage never failed.
The fifth five that was used, as I find, by this knight
was free-giving and friendliness first before all,
and chastity and chivalry ever changeless and straight,
and piety surpassing all points: these perfect five
were hasped upon him harder than on any man else.
Now these five series, in sooth, were fastened on this knight,
and each was knit with another and had no ending,
but were fixed at five points that failed not at all,
coincided in no line nor sundered either,
not ending in any angle anywhere, as I discover,
wherever the process was put in play or passed to an end.
Therefore on his shining shield was shaped now this knot,

royally with red gules upon red gold set:
this is the pure pentangle as people of learning
    have taught.
  Now Gawain in brave array
  his lance at last hath caught.
  He gave them all good day,
  for evermore as he thought.

29 He spurned his steed with the spurs and sprang on his way
so fiercely that the flint-sparks flashed out behind him.
All who beheld him so honourable in their hearts were sighing,
and assenting in sooth one said to another,
grieving for that good man: 'Before God, 'tis a shame
that thou, lord, must be lost, who art in life so noble!
To meet his match among men, Marry, 'tis not easy!
To behave with more heed would have behoved one of sense,
and that dear lord duly a duke to have made,
illustrious leader of liegemen in this land as befits him;
and that would better have been than to be butchered to death,
beheaded by an elvish man for an arrogant vaunt.
Who can recall any king that such a course ever took
as knights quibbling at court at their Christmas games!'
Many warm tears outwelling there watered their eyes,
when that lord so beloved left the castle
    that day.
  No longer he abode,
  but swiftly went his way;
  bewildering ways he rode,
  as the book I heard doth say.

30 Now he rides thus arrayed through the realm of Logres,
Sir Gawain in God's care, though no game now he found it.
Oft forlorn and alone he lodged of a night
where he found not afforded him such fare as pleased him.
He had no friend but his horse in the forests and hills,
no man on his march to commune with but God,
till anon he drew near unto Northern Wales.
All the isles of Anglesey he held on his left,
and over the fords he fared by the flats near the sea,
and then over by the Holy Head to high land again
in the wilderness of Wirral: there wandered but few
who with good will regarded either God or mortal.

And ever he asked as he went on of all whom he met
if they had heard any news of a knight that was green
in any ground thereabouts, or of the Green Chapel.
And all denied it, saying nay, and that never in their lives
a single man had they seen that of such a colour
could be.
The knight took pathways strange
by many a lonesome lea,
and oft his view did change
that chapel ere he could see.

31 Many a cliff he climbed o'er in countries unknown,
far fled from his friends without fellowship he rode.
At every wading or water on the way that he passed
he found a foe before him, save at few for a wonder;
and so foul were they and fell that fight he must needs.
So many a marvel in the mountains he met in those lands
that 'twould be tedious the tenth part to tell you thereof.
At whiles with worms he wars, and with wolves also,
at whiles with wood-trolls that wandered in the crags,
and with bulls and with bears and boars, too, at times;
and with ogres that hounded him from the heights of the fells.
Had he not been stalwart and staunch and steadfast in God,
he doubtless would have died and death had met often;
for though war wearied him much, the winter was worse,
when the cold clear water from the clouds spilling
froze ere it had fallen upon the faded earth.
Wellnigh slain by the sleet he slept ironclad
more nights than enow in the naked rocks,
where clattering from the crest the cold brook tumbled,
and hung high o'er his head in hard icicles.
Thus in peril and pain and in passes grievous
till Christmas-eve that country he crossed all alone
in need.
The knight did at that tide
his plaint to Mary plead,
her rider's road to guide
and to some lodging lead.

32 By a mount in the morning merrily he was riding
into a forest that was deep and fearsomely wild,
with high hills at each hand, and hoar woods beneath

of huge aged oaks by the hundred together;
the hazel and the hawthorn were huddled and tangled
with rough ragged moss around them trailing,
with many birds bleakly on the bare twigs sitting
that piteously piped there for pain of the cold.
The good man on Gringolet goes now beneath them
through many marshes and mires, a man all alone,
troubled lest a truant at that time he should prove
from the service of the sweet Lord, who on that selfsame night
of a maid became man our mourning to conquer.
And therefore sighing he said: 'I beseech thee, O Lord,
and Mary, who is the mildest mother most dear,
for some harbour where with honour I might hear the Mass
and thy Matins tomorrow. This meekly I ask,
and thereto promptly I pray with Pater and Ave
  and Creed.'
 In prayer he now did ride,
 lamenting his misdeed;
 he blessed him oft and cried,
 'The Cross of Christ me speed!'

33 The sign on himself he had set but thrice,
ere a mansion he marked within a moat in the forest,
on a low mound above a lawn, laced under the branches
of many a burly bole round about by the ditches:
the castle most comely that ever a king possessed
placed amid a pleasaunce with a park all about it,
within a palisade of pointed pales set closely
that took its turn round the trees for two miles or more.
Gawain from the one side gazed on the stronghold
as it shimmered and shone through the shining oaks,
and then humbly he doffed his helm, and with honour he thanked
Jesus and Saint Julian, who generous are both,
who had courtesy accorded him and to his cry harkened.
'Now bon hostel,' quoth the knight, 'I beg of you still!'
Then he goaded Gringolet with his gilded heels,
and he chose by good chance the chief pathway
and brought his master bravely to the bridge's end
  at last.
 That brave bridge was up-hauled,
 the gates were bolted fast;

the castle was strongly walled,
it feared no wind or blast.

34 Then he stayed his steed that on the steep bank halted
above the deep double ditch that was drawn round the place.
The wall waded in the water wondrous deeply,
and up again to a huge height in the air it mounted,
all of hard hewn stone to the high cornice,
fortified under the battlement in the best fashion
and topped with fair turrets set by turns about
that had many graceful loopholes with a good outlook:
that knight a better barbican had never seen built.
And inwards he beheld the hall uprising,
tall towers set in turns, and as tines clustering
the fair finials, joined featly, so fine and so long,
their capstones all carven with cunning and skill.
Many chalk-white chimneys he chanced to espy
upon the roofs of towers all radiant white;
so many a painted pinnacle was peppered about,
among the crenelles of the castle clustered so thickly
that all pared out of paper it appeared to have been.
The gallant knight on his great horse good enough thought it,
if he could come by any course that enclosure to enter,
to harbour in that hostel while the holy day lasted
with delight.
He called, and there came with speed
a porter blithe and bright;
on the wall he learned his need,
and hailed the errant knight.

35 'Good sir,' quoth Gawain, 'will you go with my message
to the high lord of this house for harbour to pray?'
'Yes, by Peter!' quoth the porter, 'and I promise indeed
that you will, sir, be welcome while you wish to stay here.'
Then quickly the man went and came again soon,
servants bringing civilly to receive there the knight.
They drew down the great drawbridge, and duly came forth,
and on the cold earth on their knees in courtesy knelt
to welcome this wayfarer with such worship as they knew.
They delivered him the broad gates and laid them wide open,
and he readily bade them rise and rode o'er the bridge.
Several servants then seized the saddle as he alighted,

and many stout men his steed to a stable then led,
while knights and esquires anon descended
to guide there in gladness this guest to the hall.
When he raised up his helm many ran there in haste
to have it from his hand, his highness to serve;
his blade and his blazon both they took charge of.
Then he greeted graciously those good men all,
and many were proud to approach him, that prince to honour.
All hasped in his harness to hall they brought him,
where a fair blaze in the fireplace fiercely was burning.
Then the lord of that land leaving his chamber
Came mannerly to meet the man on the floor.
He said: 'You are welcome at your wish to dwell here.
What is here, all is your own, to have in your rule
        and sway.'
  'Gramercy!' quoth Gawain,
  'May Christ you this repay!'
  As men that to meet were fain
  they both embraced that day.

36 Gawain gazed at the good man who had greeted him kindly,
and he thought bold and big was the baron of the castle,
very large and long, and his life at the prime:
broad and bright was his beard, and all beaver-hued,
stern, strong in his stance upon stalwart legs,
his face fell as fire, and frank in his speech;
and well it suited him, in sooth, as it seemed to the knight,
a lordship to lead untroubled over lieges trusty.
To a chamber the lord drew him, and charged men at once
to assign him an esquire to serve and obey him;
and there to wait on his word many worthy men were,
who brought him to a bright bower where the bedding was
splendid:
there were curtains of costly silk with clear-golden hems,
and coverlets cunning-wrought with quilts most lovely
of bright ermine above, embroidered at the sides,
hangings running on ropes with red-gold rings,
carpets of costly damask that covered the walls
and the floor under foot fairly to match them.
There they despoiled him, speaking to him gaily,
his byrnie doing off and his bright armour.

Rich robes then readily men ran to bring him,
for him to change, and to clothe him, having chosen the best.
As soon as he had donned one and dressed was therein,
as it sat on him seemly with its sailing skirts,
then verily in his visage a vision of Spring
to each man there appeared, and in marvellous hues
bright and beautiful was all his body beneath.
That knight more noble was never made by Christ
they thought.
He came none knew from where,
but it seemed to them he ought
to be a prince beyond compare
in the field where fell men fought.

37 A chair before the chimney where charcoal was burning
was made ready in his room, all arrayed and covered
with cushions upon quilted cloths that were cunningly made.
Then a comely cloak was cast about him
of bright silk brocade, embroidered most richly
and furred fairly within with fells of the choicest
and all edged with ermine, and its hood was to match;
and he sat in that seat seemly and noble
and warmed himself with a will, and then his woes were
amended.
Soon up on good trestles a table was raised
and clad with a clean cloth clear white to look on;
there was surnape, salt-cellar, and silvern spoons.
He then washed as he would and went to his food,
and many worthy men with worship waited upon him;
soups they served of many sorts, seasoned most choicely,
in double helpings, as was due, and divers sorts of fish;
some baked in bread, some broiled on the coals,
some seethed, some in gravy savoured with spices,
and all with condiments so cunning that it caused him delight.
A fair feast he called it frankly and often,
graciously, when all the good men together there pressed him:
'Now pray,
this penance deign to take;
'twill improve another day!'
The man much mirth did make,
for wine to his head made way.

38 Then inquiry and question were carefully put
touching personal points to that prince himself,
till he courteously declared that to the court he belonged
that high Arthur in honour held in his sway,
who was the right royal King of the Round Table,
and 'twas Gawain himself that as their guest now sat
and had come for that Christmas, as the case had turned out.
When the lord had learned whom luck had brought him,
loud laughed he thereat, so delighted he was,
and they made very merry, all the men in that castle,
and to appear in the presence were pressing and eager
of one who all profit and prowess and perfect manners
comprised in his person, and praise ever gained;
of all men on middle-earth he most was admired.
Softly each said then in secret to his friend:
'Now fairly shall we mark the fine points of manners,
and the perfect expressions of polished converse.
How speech is well spent will be expounded unasked,
since we have found here this fine father of breeding.
God has given us of His goodness His grace now indeed,
Who such a guest as Gawain has granted us to have!
When blissful men at board for His birth sing blithe
at heart,
what manners high may mean
this knight will now impart.
Who hears him will, I ween,
of love-speech learn some art.'

39 When his dinner was done and he duly had risen,
it now to the night-time very near had drawn.
The chaplains then took to the chapel their way
and rang the bells richly, as rightly they should,
for the solemn evensong of the high season.
The lord leads the way, and his lady with him;
into a goodly oratory gracefully she enters.
Gawain follows gladly, and goes there at once
and the lord seizes him by the sleeve and to a seat leads him,
kindly acknowledges him and calls him by his name,
saying that most welcome he was of all guests in the world.
And he grateful thanks gave him, and each greeted the other,
and they sat together soberly while the service lasted.
Then the lady longed to look at this knight;

and from her closet she came with many comely maidens.
She was fairer in face, in her flesh and her skin,
her proportions, her complexion, and her port than all others,
and more lovely than Guinevere to Gawain she looked.
He came through the chancel to pay court to her grace;
leading her by the left hand another lady was there
who was older than she, indeed ancient she seemed,
and held in high honour by all men about her.
But unlike in their looks those ladies appeared,
for if the younger was youthful, yellow was the elder;
with rose-hue the one face was richly mantled,
rough wrinkled cheeks rolled on the other;
on the kerchiefs of the one many clear pearls were,
her breast and bright throat were bare displayed,
fairer than white snow that falls on the hills;
the other was clad with a cloth that enclosed all her neck,
enveloped was her black chin with chalk-white veils,
her forehead folded in silk, and so fumbled all up,
so topped up and trinketed and with trifles bedecked
that naught was bare of that beldame but her brows all black,
her two eyes and her nose and her naked lips,
and those were hideous to behold and horribly bleared;
that a worthy dame she was may well, fore God,
be said!
short body and thick waist,
with bulging buttocks spread;
more delicious to the taste
was the one she by her led.

40 When Gawain glimpsed that gay lady that so gracious looked,
with leave sought of the lord towards the ladies he went;
the elder he saluted, low to her bowing,
about the lovelier he laid then lightly his arms
and kissed her in courtly wise with courtesy speaking.
His acquaintance they requested, and quickly he begged
to be their servant in sooth, if so they desired.
They took him between them, and talking they led him
to a fireside in a fair room, and first of all called
for spices, which men sped without sparing to bring them,
and ever wine therewith well to their liking.
The lord for their delight leaped up full often,
many times merry games being minded to make;

his hood he doffed, and on high he hung it on a spear,
and offered it as an honour for any to win
who the most fun could devise at that Christmas feast—
'And I shall try, by my troth, to contend with the best
ere I forfeit this hood, with the help of my friends!'
Thus with laughter and jollity the lord made his jests
to gladden Sir Gawain with games that night
in hall,
until the time was due
that the lord for lights should call;
Sir Gawain with leave withdrew
and went to bed withal.

41 On the morn when every man remembers the time
that our dear Lord for our doom to die was born,
in every home wakes happiness on earth for His sake.
So did it there on that day with the dearest delights:
at each meal and at dinner marvellous dishes
men set on the dais, the daintiest meats.
The old ancient woman was highest at table,
meetly to her side the master he took him;
Gawain and the gay lady together were seated
in the centre, where as was seemly the service began,
and so on through the hall as honour directed.
When each good man in his degree without grudge had been served,
there was food, there was festival, there was fullness of joy;
and to tell all the tale of it I should tedious find,
though pains I might take every point to detail.
Yet I ween that Wawain and that woman so fair
in companionship took such pleasure together
in sweet society soft words speaking,
their courteous converse clean and clear of all evil,
that with their pleasant pastime no prince's sport
compares.
Drums beat, and trumps men wind,
many pipers play their airs;
each man his needs did mind,
and they two minded theirs.

42 With much feasting they fared the first and the next day,
and as heartily the third came hastening after:

the gaiety of Saint John's day was glorious to hear;
[with cheer of the choicest Childermas followed,]
and that finished their revels, as folk there intended,
for there were guests who must go in the grey morning.
So a wondrous wake they held, and the wine they drank,
and they danced and danced on, and dearly they carolled.
At last when it was late their leave then they sought
to wend on their ways, each worthy stranger.
Good-day then said Gawain, but the good man stayed him,
and led him to his own chamber to the chimney-corner,
and there he delayed him, and lovingly thanked him,
for the pride and pleasure his presence had brought,
for so honouring his house at that high season
and deigning his dwelling to adorn with his favour.
'Believe me, sir, while I live my luck I shall bless
that Gawain was my guest at God's own feast.'
'Gramercy, sir,' said Gawain, 'but the goodness is yours,
all the honour is your own—may the High King repay you!
And I am under your orders what you ask to perform,
as I am bound now to be, for better or worse,
by right.'
Him longer to retain
the lord then pressed the knight;
to him replied Gawain
that he by no means might.

43 Then with courteous question he enquired of Gawain
what dire need had driven him on that festal date
with such keenness from the king's court, to come forth alone
ere wholly the holidays from men's homes had departed.
'In sooth, sir,' he said, 'you say but the truth:
a high errand and a hasty from that house brought me;
for I am summoned myself to seek for a place,
though I wonder where in the world I must wander to find it.
I would not miss coming nigh it on New Year's morning
for all the land in Logres, so our Lord help me!
And so, sir, this question I enquire of you here:
can you tell me in truth if you tale ever heard
of the Green Chapel, on what ground it may stand,
and of the great knight that guards it, all green in his colour?
For the terms of a tryst were between us established
to meet that man at that mark, if I remained alive,

and the named New Year is now nearly upon me,
and I would look on that lord, if God will allow me,
more gladly, by God's son, than gain any treasure.
So indeed, if you please, depart now I must.
For my business I have now but barely three days,
and I would fainer fall dead than fail in my errand.'
Then laughing said the lord: 'Now linger you must;
for when 'tis time to that tryst I will teach you the road.
On what ground is the Green Chapel—let it grieve you no more!
In your bed you shall be, sir, till broad is the day,
without fret, and then fare on the first of the year,
and come to the mark at midmorn, there to make what play
you know.
Remain till New Year's day,
then rise and riding go!
We'll set you on your way,
'tis but two miles or so.'

44 Then was Gawain delighted, and in gladness he laughed:
'Now I thank you a thousand times for this beyond all!
Now my quest is accomplished, as you crave it, I will
dwell a few days here, and else do what you order.'
The lord then seized him and set him in a seat beside him,
and let the ladies be sent for to delight them the more,
for their sweet pleasure there in peace by themselves.
For love of him that lord was as loud in his mirth
as one near out of his mind who scarce knew what he meant.
Then he called to the knight, crying out loudly:
'You have promised to do whatever deed I propose.
Will you hold this behest here, at this moment?'
'Yes, certainly, sir,' then said the true knight,
'while I remain in your mansion, your command I'll obey.'
'Well,' returned he, 'you have travelled and toiled from afar,
and then I've kept you awake: you're not well yet, not cured;
both sustenance and sleep 'tis certain you need.
Upstairs you shall stay, sir, and stop there in comfort
tomorrow till Mass-time, and to a meal then go
when you wish with my wife, who with you shall sit
and comfort you with her company, till to court I return.
You stay,
and I shall early rouse,

and a-hunting wend my way.'
Gawain gracefully bows:
'Your wishes I will obey.'

45 'One thing more,' said the master, 'we'll make an agreement:
whatever I win in the wood at once shall be yours,
and whatever gain you may get you shall give in exchange.
Shall we swap thus, sweet man—come, say what you think!—
whether one's luck be light, or one's lot be better?'
'By God,' quoth good Gawain, 'I agree to it all,
and whatever play you propose seems pleasant to me.'
'Done! 'Tis a bargain! Who'll bring us the drink?'
So said the lord of that land. They laughed one and all;
they drank and they dallied, and they did as they pleased,
these lords and ladies, as long as they wished,
and then with customs of France and many courtly phrases
they stood in sweet debate and soft words bandied,
and lovingly they kissed, their leave taking.
With trusty attendants and torches gleaming
they were brought at the last to their beds so soft,
one and all.
Yet ere to bed they came,
he the bargain did oft recall;
he knew how to play a game
the old governor of that hall.

III

Before the first daylight the folk uprose:
the guests that were to go for their grooms they called;
and they hurried up in haste horses to saddle,
to stow all their stuff and strap up their bags.
The men of rank arrayed them, for riding got ready,
to saddle leaped swiftly, seized then their bridles,
and went off on their ways where their wish was to go.
The liege-lord of the land was not last of them all
to be ready to ride with a rout of his men;
he ate a hurried mouthful after the hearing of Mass,
and with horn to the hunting-field he hastened at once.
When daylight was opened yet dimly on earth

he and his huntsmen were up on their high horses.
Then the leaders of the hounds leashed them in couples,
unclosed the kennel-door and cried to them 'out!',
and blew boldly on bugles three blasts full long.
Beagles bayed thereat, a brave noise making;
and they whipped and wheeled in those that wandered on a scent;
a hundred hunting-dogs, I have heard, of the best
were they.
To their stations keepers passed;
the leashes were cast away,
and many a rousing blast
woke din in the woods that day.

47 At the first burst of the baying all beasts trembled;
deer dashed through the dale by dread bewildered,
and hastened to the heights, but they hotly were greeted,
and turned back by the beaters, who boldly shouted.
They let the harts go past with their high antlers,
and the brave bucks also with their branching palms;
for the lord of the castle had decreed in the close season
that no man should molest the male of the deer.
The hinds were held back with hey! and ware!,
the does driven with great din to the deep valleys:
there could be seen let slip a sleet of arrows;
at each turn under the trees went a twanging shaft
that into brown hides bit hard with barbéd head.
Lo! they brayed, and they bled, and on the banks they died;
and ever the hounds in haste hotly pursued them,
and hunters with high horns hurried behind them
with such a clamour and cry as if cliffs had been riven.
If any beast broke away from bowmen there shooting,
it was snatched down and slain at the receiving-station;
when they had been harried from the height and hustled to the waters,
the men were so wise in their craft at the watches below,
and their greyhounds were so great that they got them at once,
and flung them down in a flash, as fast as men could see
with sight.
The lord then wild for joy
did oft spur and oft alight,
and thus in bliss employ
that day till dark of night.

48 Thus in his game the lord goes under greenwood eaves,
and Gawain the bold lies in goodly bed,
lazing, till the walls are lit by the light of day,
under costly coverlet with curtains about him.
And as in slumber he strayed, he heard stealthily come
a soft sound at his door as it secretly opened;
and from under the clothes he craned then his head,
a corner of the curtain he caught up a little,
and looked that way warily to learn what it was.
It was the lady herself, most lovely to see,
that cautiously closed the door quietly behind her,
and drew near to his bed. Then abashed was the knight,
and lay down swiftly to look as if he slept;
and she stepped silently and stole to his bed,
cast back the curtain, and crept then within,
and sat her down softly on the side of the bed,
and there lingered very long to look for his waking.
He lay there lurking a long while and wondered,
and mused in his mind how the matter would go,
to what point it might pass—to some surprise, he fancied.
Yet he said to himself: 'More seemly 'twould be
in due course with question to enquire what she wishes.'
Then rousing he rolled over, and round to her turning
he lifted his eyelids with a look as of wonder,
and signed him with the cross, thus safer to be kept
aright.
With chin and cheeks so sweet
of blended red and white,
with grace then him did greet
small lips with laughter bright.

49 'Good morning, Sir Gawain!' said that gracious lady.
'You are a careless sleeper, if one can creep on you so!
Now quickly you are caught! If we come not to terms,
I shall bind you in your bed, you may be assured.'
With laughter the lady thus lightly jested.
'Good morning to your grace!' said Gawain gaily.
'You shall work on me your will, and well I am pleased;
for I submit immediately, and for mercy I cry,
and that is best, as I deem, for I am obliged to do so.'
Thus he jested in return with much gentle laughter:
'But if you would, lady gracious, then leave grant me,

and release your prisoner and pray him to rise,
I would abandon this bed and better array me;
the more pleasant would it prove then to parley with you.'
'Nay, for sooth, fair sir,' said the sweet lady,
'you shall not go from your bed! I will govern you better:
here fast shall I enfold you, on the far side also,
and then talk with my true knight that I have taken so.
For I wot well indeed that Sir Wawain you are,
to whom all men pay homage wherever you ride;
your honour, your courtesy, by the courteous is praised,
by lords, by ladies, by all living people.
And right here you now are, and we all by ourselves;
my husband and his huntsmen far hence have ridden,
other men are abed, and my maids also,
the door closed and caught with a clasp that is strong;
and since I have in this house one that all delight in,
my time to account I will turn, while for talk I chance
have still.
To my body will you welcome be
of delight to take your fill;
for need constraineth me
to serve you, and I will.'

50 'Upon my word,' said Gawain, 'that is well, I guess;
though I am not now he of whom you are speaking—
to attain to such honour as here you tell of
I am a knight unworthy, as well indeed I know—
by God, I would be glad, if good to you seemed
whatever I could say, or in service could offer
to the pleasure of your excellence—it would be pure delight.'
'In good faith, Sir Gawain,' said the gracious lady,
'the prowess and the excellence that all others approve,
if I scorned or decried them, it were scant courtesy.
But there are ladies in number who liever would now
have thee in their hold, sir, as I have thee here,
pleasantly to play with in polished converse,
their solace to seek and their sorrows to soothe,
than great part of the goods or gold that they own.
But I thank Him who on high of Heaven is Lord
that I have here wholly in my hand what all desire,
by grace.'
She was an urgent wooer,

that lady fair of face;
the knight with speeches pure
replied in every case.

51 'Madam,' said he merrily, 'Mary reward you!
For I have enjoyed, in good faith, your generous favour,
and much honour have had else from others' kind deeds;
but as for the courtesy they accord me, since my claim is not equal,
the honour is your own, who are ever well-meaning.'
'Nay, Mary!' the lady demurred, 'as for me, I deny it.
For were I worth all the legion of women alive,
and all the wealth in the world at my will possessed,
if I should exchange at my choice and choose me a husband,
for the noble nature I know, Sir Knight, in thee here,
in beauty and bounty and bearing so gay—
of which earlier I have heard, and hold it now true—
then no lord alive would I elect before you.'
'In truth, lady,' he returned, 'you took one far better.
But I am proud of the praise you are pleased to give me,
and as your servant in earnest my sovereign I hold you,
and your knight I become, and may Christ reward you.'
Thus of many matters they spoke till midmorn was passed,
and ever the lady demeaned her as one that loved him much,
and he fenced with her featly, ever flawless in manner.
'Though I were lady most lovely,' thought the lady to herself,
'the less love would he bring here,' since he looked for his bane,
that blow
that him so soon should grieve,
and needs it must be so.
Then the lady asked for leave
and at once he let her go.

52 Then she gave him 'good day', and with a glance she laughed,
and as she stood she astonished him with the strength of her words:
'Now He that prospers all speech for this disport repay you!
But that you should be Gawain, it gives me much thought.'
'Why so?', then eagerly the knight asked her,
afraid that he had failed in the form of his converse.
But 'God bless you! For this reason', blithely she answered,

'that one so good as Gawain the gracious is held,
who all the compass of courtesy includes in his person,
so long with a lady could hardly have lingered
without craving a kiss, as a courteous knight,
by some tactful turn that their talk led to.'
Then said Wawain, 'Very well, as you wish be it done.
I will kiss at your command, as becometh a knight,
and more, lest he displease you, so plead it no longer.'
She came near thereupon and caught him in her arms,
and down daintily bending dearly she kissed him.
They courteously commended each other to Christ.
Without more ado through the door she withdrew and departed,
and he to rise up in haste made ready at once.
He calls to his chamberlain, and chooses his clothes,
and goes forth when garbed all gladly to Mass.
Then he went to a meal that meetly awaited him,
and made merry all day, till the moon arose
        o'er earth.
    Ne'er was knight so gaily engaged
    between two dames of worth,
    the youthful and the aged:
    together they made much mirth.

53 And ever the lord of the land in his delight was abroad,
hunting by holt and heath after hinds that were barren.
When the sun began to slope he had slain such a number
of does and other deer one might doubt it were true.
Then the fell folk at last came flocking all in,
and quickly of the kill they a quarry assembled.
Thither the master hastened with a host of his men,
gathered together those greatest in fat
and had them riven open rightly, as the rules require.
At the assay they were searched by some that were there,
and two fingers' breadth of fat they found in the leanest.
Next they slit the eslot, seized on the arber,
shaved it with a sharp knife and shore away the grease;
next ripped the four limbs and rent off the hide.
Then they broke open the belly, the bowels they removed
(flinging them nimbly afar) and the flesh of the knot;
they grasped then the gorge, disengaging with skill
the weasand from the windpipe, and did away with the guts.
Then they shore out the shoulders with their sharpened knives

(drawing the sinews through a small cut) the sides to keep whole;
next they burst open the breast, and broke it apart,
and again at the gorge one begins thereupon,
cuts all up quickly till he comes to the fork,
and fetches forth the fore-numbles; and following after
all the tissues along the ribs they tear away quickly.
Thus by the bones of the back they broke off with skill,
down even to the haunch, all that hung there together,
and hoisted it up all whole and hewed it off there:
and that they took for the numbles, as I trow is their name
in kind.
Along the fork of every thigh
the flaps they fold behind;
to hew it in two they hie,
down the back all to unbind.

54 Both the head and the neck they hew off after,
and next swiftly they sunder the sides from the chine,
and the bone for the crow they cast in the boughs.
Then they thrust through both thick sides with a thong by the rib,
and then by the hocks of the legs they hang them both up:
all the folk earn the fees that fall to their lot.
Upon the fell of the fair beast they fed their hounds then
on the liver and the lights and the leather of the paunches
with bread bathed in blood blended amongst them.
Boldly they blew the prise, amid the barking of dogs,
and then bearing up their venison bent their way homeward,
striking up strongly many a stout horn-call.
When daylight was done they all duly were come
into the noble castle, where quietly the knight
abode
in bliss by bright fire set.
Thither the lord now strode;
when Gawain with him met,
then free all pleasure flowed.

55 Then the master commanded his men to meet in that hall,
and both dames to come down with their damsels also;
before all the folk on that floor fair men he ordered
to fetch there forthwith his venison before him,

and all gracious in game to Gawain he called,
announced the number by tally of the nimble beasts,
and showed him the shining fat all shorn on the ribs.
'How does this play please you? Have I praise deserved?
Have I earned by mine art the heartiest thanks?'
'Yea verily,' the other averred, 'here is venison the fairest
'that I've seen in seven years in the season of winter!'
'And I give it you all, Gawain,' said the good man at once,
'for as our covenant accorded you may claim it as your own.'
'That is true,' he returned, 'and I tell you the same:
what of worth within these walls I have won also
with as good will, I warrant, 'tis awarded to you.'
His fair neck he enfolded then fast in his arms,
and kissed him with all the kindness that his courtesy knew.
'There take you my gains, sir! I got nothing more.
I would give it up gladly even if greater it were.'
'That is a good one!' quoth the good man. 'Greatly I thank you.
'Tis such, maybe, that you had better briefly now tell me
where you won this same wealth by the wits you possess.'
'That was not the covenant,' quoth he. 'Do not question me more!
For you've drawn what is due to you, no doubt can you have 'tis true.'
They laugh, and with voices fair
their merriment pursue,
and to supper soon repair
with many dainties new.

56 Later by the chimney in chamber they were seated,
abundant wine of the best was brought to them oft,
and again as a game they agreed on the morrow
to abide by the same bond as they had bargained before:
chance what might chance, to exchange all their trade,
whatever new thing they got, when they gathered at night.
They concluded this compact before the courtiers all;
the drink for the bargain was brought forth in jest;
then their leave at the last they lovingly took,
and away then at once each went to his bed.
When the cock had crowned and cackled but thrice,
the lord had leaped from his bed, and his lieges each one;

so that their meal had been made, and the Mass was over,
and folk bound for the forest, ere the first daybreak,
to chase.
Loud with hunters and horns
o'er plains they passed apace,
and loosed there among the thorns
the running dogs to race.

57 Soon these cried for a quest in a covert by a marsh;
the huntsman hailed the hound that first heeded the scent,
stirring words he spoke to him with a strident voice.
The hounds then that heard it hastened thither swiftly,
and fell fast on the line, some forty at once.
Then such a baying and babel of bloodhounds together
arose that the rock-wall rang all about them.
Hunters enheartened them with horn and with mouth,
and then all in a rout rushed on together
between a fen-pool in that forest and a frowning crag.
In a tangle under a tall cliff at the tarn's edges,
where the rough rock ruggedly in ruin was fallen,
they fared to the find, followed by hunters
who made a cast round the crag and the clutter of stones,
till well they were aware that it waited within:
the very beast that the baying bloodhounds had spoken.
Then they beat on the bushes and bade him uprise,
and forth he came to their peril against folk in his path.
'Twas a boar without rival that burst out upon them;
long the herd he had left, that lone beast aged,
for savage was he, of all swine the hugest,
grim indeed when he grunted. Then aghast were many;
for three at the first thrust he threw to the ground,
and sprang off with great speed, sparing the others;
and they hallooed on high, and ha! ha! shouted,
and held horn to mouth, blowing hard the rally.
Many were the wild mouthings of men and of dogs,
as they bounded after this boar, him with blare and with din
to quell.
Many times he turns to bay,
and maims the pack pell-mell;
he hurts many hounds, and they
grievously yowl and yell.

58 Hunters then hurried up eager to shoot him,
aimed at him their arrows, often they hit him;
but poor at core proved the points that pitched on his shields,
and the barbs on his brows would bite not at all;
though the shaven shaft shivered in pieces,
back the head came hopping, wherever it hit him.
But when the hurts went home of their heavier strokes,
then with brain wild for battle he burst out upon them,
ruthless he rent them as he rushed forward,
and many quailed at his coming and quickly withdrew.
But the lord on a light horse went leaping after him;
as bold man on battle-field with his bugle he blew
the rally-call as he rode through the rough thickets,
pursuing this wild swine till the sunbeams slanted.
This day in such doings thus duly they passed,
while our brave knight beloved there lies in his bed
at home in good hap, in housings so costly
and gay.
The lady did not forget:
she came to bid good day;
early she on him set,
his will to wear away.

59 She passed to the curtain and peeped at the knight.
Sir Wawain graciously then welcomed her first,
and she answered him alike, eagerly speaking,
and sat her softly by his side; and suddenly she laughed,
and with a look full of love delivered these words:
'Sir, if you are Wawain, a wonder I think it
that a man so well-meaning, ever mindful of good,
yet cannot comprehend the customs of the gentle;
and if one acquaints you therewith, you do not keep them in mind:
thou hast forgot altogether what a day ago I taught
by the plainest points I could put into words!'
'What is that?' he said at once. 'I am not aware of it at all.
But if you are telling the truth, I must take all the blame.'
'And yet as to kisses', she quoth, 'this counsel I gave you:
wherever favour is found, defer not to claim them:
that becomes all who care for courteous manners.'
'Take back', said the true knight, 'that teaching, my dear!
For that I dared not do, for dread of refusal.

Were I rebuffed, I should be to blame for so bold an offer.'
'Ma fay!' said the fair lady, 'you may not be refused;
you are stout enough to constrain one by strength, if you like,
if any were so ill bred as to answer you nay.'
'Indeed, by God', quoth Gawain, 'you graciously speak;
but force finds no favour among the folk where I dwell,
and any gift not given gladly and freely.
I am at your call and command to kiss when you please.
You may receive as you desire, and cease as you think
in place.'
Then down the lady bent,
and sweetly kissed his face.
Much speech then there they spent
of lovers' grief and grace.

60 'I would learn from you, lord,' the lady then said,
'if you would not mind my asking, what is the meaning of this:
that one so young as are you in years, and so gay,
by renown so well known for knighthood and breeding,
while of all chivalry the choice, the chief thing to praise,
is the loyal practice of love: very lore of knighthood—
for, talking of the toils that these true knights suffer,
it is the title and contents and text of their works:
how lovers for their true love their lives have imperilled,
have endured for their dear one dolorous trials,
until avenged by their valour, their adversity passed,
they have brought bliss into her bower by their own brave virtues—
and you are the knight of most noble renown in our age,
and your fame and fair name afar is published,
and I have sat by your very self now for the second time,
yet your mouth has never made any remark I have heard
that ever belonged to love-making, lesser or greater.
Surely, you that are so accomplished and so courtly in your vows
should be prompt to expound to a young pupil
by signs and examples the science of lovers.
Why? Are you ignorant who all honour enjoy?
Or else you esteem me too stupid to understand your courtship?
But nay!
Here single I come and sit,

a pupil for your play;
come, teach me of your wit,
while my lord is far away.'

61 'In good faith', said Gawain, 'may God reward you!
Great delight I gain, and am glad beyond measure
that one so worthy as you should be willing to come here
and take pains with so poor a man: as for playing with your knight,
showing favour in any form, it fills me with joy.
But for me to take up the task on true love to lecture,
to comment on the text and tales of knighthood
to you, who I am certain possess far more skill
in that art by the half than a hundred of such
as I am, or shall ever be while on earth I remain,
it would be folly manifold, in faith, my lady!
All your will I would wish to work, as I am able,
being so beholden in honour, and, so help me the Lord,
desiring ever the servant of yourself to remain.'
Thus she tested and tried him, tempting him often,
so as to allure him to love-making, whatever lay in her heart.
But his defence was so fair that no fault could be seen,
nor any evil upon either side, nor aught but joy
they wist.
They laughed and long they played;
at last she him then kissed,
with grace adieu him bade,
and went whereso she list.

62 Then rousing from his rest he rose to hear Mass,
and then their dinner was laid and daintily served.
The livelong day with the ladies in delight he spent,
but the lord o'er the lands leaped to and fro,
pursuing his fell swine that o'er the slopes hurtled
and bit asunder the backs of the best of his hounds,
wherever to bay he was brought, until bowmen dislodged him,
and made him, maugre his teeth, move again onward,
so fast the shafts flew when the folk were assembled.
And yet the stoutest of them still he made start there aside,
till at last he was so spent he could speed no further,
but in such haste as he might he made for a hollow
on a reef beside a rock where the river was flowing.

He put the bank at his back, began then to paw;
fearfully the froth of his mouth foamed from the corners;
he whetted his white tusks. Then weary were all
the brave men so bold as by him to stand
of plaguing him from afar, yet for peril they dared not
come nigher.
He had hurt so many before,
that none had now desire
to be torn with the tusks once more
of a beast both mad and dire.

63 Till the knight himself came, his courser spurring,
and saw him brought there to bay, and all about him his men.
Nothing loth he alighted, and leaving his horse,
brandished a bright blade and boldly advanced,
striding stoutly through the ford to where stood the felon.
The wild beast was aware of him with his weapon in hand,
and high raised his hair; with such hate he snorted
that folk feared for the knight, lest his foe should worst him.
Out came the swine and set on him at once,
and the boar and the brave man were both in a mellay
in the wildest of the water. The worse had the beast,
for the man marked him well, and as they met he at once
struck steadily his point straight in the neck-slot,
and hit him up to the hilts, so that his heart was riven,
and with a snarl he succumbed, and was swept down the water
straightway.
A hundred hounds him caught,
and fiercely bit their prey;
the men to the bank him brought,
and dogs him dead did lay.

64 There men blew for the prise in many a blaring horn,
and high and loud hallooed all the hunters that could;
bloodhounds bayed for the beast, as bade the masters,
who of that hard-run chase were the chief huntsmen.
Then one that was well learnéd in woodmen's lore
with pretty cunning began to carve up this boar.
First he hewed off his head and on high set it,
then he rent him roughly down the ridge of the back,
brought out the bowels, burned them on gledes,
and with them, blended with blood, the bloodhounds rewarded.

Next he broke up the boar-flesh in broad slabs of brawn,
and haled forth the hastlets in order all duly,
and yet all whole he fastened the halves together,
and strongly on a stout pole he strung them then up.
Now with this swine homeward swiftly they hastened,
and the boar's head was borne before the brave knight himself
who felled him in the ford by force of his hand
so great.
Until he saw Sir Gawain
in the hall he could hardly wait.
He called, and his pay to gain
the other came there straight.

65 The lord with his loud voice and laughter merry
gaily he greeted him when Gawain he saw.
The fair ladies were fetched and the folk all assembled,
and he showed them the shorn slabs, and shaped his report
of the width and wondrous length, and the wickedness also
in war, of the wild swine, as in the woods he had fled.
With fair words his friend the feat then applauded,
and praised the great prowess he had proved in his deeds;
for such brawn on a beast, the brave knight declared,
or such sides on a swine he had never seen before.
They then handled the huge head, and highly he praised it,
showing horror at the hideous thing to honour the lord.
Now, Gawain,' said the good man, 'this game is your own
by close covenant we concluded, as clearly you know.'
That is true,' he returned, 'and as truly I assure you
all my winnings, I warrant, I shall award you in exchange.'
He clasped his neck, and courteously a kiss he then gave him
and swiftly with a second he served him on the spot.
'Now we are quits,' he quoth, 'and clear for this evening
of all covenants we accorded, since I came to this house,
as is due.'
The lord said: 'By Saint Gile,
your match I never knew!
You'll be wealthy in a while,
such trade if you pursue.'

66 Then on top of the trestles the tables they laid,
cast the cloths thereon, and clear light then

wakened along the walls; waxen torches
men set there, and servants went swift about the hall.
Much gladness and gaiety began then to spring
round the fire on the hearth, and freely and oft
at supper and later: many songs of delight,
such as canticles of Christmas, and new carol-dances,
amid all the mannerly mirth that men can tell of;
and ever our noble knight was next to the lady.
Such glances she gave him of her gracious favour,
secretly stealing sweet looks that strong man to charm,
that he was passing perplexed, and ill-pleased at heart.
Yet he would fain not of his courtesy coldly refuse her,
but graciously engaged her, however against the grain
the play.
When mirth they had made in hall
as long as they wished to stay,
to a room did the lord them call
and to the ingle they made their way.

67 There amid merry words and wine they had a mind once more
to harp on the same note on New Year's Eve.
But said Gawain: 'Grant me leave to go on the morrow!
For the appointment approaches that I pledged myself to.'
The lord was loth to allow it, and longer would keep him,
and said: 'As I am a true man I swear on my troth
the Green Chapel thou shalt gain, and go to your business
in the dawn of New Year, sir, ere daytime begins.
So still lie upstairs and stay at thine ease,
and I shall hunt in the holt here, and hold to my terms
with thee truly, when I return, to trade all our gains.
For I have tested thee twice, and trusty I find thee.
Now 'third time pays for all', bethink thee tomorrow!
Make we merry while we may and be mindful of joy,
for the woe one may win whenever one wishes!'
This was graciously agreed, and Gawain would linger.
Then gaily drink is given them and they go to their beds
with light.
Sir Gawain lies and sleeps
soft and sound all night;
his host to his hunting keeps,
and is early arrayed aright.

68 After Mass of a morsel he and his men partook.
Merry was the morning. For his mount then he called.
All the huntsmen that on horse behind him should follow
were ready mounted to ride arrayed at the gates.
Wondrous fair were the fields, for the frost clung there;
in red rose-hued o'er the wrack arises the sun,
sailing clear along the coasts of the cloudy heavens.
The hunters loosed hounds by a holt-border;
the rocks rang in the wood to the roar of their horns.
Some fell on the line to where the fox was lying,
crossing and re-crossing it in the cunning of their craft.
A hound then gives tongue, the huntsman names him,
round him press his companions in a pack all snuffling,
running forth in a rabble then right in his path.
The fox flits before them. They find him at once,
and when they see him by sight they pursue him hotly,
decrying him full clearly with a clamour of wrath.
He dodges and ever doubles through many a dense coppice,
and looping oft he lurks and listens under fences.
At last at a little ditch he leaps o'er a thorn-hedge,
sneaks out secretly by the side of a thicket,
weens he is out of the wood and away by his wiles from the hounds.
Thus he went unawares to a watch that was posted,
where fierce on him fell three foes at once
all grey.
He swerves then swift again,
and dauntless darts astray;
in grief and in great pain
to the wood he turns away.

69 Then to hark to the hounds it was heart's delight,
when all the pack came upon him, there pressing together.
Such a curse at the view they called down on him
that the clustering cliffs might have clattered in ruin.
Here he was hallooed when hunters came on him,
yonder was he assailed with snarling tongues;
there he was threatened and oft thief was he called,
with ever the trailers at his tail so that tarry he could not.
Oft was he run at, if he rushed outwards;
oft he swerved in again, so subtle was Reynard.
Yea! he led the lord and his hunt as laggards behind him

thus by mount and by hill till mid-afternoon.
Meanwhile the courteous knight in the castle in comfort slumbered
behind the comely curtains in the cold morning.
But the lady in love-making had no liking to sleep
nor to disappoint the purpose she had planned in her heart;
but rising up swiftly his room now she sought
in a gay mantle that to the ground was measured
and was fur-lined most fairly with fells well trimmed,
with no comely coif on her head, only the clear jewels
that were twined in her tressure by twenties in clusters;
her noble face and her neck all naked were laid,
her breast bare in front and at the back also.
She came through the chamber-door and closed it behind her,
wide set a window, and to wake him she called,
thus greeting him gaily with her gracious words
of cheer:
'Ah! man, how canst thou sleep,
the morning is so clear!'
He lay in darkness deep,
but her call he then could hear.

70 In heavy darkness drowsing he dream-words muttered,
as a man whose mind was bemused with many mournful thoughts,
how destiny should his doom on that day bring him
when he at the Green Chapel the great man would meet,
and be obliged his blow to abide without debate at all.
But when so comely she came, he recalled then his wits,
swept aside his slumbers, and swiftly made answer.
The lady in lovely guise came laughing sweetly,
bent down o'er his dear face, and deftly kissed him.
He greeted her graciously with a glad welcome,
seeing her so glorious and gaily attired,
so faultless in her features and so fine in her hues
that at once joy up-welling went warm to his heart.
With smiles sweet and soft they turned swiftly to mirth,
and only brightness and bliss was broached there between them
so gay.
They spoke then speeches good,
much pleasure was in that play;
great peril between them stood,
unless Mary for her knight should pray.

71 For she, queenly and peerless, pressed him so closely,
led him so near the line, that at last he must needs
either refuse her with offence or her favours there take.
He cared for his courtesy, lest a caitiff he proved,
yet more for his sad case, if he should sin commit
and to the owner of the house, to his host, be a traitor.
'God help me!' said he. 'Happen that shall not!'
Smiling sweetly aside from himself then he turned
all the fond words of favour that fell from her lips.
Said she to the knight then: 'Now shame you deserve,
if you love not one that lies alone here beside you,
who beyond all women in the world is wounded in heart,
unless you have a lemman, more beloved, whom you like better,
and have affianced faith to that fair one so fast and so true
that your release you desire not—and so I believe now;
and to tell me if that be so truly, I beg you.
For all sakes that men swear by conceal not the truth
in guile.'
The knight said: 'By Saint John,'
and softly gave a smile,
'Nay! lover have I none,
and none will have meanwhile.'

72 'Those words', said the woman, 'are the worst that could be.
But I am answered indeed, and 'tis hard to endure.
Kiss me now kindly, and I will quickly depart.
I may but mourn while I live as one that much is in love.'
Sighing she sank down, and sweetly she kissed him;
then soon she left his side, and said as she stood there:
'Now, my dear, at this parting do me this pleasure,
give me something as thy gift, thy glove it might be,
that I may remember thee, dear man, my mourning to lessen.'
'Now on my word,' then said he, 'I wish I had here
the loveliest thing for thy delight that in my land I possess;
for worthily have you earned wondrously often
more reward by rights than within my reach would now be,
save to allot you as love-token thing of little value.
Beneath your honour it is to have here and now
a glove for a guerdon as the gift of Sir Gawain:

and I am here on an errand in unknown lands,
and have no bearers with baggage and beautiful things
(unluckily, dear lady) for your delight at this time.
A man must do as he is placed; be not pained nor aggrieved,'
said he.
Said she so comely clad:
'Nay, noble knight and free,
though naught of yours I had,
you should get a gift from me.'

73 A rich ring she offered him of red gold fashioned,
with a stone like a star standing up clear
that bore brilliant beams as bright as the sun:
I warrant you it was worth wealth beyond measure.
But the knight said nay to it, and announced then at once:
'I will have no gifts, fore God, of your grace at this time.
I have none to return you, and naught will I take.'
She proffered it and pressed him, and he her pleading refused,
and swore swiftly upon his word that accept it he would not.
And she, sorry that he refused, said to him further:
'If to my ring you say nay, since too rich it appears,
and you would not so deeply be indebted to me,
I shall give you my girdle, less gain will that be.'
She unbound a belt swiftly that embracing her sides
was clasped above her kirtle under her comely mantle.
Fashioned it was of green silk, and with gold finished,
though only braided round about, embroidered by hand;
and this she would give to Gawain, and gladly besought him,
of no worth though it were, to be willing to take it.
And he said nay, he would not, he would never receive
either gold or jewelry, ere God the grace sent him
to accomplish the quest on which he had come thither.
'And therefore I pray you, please be not angry,
and cease to insist on it, for to your suit I will ever
say no.
I am deeply in debt to you
for the favour that you show,
to be your servant true
for ever in weal or woe.'

74 'Do you refuse now this silk,' said the fair lady,
'because in itself it is poor? And so it appears.
See how small 'tis in size, and smaller in value!

But one who knew of the nature that is knit therewithin
would appraise it probably at a price far higher.
For whoever goes girdled with this green riband,
while he keeps it well clasped closely about him,
there is none so hardy under heaven that to hew him were able;
for he could not be killed by any cunning of hand.'
The knight then took note, and thought now in his heart,
'twould be a prize in that peril that was appointed to him.
When he gained the Green Chapel to get there his sentence,
if by some sleight he were not slain, 'twould be a sovereign device.
Then he bore with her rebuke, and debated not her words;
and she pressed on him the belt, and proffered it in earnest;
and he agreed, and she gave it very gladly indeed,
and prayed him for her sake to part with it never,
but on his honour hide it from her husband; and he then agreed
that no one ever should know, nay, none in the world
but they.
With earnest heart and mood
great thanks he oft did say.
She then the knight so good
a third time kissed that day.

75 Then she left him alone, her leave taking,
for amusement from the man no more could she get.
When she was gone Sir Gawain got him soon ready,
arose and robed himself in raiment noble.
He laid up the love-lace that the lady had given,
hiding it heedfully where he after might find it.
Then first of all he chose to fare to the chapel,
privately approached a priest, and prayed that he there
would uplift his life, that he might learn better
how his soul should be saved, when he was sent from the world.
There he cleanly confessed him and declared his misdeeds,
both the more and the less, and for mercy he begged,
to absolve him of them all he besought the good man;
and he assoiled him and made him as safe and as clean
as for Doom's Day indeed, were it due on the morrow.
Thereafter more merry he made among the fair ladies,
with carol-dances gentle and all kinds of rejoicing,
than ever he did ere that day, till the darkness of night,
in bliss.

Each man there said: 'I vow
a delight to all he is!
Since hither he came till now,
he was ne'er so gay as this.'

76 Now indoors let him dwell and have dearest delight,
while the free lord yet fares afield in his sports!
At last the fox he has felled that he followed so long;
for, as he spurred through a spinney to espy there the villain,
where the hounds he had heard that hard on him pressed,
Reynard on his road came through a rough thicket,
and all the rabble in a rush were right on his heels.
The man is aware of the wild thing, and watchful awaits him,
brings out his bright brand and at the beast hurls it;
and he blenched at the blade, and would have backed if he could.
A hound hastened up, and had him ere he could;
and right before the horse's feet they fell on him all,
and worried there the wily one with a wild clamour.
The lord quickly alights and lifts him at once,
snatching him swiftly from their slavering mouths,
holds him high o'er his head, hallooing loudly;
and there bay at him fiercely many furious hounds.
Huntsmen hurried thither, with horns full many
ever sounding the assembly, till they saw the master.
When together had come his company noble,
all that ever bore bugle were blowing at once,
and all the others hallooed that had not a horn:
it was the merriest music that ever men harkened,
the resounding song there raised that for Reynard's soul awoke.
To hounds they pay their fees,
their heads they fondly stroke,
and Reynard then they seize,
and off they skin his cloak.

77 And then homeward they hastened, for at hand was now night,
making strong music on their mighty horns.
The lord alighted at last at his beloved abode,
found a fire in the hall, and fair by the hearth
Sir Gawain the good, and gay was he too,
among the ladies in delight his lot was most joyful.

He was clad in a blue cloak that came to the ground;
his surcoat well beseemed him with its soft lining,
and its hood of like hue that hung on his shoulder:
all fringed with white fur very finely were both.
He met indeed the master in the midst of the floor,
and in gaiety greeted him, and graciously said:
'In this case I will first our covenant fulfil
that to our good we agreed, when ungrudged went the drink.'
He clasps then the knight and kisses him thrice,
as long and deliciously as he could lay them upon him.
'By Christ!' the other quoth, 'you've come by a fortune
in winning such wares, were they worth what you paid.'
'Indeed, the price was not important,' promptly he answered,
'whereas plainly is paid now the profit I gained.'
'Marry!' said the other man, 'mine is not up to't;
for I have hunted all this day, and naught else have I got
but this foul fox-fell—the Fiend have the goods!—
and that is price very poor to pay for such treasures
as these you have thrust upon me, three such kisses
so good.'
' 'Tis enough,' then said Gawain.
'I thank you, by the Rood,'
and how the fox was slain
he told him as they stood.

78 With mirth and minstrelsy and meats at their pleasure
as merry they made as any men could be;
amid the laughter of ladies and light words of jest
both Gawain and the good man could no gayer have proved,
unless they had doted indeed or else drunken had been.
Both the host and his household went on with their games,
till the hour had approached when part must they all;
to bed were now bound the brave folk at last.
Bowing low his leave of the lord there first
the good knight then took, and graciously thanked him:
'For such a wondrous welcome as within these walls I have had,
for your honour at this high feast the High King reward you!
In your service I set myself, your servant, if you will.
For I must needs make a move tomorrow, as you know,
if you give me some good man to go, as you promised,
and guide me to the Green Chapel, as God may permit me

to face on New Year's day such doom as befalls me.'
'On my word,' said his host, 'with hearty good will
to all that ever I promised I promptly shall hold.'
Then a servant he assigns him to set him on the road,
and by the downs to conduct him, that without doubt or delay
he might through wild and through wood ways most straight
pursue.
Said Gawain, 'My thanks receive,
such a favour you will do!'
The knight then took his leave
of those noble ladies two.

79 Sadly he kissed them and said his farewells,
and pressed oft upon them in plenty his thanks,
and they promptly the same again repaid him;
to God's keeping they gave him, grievously sighing.
Then from the people of the castle he with courtesy parted;
all the men that he met he remembered with thanks
for their care for his comfort and their kind service,
and the trouble each had taken in attendance upon him;
and every one was as woeful to wish him adieu
as had they lived all their lives with his lordship in honour.
Then with link-men and lights he was led to his chamber
and brought sweetly to bed, there to be at his rest.
That soundly he slept then assert will I not,
for he had many matters in the morning to mind, if he would,
in thought.
There let him lie in peace,
near now is the tryst he sought.
If a while you will hold your peace,
I will tell the deeds they wrought!

IV

Now New Year draws near and the night passes,
day comes driving the dark, as ordained by God;
but wild weathers of the world awake in the land,
clouds cast keenly the cold upon earth
with bitter breath from the North biting the naked.
Snow comes shivering sharp to shrivel the wild things,

the whistling wind whirls from the heights
and drives every dale full of drifts very deep.
Long the knight listens as he lies in his bed;
though he lays down his eyelids, very little he sleeps:
at the crow of every cock he recalls well his tryst.
Briskly he rose from his bed ere the break of day,
for there was light from a lamp that illumined his chamber.
He called to his chamberlain, who quickly him answered,
and he bade him bring his byrnie and his beast saddle.
The man got him up and his gear fetched him,
and garbed then Sir Gawain in great array;
first he clad him in his clothes to keep out the cold,
and after that in his harness that with heed had been tended,
both his pauncer and his plates polished all brightly,
the rings rid of the rust on his rich byrnie:
all was neat as if new, and the knight him thanked
with delight.
He put on every piece
all burnished well and bright;
most gallant from here to Greece
for his courser called the knight.

81 While the proudest of his apparel he put on himself:
his coat-armour, with the cognisance of the clear symbol
upon velvet environed with virtuous gems
all bound and braided about it, with broidered seams
and with fine furs lined wondrous fairly within,
yet he overlooked not the lace that the lady had given him;
that Gawain forgot not, of his own good thinking;
when he had belted his brand upon his buxom haunches,
he twined the love-token twice then about him,
and swiftly he swathed it sweetly about his waist,
that girdle of green silk, and gallant it looked
upon the royal red cloth that was rich to behold.
But he wore not for worth nor for wealth this girdle,
not for pride in the pendants, though polished they were,
not though the glittering gold there gleamed at the ends,
but so that himself he might save when suffer he must,
must abide bane without debating it with blade or with brand
of war.
When arrayed the knight so bold
came out before the door,

to all that high household
great thanks he gave once more.

82 Now Gringolet was groomed, the great horse and high,
who had been lodged to his liking and loyally tended:
fain to gallop was that gallant horse for his good fettle.
His master to him came and marked well his coat,
and said: 'Now solemnly myself I swear on my troth
there is a company in this castle that is careful of honour!
Their lord that them leads, may his lot be joyful!
Their beloved lady in life may delight befall her!
If they out of charity thus cherish a guest,
upholding their house in honour, may He them reward
that upholds heaven on high, and all of you too!
And if life a little longer I might lead upon earth,
I would give you some guerdon gladly, were I able.'
Then he steps in the stirrup and strides on his horse;
his shield his man showed him, and on shoulder he slung it,
Gringolet he goaded with his gilded heels,
and he plunged forth on the pavement, and prancing no more
stood there.
Ready now was his squire to ride
that his helm and lance would bear.
'Christ keep this castle!' he cried
and wished it fortune fair.

83 The bridge was brought down and the broad gates then
unbarred and swung back upon both hinges.
The brave man blessed himself, and the boards crossing,
bade the porter up rise, who before the prince kneeling
gave him 'Good day, Sir Gawain!', and 'God save you!'
Then he went on his way with the one man only
to guide him as he goes to that grievous place
where he is due to endure the dolorous blow.
They go by banks and by braes where branches are bare,
they climb along cliffs where clingeth the cold;
the heavens are lifted high, but under them evilly
mist hangs moist on the moor, melts on the mountains;
every hill has a hat, a mist-mantle huge.
Brooks break and boil on braes all about,
bright bubbling on their banks where they bustle downwards.
Very wild through the wood is the way they must take,

until soon comes the season when the sun rises
        that day.
    On a high hill they abode,
    white snow beside them lay;
    the man that by him rode
    there bade his master stay.

84 'For so far I have taken you, sir, at this time,
and now you are near to that noted place
that you have enquired and questioned so curiously after.
But I will announce now the truth, since you are known to me,
and you are a lord in this life that I love greatly,
if you would follow my advice you would fare better.
The place that you pass to, men perilous hold it,
the worst wight in the world in that waste dwelleth;
for he is stout and stern, and to strike he delights,
and he mightier than any man upon middle-earth is,
and his body is bigger than the four best men
that are in Arthur's house, either Hestor or others.
All goes as he chooses at the Green Chapel;
no one passes by that place so proud in his arms
that he hews not to death by dint of his hand.
For he is a man monstrous, and mercy he knows not;
for be it a churl or a chaplain that by the Chapel rideth,
a monk or a mass-priest or any man besides,
he would as soon have him slain as himself go alive.
And so I say to you, as sure as you sit in your saddle,
if you come there, you'll be killed, if the carl has his way.
Trust me, that is true, though you had twenty lives
        to yield.
    He here has dwelt now long
    and stirred much strife on field;
    against his strokes so strong
    yourself you cannot shield.

85 And so, good Sir Gawain, now go another way,
and let the man alone, for the love of God, sir!
Come to some other country, and there may Christ keep you!
And I shall haste me home again, and on my honour I promise
that I swear will by God and all His gracious saints,
so help me God and the Halidom, and other oaths a plenty,
that I will safe keep your secret, and say not a word

that ever you fain were to flee for any foe that I knew of.'
'Gramercy!' quoth Gawain, and regretfully answered:
'Well, man, I wish thee, who wishest my good,
and keep safe my secret, I am certain thou wouldst.
But however heedfully thou hid it, if I here departed,
fain in fear now to flee, in the fashion thou speakest,
I should a knight coward be, I could not be excused.
Nay, I'll fare to the Chapel, whatever chance may befall,
and have such words with that wild man as my wish is to say,
come fair or come foul, as fate will allot
me there.
He may be a fearsome knave
to tame, and club may bear;
but His servants true to save
the Lord can well prepare.'

86 'Marry!' quoth the other man, 'now thou makest it so clear
that thou wishest thine own bane to bring on thyself,
and to lose thy life hast a liking, to delay thee I care not!
Have here thy helm on thy head, thy spear in thy hand,
and ride down by yon rock-side where runs this same track,
till thou art brought to the bottom of the baleful valley.
A little to thy left hand then look o'er the green,
and thou wilt see on the slope the selfsame chapel,
and the great man and grim on ground that it keeps.
Now farewell in God's name, Gawain the noble!
For all the gold in the world I would not go with thee,
nor bear thee fellowship through this forest one foot further!'
With that his bridle towards the wood back the man turneth,
hits his horse with his heels as hard as he can,
gallops on the greenway, and the good knight there leaves
alone,
Quoth Gawain: 'By God on high
I will neither grieve nor groan.
With God's will I comply,
Whose protection I do own.'

87 Then he put spurs to Gringolet, and espying the track,
thrust in along a bank by a thicket's border,
rode down the rough brae right to the valley;
and then he gazed all about: a grim place he thought it,
and saw no sign of shelter on any side at all,

only high hillsides sheer upon either hand,
and notched knuckled crags with gnarled boulders;
the very skies by the peaks were scraped, it appeared.
Then he halted and held in his horse for the time,
and changed oft his front the Chapel to find.
Such on no side he saw, as seemed to him strange,
save a mound as it might be near the marge of a green,
a worn barrow on a brae by the brink of a water,
beside falls in a flood that was flowing down;
the burn bubbled therein, as if boiling it were.
He urged on his horse then, and came up to the mound,
there lightly alit, and lashed to a tree
his reins, with a rough branch rightly secured them.
Then he went to the barrow and about it he walked,
debating in his mind what might the thing be.
It had a hole at the end and at either side,
and with grass in green patches was grown all over,
and was all hollow within: nought but an old cavern,
or a cleft in an old crag; he could not it name
aright.
'Can this be the Chapel Green,
O Lord?' said the gentle knight.
'Here the Devil might say, I ween,
his matins about midnight!'

88 'On my word,' quoth Wawain, ' 'tis a wilderness here!
This oratory looks evil. With herbs overgrown
it fits well that fellow transformed into green
to follow here his devotions in the Devil's fashion.
Now I feel in my five wits the Fiend 'tis himself
that has trapped me with this tryst to destroy me here.
This is a chapel of mischance, the church most accursed
that ever I entered. Evil betide it!'
With high helm on his head, his lance in his hand,
he roams up to the roof of that rough dwelling.
Then he heard from the high hill, in a hard rock-wall
beyond the stream on a steep, a sudden startling noise.
How it clattered in the cliff, as if to cleave it asunder,
as if one upon a grindstone were grinding a scythe!
How it whirred and it rasped as water in a mill-race!
How it rushed, and it rang, rueful to harken!
Then 'By God,' quoth Gawain, 'I guess this ado

is meant for my honour, meetly to hail me
as knight!
As God wills! Waylaway!
That helps me not a mite.
My life though down I lay,
no noise can me affright.'

89 Then clearly the knight there called out aloud:
'Who is master in this place to meet me at tryst?
For now 'tis good Gawain on ground that here walks.
If any aught hath to ask, let him hasten to me,
either now or else never, his needs to further!'
'Stay!' said one standing above on the steep o'er his head,
'and thou shalt get in good time what to give thee I vowed.'
Still with that rasping and racket he rushed on a while,
and went back to his whetting, till he wished to descend.
And then he climbed past a crag, and came from a hole,
hurtling out of a hid nook with a horrible weapon:
a Danish axe newly dressed the dint to return,
with cruel cutting-edge curved along the handle—
filed on a whetstone, and four feet in width,
'twas no less—along its lace of luminous hue;
and the great man in green still guised as before,
his locks and long beard, his legs and his face,
save that firm on his feet he fared on the ground,
steadied the haft on the stones and stalked beside it.
When he walked to the water, where he wade would not,
he hopped over on his axe and haughtily strode,
fierce and fell on a field where far all about
lay snow.
Sir Gawain the man met there,
neither bent nor bowed he low.
The other said: 'Now, sirrah fair,
I true at tryst thee know!'

90 'Gawain,' said that green man, 'may God keep thee!
On my word, sir, I welcome thee with a will to my place,
and thou hast timed thy travels as trusty man should,
and thou hast forgot not the engagement agreed on between us:
at this time gone a twelvemonth thou took'st thy allowance,
and I should now this New Year nimbly repay thee.
And we are in this valley now verily on our own,

there are no people to part us—we can play as we like.
Have thy helm off thy head, and have here thy pay!
Bandy me no more debate than I brought before thee
when thou didst sweep off my head with one swipe only!'
'Nay,' quoth Gawain, 'by God that gave me my soul,
I shall grudge thee not a grain any grief that follows.
Only restrain thee to one stroke, and still shall I stand
and offer thee no hindrance to act as thou likest
right here.'
With a nod of his neck he bowed,
let bare the flesh appear;
he would not by dread be cowed,
no sign he gave of fear.

91 Then the great man in green gladly prepared him,
gathered up his grim tool there Gawain to smite;
with all the lust in his limbs aloft he heaved it,
shaped as mighty a stroke as if he meant to destroy him.
Had it driving come down as dour as he aimed it,
under his dint would have died the most doughty man ever.
But Gawain on that guisarm then glanced to one side,
as down it came gliding on the green there to end him,
and he shrank a little with his shoulders at the sharp iron.
With a jolt the other man jerked back the blade,
and reproved then the prince, proudly him taunting.
'Thou'rt not Gawain,' said the green man, 'who is so good reported,
who never flinched from any foes on fell or in dale;
and now thou fleest in fear, ere thou feelest a hurt!
Of such cowardice that knight I ne'er heard accused.
Neither blenched I nor backed, when thy blow, sir, thou aimedst,
nor uttered any cavil in the court of King Arthur.
My head flew to my feet, and yet fled I never;
but thou, ere thou hast any hurt, in thy heart quailest,
and so the nobler knight to be named I deserve
therefore.'
'I blenched once,' Gawain said,
'and I will do so no more.
But if on floor now falls my head,
I cannot it restore.

92 'But get busy, I beg, sir, and bring me to the point.
Deal me my destiny, and do it out of hand!
For I shall stand from thee a stroke and stir not again
till thine axe hath hit me, have here my word on't!'
'Have at thee then!' said the other, and heaved it aloft,
and wratched him as wrathfully as if he were wild with rage.
He made at him a mighty aim, but the man he touched not,
holding back hastily his hand, ere hurt it might do.
Gawain warily awaited it, and winced with no limb,
but stood as still as a stone or the stump of a tree
that with a hundred ravelled roots in rocks is embedded.
This time merrily remarked then the man in the green:
'So, now thou hast thy heart whole, a hit I must make.
May the high order now keep thee that Arthur gave thee,
and guard thy gullet at this go, if it can gain thee that.'
Angrily with ire then answered Sir Gawain:
'Why! lash away, thou lusty man! Too long dost thou threaten.
'Tis thy heart methinks in thee that now quaileth!'
'In faith,' said the fellow, 'so fiercely thou speakest,
I no longer will linger delaying thy errand
right now.'
Then to strike he took his stance
and grimaced with lip and brow.
He that of rescue saw no chance
was little pleased, I trow.

93 Lightly his weapon he lifted, and let it down neatly
with the bent horn of the blade towards the neck that was bare;
though he hewed with a hammer-swing, he hurt him no more
than to snick him on one side and sever the skin.
Through the fair fat sank the edge, and the flesh entered,
so that the shining blood o'er his shoulders was shed on the earth;
and when the good knight saw the gore that gleamed on the snow,
he sprang out with spurning feet a spear's length and more,
in haste caught his helm and on his head cast it,
under his fair shield he shot with a shake of his shoulders,
brandished his bright sword, and boldly he spake—
never since he as manchild of his mother was born
was he ever on this earth half so happy a man:

'Have done, sir, with thy dints! Now deal me no more!
I have stood from thee a stroke without strife on this spot,
and if thou offerest me others, I shall answer thee promptly,
and give as good again, and as grim, be assured,
shall pay.
But one stroke here's my due,
as the covenant clear did say
that in Arthur's halls we drew.
And so, good sir, now stay!'

94 From him the other stood off, and on his axe rested,
held the haft to the ground, and on the head leaning,
gazed at the good knight as on the green he there strode.
To see him standing so stout, so stern there and fearless,
armed and unafraid, his heart it well pleased.
Then merrily he spoke with a mighty voice,
and loudly it rang, as to that lord he said:
'Fearless knight on this field, so fierce do not be!
No man here unmannerly hath thee maltreated,
nor aught given thee not granted by agreement at court.
A hack I thee vowed, and thou'st had it, so hold thee content;
I remit thee the remnant of all rights I might claim.
If I brisker had been, a buffet, it may be,
I could have handed thee more harshly, and harm could have done thee.
First I menaced thee in play with no more than a trial,
and clove thee with no cleft: I had a claim to the feint,
for the fast pact we affirmed on the first evening,
and thou fairly and unfailing didst faith with me keep,
all thy gains thou me gavest, as good man ought.
The other trial for the morning, man, I thee tendered
when thou kissedst my comely wife, and the kisses didst render.
For the two here I offered only two harmless feints
to make.
The true shall truly repay,
for no peril then need he quake.
Thou didst fail on the third day,
and so that tap now take!

95 For it is my weed that thou wearest, that very woven girdle:
my own wife it awarded thee, I wot well indeed.

Now I am aware of thy kisses, and thy courteous ways,
and of thy wooing by my wife: I worked that myself!
I sent her to test thee, and thou seem'st to me truly
the fair knight most faultless that e'er foot set on earth!
As a pearl than white pease is prized more highly,
so is Gawain, in good faith, than other gallant knights.
But in this you lacked, sir, a little, and of loyalty came short.
But that was for no artful wickedness, nor for wooing either,
but because you loved your own life: the less do I blame you.'
The other stern knight in a study then stood a long while,
in such grief and disgust he had a grue in his heart;
all the blood from his breast in his blush mingled,
and he shrank into himself with shame at that speech.
The first words on that field that he found then to say
were: 'Cursed be ye, Coveting, and Cowardice also!
In you is vileness, and vice that virtue destroyeth.'
He took then the treacherous thing, and untying the knot
fiercely flung he the belt at the feet of the knight:
'See there the falsifier, and foul be its fate!
Through care for thy blow Cowardice brought me
to consent to Coveting, my true kind to forsake,
which is free-hand and faithful word that are fitting to knights.
Now I am faulty and false, who afraid have been ever
of treachery and troth-breach: the two now my curse
may bear!
I confess, sir, here to you
all faulty has been my fare.
Let me gain your grace anew,
and after I will beware.'

96 Then the other man laughed and lightly answered:
'I hold it healed beyond doubt, the harm that I had.
Thou hast confessed thee so clean and acknowledged thine errors,
and hast the penance plain to see from the point of my blade,
that I hold thee purged of that debt, made as pure and as clean
as hadst thou done no ill deed since the day thou wert born.
And I give thee, sir, the girdle with gold at its hems,
for it is green like my gown. So, Sir Gawain, you may
think of this our contest when in the throng thou walkest
among princes of high praise; 'twill be a plain reminder
of the chance of the Green Chapel between chivalrous knights.

And now you shall in this New Year come anon to my house,
and in our revels the rest of this rich season
shall go.'
The lord pressed him hard to wend,
and said, 'my wife, I know,
we soon shall make your friend,
who was your bitter foe.'

97 'Nay forsooth!' the knight said, and seized then his helm,
and duly it doffed, and the doughty man thanked:
'I have lingered too long! May your life now be blest,
and He promptly repay you Who apportions all honours!
And give my regards to her grace, your goodly consort,
both to her and to the other, to mine honoured ladies,
who thus their servant with their designs have subtly beguiled.
But no marvel it is if mad be a fool,
and by the wiles of women to woe be brought.
For even so Adam by one on earth was beguiled,
and Solomon by several, and to Samson moreover
his doom by Delilah was dealt; and David was after
blinded by Bathsheba, and he bitterly suffered.
Now if these came to grief through their guile, a gain 'twould be vast
to love them well and believe them not, if it lay in man's power!
Since these were aforetime the fairest, by fortune most blest,
eminent among all the others who under heaven bemused
were too,
and all of them were betrayed
by women that they knew,
though a fool I now am made,
some excuse I think my due.'

98 'But for your girdle,' quoth Gawain, 'may God you repay!
That I will gain with good will, not for the gold so joyous
of the cincture, nor the silk, nor the swinging pendants,
nor for wealth, nor for worth, nor for workmanship fine;
but as a token of my trespass I shall turn to it often
when I ride in renown, ruefully recalling
the failure and the frailty of the flesh so perverse,
so tender, so ready to take taints of defilement.
And thus, when pride my heart pricks for prowess in arms,

one look at this love-lace shall lowlier make it.
But one thing I would pray you, if it displeaseth you not,
since you are the lord of yonder land, where I lodged for a while
in your house and in honour—may He you reward
Who upholdeth the heavens and on high sitteth!—
how do you announce your true name? And then nothing further.'
'That I will tell thee truly,' then returned the other.
'Bertilak de Hautdesert hereabouts I am called,
[who thus have been enchanted and changed in my hue]
by the might of Morgan le Fay that in my mansion dwelleth,
and by cunning of lore and crafts well learned.
The magic arts of Merlin she many hath mastered;
for deeply in dear love she dealt on a time
with that accomplished clerk, as at Camelot runs
the fame;
and Morgan the Goddess
is therefore now her name.
None power and pride possess
too high for her to tame.

99 She made me go in this guise to your goodly court
to put its pride to the proof, if the report were true
that runs of the great renown of the Round Table.
She put this magic upon me to deprive you of your wits,
in hope Guinevere to hurt, that she in horror might die
aghast at that glamoury that gruesomely spake
with its head in its hand before the high table.
She it is that is at home, that ancient lady;
she is indeed thine own aunt, Arthur's half-sister,
daughter of the Duchess of Tintagel on whom doughty Sir Uther
after begat Arthur, who in honour is now.
Therefore I urge thee in earnest, sir, to thine aunt return!
In my hall make merry! My household thee loveth,
and I wish thee as well, upon my word, sir knight,
as any that go under God, for thy great loyalty.'
But he denied him with a 'Nay! by no means I will!'
They clasp then and kiss and to the care give each other
of the Prince of Paradise; and they part on that field
so cold,

To the king's court on courser keen
then hastened Gawain the bold,
and the knight in the glittering green
to ways of his own did hold.

100 Wild ways in the world Wawain now rideth
on Gringolet: by the grace of God he still lived.
Oft in house he was harboured and lay oft in the open,
oft vanquished his foe in adventures as he fared
which I intend not this time in my tale to recount.
The hurt was healed that he had in his neck,
and the bright-hued belt he bore now about it
obliquely like a baldric bound at his side,
under his left arm with a knot that lace was fastened
to betoken he had been detected in the taint of a fault;
and so at last he came to the Court again safely.
Delight there was awakened, when the lords were aware
that good Gawain had returned; glad news they thought it.
The king kissed the knight, and the queen also,
and then in turn many a true knight that attended to greet him.
About his quest they enquire, and he recounts all the marvels,
declares all the hardships and care that he had,
what chanced at the Chapel, what cheer made the knight,
the love of the lady, and the lace at the last.
The notch in his neck naked he showed them
that he had for his dishonesty from the hands of the knight
in blame.
It was torment to tell the truth:
in his face the blood did flame;
he groaned for grief and ruth
when he showed it, to his shame.

101 'Lo! Lord,' he said at last, and the lace handled,
'This is the band! For this a rebuke I bear in my neck!
This is the grief and disgrace I have got for myself
from the covetousness and cowardice that o'ercame me there!
This is the token of the troth-breach that I am detected in,
and needs must I wear it while in the world I remain;
for a man may cover his blemish, but unbind it he cannot,
for where once 'tis applied, thence part will it never.'
The king comforted the knight, and all the Court also
laughed loudly thereat, and this law made in mirth

the lords and the ladies that whoso belonged to the Table,
every knight of the Brotherhood, a baldric should have,
a band of bright green obliquely about him,
and this for love of that knight as a livery should wear.
For that was reckoned the distinction of the Round Table,
and honour was his that had it evermore after,
as it is written in the best of the books of romance.
Thus in Arthur his days happened this marvel,
as the Book of the Brut beareth us witness;
since Brutus the bold knight to Britain came first,
after the siege and the assault had ceased at Troy,
I trow,
many a marvel such before,
has happened here ere now.
To His bliss us bring Who bore
the Crown of Thorns on brow! AMEN

HONY SOYT QUI MAL PENCE

PEARL

Pearl of delight that a prince doth please
To grace in gold enclosed so clear,
I vow that from over orient seas
Never proved I any in price her peer.
So round, so radiant ranged by these,
So fine, so smooth did her sides appear
That ever in judging gems that please
Her only alone I deemed as dear.
Alas! I lost her in garden near:
Through grass to the ground from me it shot;
I pine now oppressed by love-wound drear
For that pearl, mine own, without a spot.

2 Since in that spot it sped from me,
I have looked and longed for that precious thing
That me once was wont from woe to free,
to uplift my lot and healing bring,
But my heart doth hurt now cruelly,
My breast with burning torment sting.
Yet in secret hour came soft to me
The sweetest song I e'er heard sing;
Yea, many a thought in mind did spring
To think that her radiance in clay should rot.
O mould! Thou marrest a lovely thing,
My pearl, mine own, without a spot.

3 In that spot must needs be spices spread
Where away such wealth to waste hath run;
Blossoms pale and blue and red
There shimmer shining in the sun;
No flower nor fruit their hue may shed
Where it down into darkling earth was done,
For all grass must grow from grains that are dead,
No wheat would else to barn be won.
From good all good is ever begun,
And fail so fair a seed could not,

So that sprang and sprouted spices none
From that precious pearl without a spot.

4 That spot whereof I speak I found
When I entered in that garden green,
As August's season high came round
When corn is cut with sickles keen.
There, where that pearl rolled down, a mound
With herbs was shadowed fair and sheen,
With gillyflower, ginger, and gromwell crowned,
And peonies powdered all between.
If sweet was all that there was seen,
Fair, too, a fragrance flowed I wot,
Where dwells that dearest, as I ween,
My precious pearl without a spot.

5 By that spot my hands I wrung dismayed;
For care full cold that had me caught
A hopeless grief on my heart was laid.
Though reason to reconcile me sought,
For my pearl there prisoned a plaint I made,
In fierce debate unmoved I fought;
Be comforted Christ Himself me bade,
But in woe my will ever strove distraught.
On the flowery plot I fell, methought;
Such odour through my senses shot,
I slipped and to sudden sleep was brought,
O'er that precious pearl without a spot.

6 From that spot my spirit sprang apace,
On the turf my body abode in trance;
My soul was gone by God's own grace
Adventuring where marvels chance.
I knew not where in the world was that place
Save by cloven cliffs was set my stance;
And towards a forest I turned my face,
Where rocks in splendour met my glance;
From them did a glittering glory lance,
None could believe the light they lent;
Never webs were woven in mortal haunts
Of half such wealth and wonderment.

7 Wondrous was made each mountain-side
With crystal cliffs so clear of hue;
About them woodlands bright lay wide,
As Indian dye their boles were blue;
The leaves did as burnished silver slide
That thick upon twigs there trembling grew.
When glades let light upon them glide
They shone with a shimmer of dazzling hue.
The gravel on ground that I trod with shoe
Was of precious pearls of the Orient:
Sunbeams are blear and dark to view
Compared with that fair wonderment.

8 In wonder at those fells so fair
My soul all grief forgot let fall;
Odours so fresh of fruits there were,
I was fed as by food celestial.
In the woods the birds did wing and pair,
Of flaming hues, both great and small;
But cithern-string and gittern-player
Their merry mirth could ne'er recall,
For when they beat their pinions all
In harmony their voices blent:
No delight more lovely could men enthrall
Than behold and hear that wonderment.

9 Thus arrayed was all in wonderment
That forest where forth my fortune led;
No man its splendour to present
With tongue could worthy words have said.
I walked ever onward well-content;
No hill was so tall that it stayed my tread;
More fair the further afield I went
Were plants, and fruits, and spices spread;
Through hedge and mead lush waters led
As in strands of gold there steeply pent.
A river I reached in cloven bed:
O Lord! the wealth of its wonderment!

10 The adornments of that wondrous deep
Were beauteous banks of beryl bright:

Swirling sweetly its waters sweep,
Ever rippling on in murmurous flight.
In the depths stood dazzling stones aheap
As a glitter through glass that glowed with light,
As streaming stars when on earth men sleep
Stare in the welkin in winter night;
For emerald, sapphire, or jewel bright
Was every pebble in pool there pent,
And the water was lit with rays of light,
Such wealth was in its wonderment.

11 The wondrous wealth of down and dales,
of wood and water and lordly plain,
My mirth makes mount: my mourning fails,
My care is quelled and cured my pain.
Then down a stream that strongly sails
I blissful turn with teeming brain;
The further I follow those flowing vales
The more strength of joy my heart doth strain.
As fortune fares where she doth deign,
Whether gladness she gives or grieving sore,
So he who may her graces gain,
His hap is to have ever more and more.

12 There more was of such marvels thrice
Than I could tell, though I long delayed;
For earthly heart could not suffice
For a tithe of the joyful joys displayed.
Therefore I thought that Paradise
Across those banks was yonder laid;
I weened that the water by device
As bounds between pleasances was made;
Beyond that stream by steep or slade
That city's walls I weened must soar;
But the water was deep, I dared not wade,
And ever I longed to, more and more.

13 More and more, and yet still more,
I fain beyond the stream had scanned,
For fair as was this hither shore,
Far lovelier was the further land.
To find a ford I did then explore,

And round about did stare and stand;
But perils pressed in sooth more sore
The further I strode along the strand.
I should not, I thought, by fear be banned
From delights so lovely that lay in store;
But a happening new then came to hand
That moved my mind ever more and more.

14 A marvel more did my mind amaze:
I saw beyond that border bright
From a crystal cliff the lucent rays
And beams in splendour lift their light.
A child abode there at its base:
She wore a gown of glistening white,
A gentle maid of courtly grace;
Erewhile I had known her well by sight.
As shredded gold that glistered bright
She shone in beauty upon the shore;
Long did my glance on her alight,
And the longer I looked I knew her more.

15 The more I that face so fair surveyed,
When upon her gracious form I gazed,
Such gladdening glory upon me played
As my wont was seldom to see upraised.
Desire to call her then me swayed,
But dumb surprise my mind amazed;
In place so strange I saw that maid,
The blow might well my wits have crazed.
Her forehead fair then up she raised
That hue of polished ivory wore.
It smote my heart distraught and dazed,
And ever the longer, the more and more.

16 More than I would my dread did rise.
I stood there still and dared not call
With closéd mouth and open eyes,
I stood as tame as hawk in hall.
A ghost was present, I did surmise,
And feared for what might then befall,
Lest she should flee before mine eyes
Ere I to tryst could her recall.

So smooth, so seemly, slight and small,
That flawless fair and mirthful maid
Arose in robes majestical,
A precious gem in pearls arrayed.

17 There pearls arrayed and royally dight
Might one have seen by fortune graced
When fresh as flower-de-luces bright
She down to the water swiftly paced
In linen robe of glistening white,
With open sides that seams enlaced
With the merriest margery-pearls my sight
Ever before, I vow, had traced.
Her sleeves hung long below her waist
Adorned with pearls in double braid;
Her kirtle matched her mantle chaste
All about with precious pearls arrayed.

18 A crown arrayed too wore that girl
Of margery-stones and others none,
With pinnacles of pure white pearl
That perfect flowers were figured on.
On head nought else her hair did furl,
And it framed, as it did round her run,
Her countenance grave for duke or earl,
And her hue as rewel ivory wan.
As shredded sheen of gold then shone
Her locks on shoulder loosely laid.
Her colour pure was surpassed by none
Of the pearls in purfling rare arrayed.

19 Arrayed was wristlet, and the hems were dight
At hands, at sides, at throat so fair
With no gem but the pearl all white
And burnished white her garments were;
But a wondrous pearl unstained and bright
She amidst her breast secure did bear;
Ere mind could fathom its worth and might
Man's reason thwarted would despair.
No tongue could in worthy words declare
The beauty that was there displayed,

It was so polished, pure, and fair,
That precious pearl on her arrayed.

20 In pearls arrayed that maiden free
Beyond the stream came down the strand.
From here to Greece none as glad could be
As I on shore to see her stand,
Than aunt or niece more near to me:
The more did joy my heart expand.
She deigned to speak, so sweet was she,
Bowed low as ladies' ways demand.
With her crown of countless worth in hand
A gracious welcome she me bade.
My birth I blessed, who on the strand
To my love replied in pearls arrayed.

21 'O Pearl!' said I, 'in pearls arrayed,
Are you my pearl whose loss I mourn?
Lament alone by night I made,
Much longing I have hid for thee forlorn,
Since to the grass you from me strayed.
While I pensive waste by weeping worn,
Your life of joy in the land is laid
Of Paradise by strife untorn.
What fate hath hither my jewel borne
And made me mourning's prisoner?
Since asunder we in twain were torn,
I have been a joyless jeweller.'

22 That jewel in gems so excellent
Lifted her glance with eyes of grey,
Put on her crown of pearl-orient,
And gravely then began to say:
'Good sir, you have your speech mis-spent
To say your pearl is all away
That is in chest so choicely pent,
Even in this gracious garden gay,
Here always to linger and to play
Where regret nor grief e'er trouble her.
"Here is a casket safe" you would say,
If you were a gentle jeweller.

23 But, jeweller gentle, if from you goes
Your joy through a gem that you held lief,
Methinks your mind toward madness flows
And frets for a fleeting cause of grief.
For what you lost was but a rose
That by nature failed after flowering brief;
Now the casket's virtues that it enclose
Prove it a pearl of price in chief;
And yet you have called your fate a thief
That of naught to aught hath fashioned her,
You grudge the healing of your grief,
You are no grateful jeweller.'

24 Then a jewel methought had now come near,
And jewels the courteous speech she made.
'My blissful one,' quoth I, 'most dear,
My sorrows deep you have all allayed.
To pardon me I pray you here!
In the darkness I deemed my pearl was laid;
I have found it now, and shall make good cheer,
With it dwell in shining grove and glade,
And praise all the laws that my Lord hath made,
Who hath brought me near such bliss with her.
Now could I to reach you these waters wade,
I should be a joyful jeweller.'

25 'Jeweller', rejoined that jewel clean,
'Why jest ye men? How mad ye be!
Three things at once you have said, I ween:
Thoughtless, forsooth, were all the three.
You know not on earth what one doth mean;
Your words from your wits escaping flee:
You believe I live here on this green,
Because you can with eyes me see;
Again, you will in this land with me
Here dwell yourself, you now aver;
And thirdly, pass this water free:
That may no joyful jeweller.

26 I hold that jeweller worth little praise
Who well esteems what he sees with eye,
And much to blame his graceless ways

Who believes our Lord would speak a lie.
He promised faithfully your lives to raise
Though fate decreed your flesh should die;
His words as nonsense ye appraise
Who approve of naught not seen with eye;
And that presumption doth imply,
Which all good men doth ill beseem,
On tale as true ne'er to rely
Save private reason right it deem.

27 Do you deem that you yourself maintain
Such words as man to God should dare?
You will dwell, you say, in this domain:
'Twere best for leave first offer prayer,
And yet that grace you might not gain.
Now over this water you wish to fare:
By another course you must that attain;
Your flesh shall in clay find colder lair,
For our heedless father did of old prepare
Its doom by Eden's grove and stream;
Through dismal death must each man fare,
Ere o'er this deep him God redeem.'

28 'If my doom you deem it, maiden sweet,
To mourn once more, then I must pine.
Now my lost one found again I greet,
Must bereavement new till death be mine?
Why must I at once both part and meet?
My precious pearl doth my pain design!
What use hath treasure but tears to repeat,
When one at its loss must again repine?
Now I care not though my days decline
Outlawed afar o'er land and stream;
When in my pearl no part is mine,
Only endless dolour one that may deem.'

29 'But of woe, I deem, and deep distress
You speak', she said. 'Why do you so?
Through loud lament when they lose the less
Oft many men the more forgo.
'Twere better with cross yourself to bless,
Ever praising God in weal and woe;

For resentment gains you not a cress:
Who must needs endure, he may not say no!
For though you dance as any doe,
Rampant bray or raging scream,
When escape you cannot, to nor fro,
His doom you must abide, I deem.

30 Deem God unjust, the Lord indict,
From his way a foot He will not wend;
The relief amounts not to a mite,
Though gladness your grief may never end.
Cease then to wrangle, to speak in spite,
And swiftly seek Him as your friend.
Your prayer His pity may excite,
So that Mercy shall her powers expend.
To your languor He may comfort lend,
And swiftly your griefs removed may seem;
For lament or rave, to submit pretend,
'Tis His to ordain what He right may deem.'

31 Then I said, I deem, to that damosel:
'May I give no grievance to my Lord,
Rash fool, though blundering tale I tell.
My heart the pain of loss outpoured,
Gushing as water springs from well.
I commit me ever to His mercy's ward.
Rebuke me not with words so fell,
Though I erring stray, my dear adored!
But your comfort kindly to me accord,
In pity bethinking you of this:
For partner you did me pain award
On whom was founded all my bliss.

32 Both bliss and grief you have been to me,
But of woe far greater hath been my share.
You were caught away from all perils free,
But my pearl was gone, I knew not where;
My sorrow is softened now I it see.
When we parted, too, at one we were;
Now God forbid that we angry be!
We meet on our roads by chance so rare.
Though your converse courtly is and fair,

I am but mould and good manners miss.
Christ's mercy, Mary and John: I dare
Only on these to found my bliss.

33 In bliss you abide and happiness,
And I with woe am worn and grey;
Oft searing sorrows I possess,
Yet little heed to that you pay.
But now I here yourself address,
Without reproach I would you pray
To deign in sober words express
What life you lead the livelong day.
For delighted I am that your lot, you say,
So glorious and so glad now is;
There finds my joy its foremost way,
On that is founded all my bliss.'

34 'Now bliss you ever bless!' she cried,
Lovely in limb, in hue so clear,
'And welcome here to walk and bide;
For now your words are to me dear.
Masterful mood and haughty pride,
I warn you, are bitterly hated here.
It doth not delight my Lord to chide,
For meek are all that dwell Him near.
So, when in His place you must appear,
Be devout in humble lowliness:
To my Lord, the Lamb, such a mien is dear,
On whom is founded all my bliss.

35 A blissful life you say is mine;
You wish to know in what degree.
Your pearl you know you did resign
When in young and tender years was she;
Yet my Lord, the Lamb, through power divine
Myself He chose His bride to be,
And crowned me queen in bliss to shine,
While days shall endure eternally.
Dowered with His heritage all is she
That is His love. I am wholly His:
On His glory, honour, and high degree
Are built and founded all my bliss.'

36 'O Blissful!' said I, 'can this be true?
Be not displeased if in speech I err!
Are you the queen of heavens blue,
Whom all must honour on earth that fare?
We believe that our Grace of Mary grew,
Who in virgin-bloom a babe did bear;
And claim her crown: who could this do
But one that surpassed her in favour fair?
And yet for unrivalled sweetness rare
We call her the Phoenix of Araby,
That her Maker let faultless wing the air,
Like to the Queen of Courtesy.'

37 'O courteous Queen', that damsel said,
Kneeling on earth with uplifted face,
'Mother immaculate, and fairest maid,
Blessed beginner of every grace!'
Uprising then her prayer she stayed,
And there she spoke to me a space:
'Here many the prize they have gained are paid,
But usurpers, sir, here have no place.
That empress' realm doth heaven embrace,
And earth and hell she holds in fee,
From their heritage yet will none displace,
For she is the Queen of Courtesy.

38 The court where the living God doth reign
Hath a virtue of its own being,
That each who may thereto attain
Of all the realm is queen or king,
Yet never shall other's right obtain,
But in other's good each glorying
And wishing each crown worth five again,
If amended might be so fair a thing.
But my Lady of whom did Jesu spring,
O'er us high she holds her empery,
And none that grieves of our following,
For she is the Queen of Courtesy.

39 In courtesy we are members all
Of Jesus Christ, Saint Paul doth write:
As head, arm, leg, and navel small

To their body doth loyalty true unite,
So as limbs to their Master mystical
All Christian souls belong by right.
Now among your limbs can you find at all
Any tie or bond of hate or spite?
Your head doth not feel affront or slight
On your arm or finger though ring it see;
So we all proceed in love's delight
To king and queen by courtesy.'

40 'Courtesy,' I said, 'I do believe
And charity great dwells you among,
But may my words no wise you grieve,
. . . .
You in heaven too high yourself conceive
To make you a queen who were so young.
What honour more might he achieve
Who in strife on earth was ever strong,
And lived his life in penance long
With his body's pain to get bliss for fee?
What greater glory could to him belong
Than king to be crowned by courtesy?

41 That courtesy gives its gifts too free,
If it be sooth that you now say.
Two years you lived not on earth with me,
And God you could not please, nor pray
With Pater and Creed upon your knee—
And made a queen that very day!
I cannot believe, God helping me,
That God so far from right would stray.
Of a countess, damsel, I must say,
'Twere fair in heaven to find the grace,
Or of lady even of less array,
But a queen! It is too high a place.'

42 'Neither time nor place his grace confine',
Then said to me that maiden bright,
'For just is all that He doth assign,
And nothing can He work but right.
In God's true gospel, in words divine
That Matthew in your mass doth cite,

A tale he aptly doth design,
In parable saith of heaven's light:
"My realm on high I liken might
To a vineyard owner in this case.
The year had run to season right;
To dress the vines 'twas time and place.

43 All labourers know when that time is due.
The master up full early rose
To hire him vineyard workers new;
And some to suit his needs he chose.
Together they pledge agreement true
For a penny a day, and forth each goes,
Travails and toils to tie and hew,
Binds and prunes and in order stows.
In forenoon the master to market goes,
And there finds men that idle laze.
'Why stand ye idle?' he said to those.
'Do ye know not time of day nor place?'

44 'This place we reached betimes ere day',
This answer from all alike he drew,
'Since sunrise standing here we stay,
And no man offers us work to do.'
'Go to my vineyard! Do what ye may!'
Said the lord, and made a bargain true:
'In deed and intent I to you will pay
What hire may justly by night accrue.'
They went to his vines and laboured too,
But the lord all day that way did pace,
And brought to his vineyard workers new,
Till daytime almost passed that place.

45 In that place at time of evensong,
One hour before the set of sun,
He saw there idle labourers strong
And thus his earnest words did run:
'Why stand ye idle all day long?'
They said they chance of hire had none.
'Go to my vineyard, yeomen young,
And work and do what may be done!'
The hour grew late and sank the sun,

Dusk came o'er the world apace;
He called them to claim the wage they had won,
For time of day had passed that place.

46 The time in that place he well did know;
He called: 'Sir steward, the people pay!
Give them the hire that I them owe.
Moreover, that none reproach me may,
Set them all in a single row,
And to each alike give a penny a day;
Begin at the last that stands below,
Till to the first you make your way.'
Then the first began to complain and say
That they had laboured long and sore:
'These but one hour in stress did stay;
It seems to us we should get more.

47 More have we earned, we think it true,
Who have borne the daylong heat indeed,
Than these who hours have worked not two,
And yet you our equals have decreed.'
One such the lord then turned him to:
'My friend, I will not curtail your meed.
Go now and take what is your due!
For a penny I hired you as agreed,
Why now to wrangle do you proceed?
Was it not a penny you bargained for?
To surpass his bargain may no man plead.
Why then will you ask for more?

48 Nay, more—am I not allowed in gift
To dispose of mine as I please to do?
Or your eye to evil, maybe, you lift,
For I none betray and I am true?'
Thus I", said Christ, "shall the order shift:
The last shall come first to take his due,
And the first come last, be he never so swift;
For many are called, but the favourites few."
Thus the poor get ever their portion too,
Though late they came and little bore;
And though to their labour little accrue,
The mercy of God is much the more.

49 More is my joy and bliss herein,
The flower of my life, my lady's height,
Than all the folk in the world might win,
Did they seek award on ground of right.
Though 'twas but now that I entered in,
And came to the vineyard by evening's light,
First with my hire did my Lord begin;
I was paid at once to the furthest mite.
Yet others in toil without respite
That had laboured and sweated long of yore,
He did not yet with hire requite,
Nor will, perchance, for years yet more.'

50 Then more I said and spoke out plain:
'Unreasonable is what you say.
Ever ready God's justice on high doth reign,
Or a fable doth Holy Writ purvey.
The Psalms a cogent verse contain,
Which puts a point that one must weigh:
"High King, who all dost foreordain,
His deserts Thou dost to each repay."
Now if daylong one did steadfast stay,
And you to payment came him before,
Then lesser work can earn more pay;
And the longer you reckon, the less hath more.'

51 'Of more and less in God's domains
No question arises', said that maid,
'For equal hire there each one gains,
Be guerdon great or small him paid.
No churl is our Chieftain that in bounty reigns,
Be soft or hard by Him purveyed;
As water of dike His gifts He drains,
Or streams from a deep by drought unstayed.
Free is the pardon to him conveyed
Who in fear to the Saviour in sin did bow;
No bars from bliss will for such be made,
For the grace of God is great enow.

52 But now to defeat me you debate
That wrongly my penny I have taken here;
You say that I who came too late

Deserve not hire at price so dear.
Where heard you ever of man relate
Who, pious in prayer from year to year,
Did not somehow forfeit the guerdon great
Sometime of Heaven's glory clear?
Nay, wrong men work, from right they veer,
And ever the ofter the older, I trow.
Mercy and grace must then them steer,
For the grace of God is great enow.

53 But enow have the innocent of grace.
As soon as born, in lawful line
Baptismal waters them embrace;
Then they are brought unto the vine.
Anon the day with darkened face
Doth toward the night of death decline.
They wrought no wrong while in that place,
And his workmen then pays the Lord divine.
They were there; they worked at his design;
Why should He not their toil allow,
Yea, first to them their hire assign?
For the grace of God is great enow.

54 Enow 'tis known that Man's high kind
At first for perfect bliss was bred.
Our eldest father that grace resigned
Through an apple upon which he fed.
We were all damned, for that food assigned
To die in grief, all joy to shed,
And after in flames of hell confined
To dwell for ever unréspited
But soon a healing hither sped:
Rich blood ran on rough rood-bough,
And water fair. In that hour of dread
The grace of God grew great enow.

55 Enow there went forth from that well
Water and blood from wounds so wide:
The blood redeemed us from pains of hell,
Of the second death the bond untied;
The water is baptism, truth to tell,
That the spear so grimly ground let glide.

It washes away the trespass fell
By which Adam drowned us in deathly tide.
No bars in the world us from Bliss divide
In blessed hour restored, I trow,
Save those that He hath drawn aside;
And the grace of God is great enow.

56 Grace enow may the man receive
Who sins anew, if he repent;
But craving it he must sigh and grieve
And abide what pains are consequent.
But reason that right can never leave
Evermore preserves the innocent;
'Tis a judgement God did never give
That the guiltless should ever have punishment.
The guilty, contrite and penitent,
Through mercy may to grace take flight;
But he that to treachery never bent
In innocence is saved by right.

57 It is right thus by reason, as in this case
I learn, to save these two from ill;
The righteous man shall see His face,
Come unto him the harmless will.
This point the Psalms in a passage raise;
"Who, Lord, shall climb Thy lofty hill,
Or rest within Thy holy place?"
He doth the answer swift fulfil:
"Who wrought with hands no harm nor ill,
Who is of heart both clean and bright,
His steps shall there be steadfast still":
The innocent ever is saved by right.

58 The righteous too, one may maintain,
He shall to that noble tower repair,
Who leads not his life in folly vain,
Nor guilefully doth to neighbour swear.
That Wisdom did honour once obtain
For such doth Solomon declare:
She pressed him on by ways made plain
And showed him afar God's kingdom fair,
As if saying: "That lovely island there

That mayst thou win, be thou brave in fight."
But to say this doubtless one may dare:
The innocent ever is saved by right.

59 To righteous men—have you seen it there?—
In the Psalter David a verse applied:
"Do not, Lord, Thy servant to judgement bear;
For to Thee none living is justified."
So when to that Court you must repair
Where all our cases shall be tried,
If on right you stand, lest you trip beware,
Warned by these words that I espied.
But He on rood that bleeding died,
Whose hands the nails did harshly smite,
Grant you may pass, when you are tried,
By innocence and not by right.

60 Let him that can rightly read in lore,
Look in the Book and learn thereby
How Jesus walked the world of yore,
And people pressed their babes Him nigh,
For joy and health from Him did pour.
"Our children touch!" they humbly cry.
"Let be!" his disciples rebuked them sore,
And to many would approach deny.
Then Jesus sweetly did reply:
"Nay! let children by me alight;
For such is heaven prepared on high!"
The innocent ever is saved by right.

61 Then Jesus summoned his servants mild,
And said His realm no man might win,
Unless he came there as a child;
Else never should he come therein.
Harmless, true, and undefiled,
Without mark or mar of soiling sin,
When such knock at those portals piled,
Quick for them men will the gate unpin.
That bliss unending dwells therein
That the jeweller sought, above gems did rate,
And sold all he had to clothe him in,
To purchase a pearl immaculate.

62 This pearl immaculate purchased dear
The jeweller gave all his goods to gain
Is like the realm of heaven's sphere:
So said the Lord of land and main;
For it is flawless, clean and clear,
Endlessly round, doth joy contain,
And is shared by all the righteous here.
Lo! amid my breast it doth remain;
There my Lord, the Lamb that was bleeding slain,
In token of peace it placed in state.
I bid you the wayward world disdain
And procure your pearl immaculate!'

63 'Immaculate Pearl in pearls unstained,
Who bear of precious pearls the prize,
Your figure fair for you who feigned?
Who wrought your robe, he was full wise!
Your beauty was never from nature gained;
Pygmalion did ne'er your face devise;
In Aristotle's learning is contained
Of these properties' nature no surmise;
Your hue the flower-de-luce defies,
Your angel-bearing is of grace so great.
What office, purest, me apprise
Doth bear this pearl immaculate?'

64 'My immaculate Lamb, my final end
Beloved, Who all can heal', said she,
'Chose me as spouse, did to bridal bend
That once would have seemed unmeet to be.
From your weeping world when I did wend
He called me to his felicity:
"Come hither to me, sweetest friend,
For no blot nor spot is found in thee!"
Power and beauty he gave to me;
In his blood he washed my weeds in state,
Crowned me clean in virginity,
And arrayed me in pearls immaculate.'

65 'Why, immaculate bride of brightest flame,
Who royalty have so rich and rare,
Of what kind can He be, the Lamb you name,

Who would you His wedded wife declare?
Over others all hath climbed your fame,
In lady's life with Him to fare.
For Christ have lived in care and blame
Many comely maids with comb in hair;
Yet the prize from all those brave you bear,
And all debar from bridal state,
All save yourself so proud and fair,
A matchless maid immaculate.'

66 'Immaculate, without a stain,
Flawless I am', said that fair queen;
'And that I may with grace maintain,
But "matchless" I said not nor do mean.
As brides of the Lamb in bliss we reign,
Twelve times twelve thousand strong, I ween,
As Apocalypse reveals it plain:
In a throng they there by John were seen;
On Zion's hill, that mount serene,
The apostle had dream divine of them
On that summit for marriage robed all clean
In the city of New Jerusalem.

67 Of Jerusalem my tale doth tell,
If you will know what His nature be,
My Lamb, my Lord, my dear Jewel,
My Joy, my Bliss, my Truelove free.
Isaiah the prophet once said well
In pity for His humility:
"That glorious Guiltless they did fell
Without cause or charge of felony,
As sheep to the slaughter led was He,
And as lamb the shearer in hand doth hem
His mouth he closed without plaint or plea,
When the Jews Him judged in Jerusalem."

68 In Jerusalem was my Truelove slain,
On the rood by ruffians fierce was rent;
Willing to suffer all our pain
To Himself our sorrows sad He lent.
With cruel blows His face was flain
That was to behold so excellent:

He for sin to be set at naught did deign,
Who of sin Himself was innocent.
Beneath the scourge and thorns He bent,
And stretched on a cross's brutal stem
As meek as lamb made no lament,
And died for us in Jerusalem.

69 In Jerusalem, Jordan, and Galilee,
As there baptized the good Saint John,
With Isaiah well did his words agree.
When to meet him once had Jesus gone
He spake of Him this prophecy:
"Lo, the Lamb of God whom our trust is on!
From the grievous sins He sets us free
That all this world hath daily done."
He wrought himself yet never one,
Though He smirched himself with all of them.
Who can tell the Fathering of that Son
That died for us in Jerusalem?

70 In Jerusalem as lamb they knew
And twice thus took my Truelove dear,
As in prophets both is record true,
For his meekness and His gentle cheer.
The third time well is matched thereto,
In Apocalypse 'tis written clear:
Where sat the saints, Him clear to view
Amidst the throne the Apostle dear
Saw loose the leaves of the book and shear
The seven signets sewn on them.
At that sight all folk there bowed in fear
In hell, in earth, and Jerusalem.

71 Jerusalem's Lamb had never stain
Of other hue than whiteness fair;
There blot nor blemish could remain,
So white the wool, so rich and rare.
Thus every soul that no soil did gain
His comely wife doth the Lamb declare;
Though each day He a host obtain,
No grudge nor grievance do we bear,
But for each one five we wish there were.

The more the merrier, so God me bless!
Our love doth thrive where many fare
In honour more and never less.

72 To less of bliss may none us bring
Who bear this pearl upon each breast,
For ne'er could they think of quarrelling
Of spotless pearls who bear the crest.
Though the clods may to our corses cling,
And for woe ye wail bereaved of rest,
From one death all our trust doth spring
In knowledge complete by us possessed.
The Lamb us gladdens, and, our grief redressed,
Doth at every Mass with joy us bless.
Here each hath bliss supreme and best,
Yet no one's honour is ever the less.

73 Lest less to trust my tale you hold,
In Apocalypse 'tis writ somewhere:
"The Lamb", saith John, "I could behold
On Zion standing proud and fair;
With him maidens a hundred-thousand fold,
And four and forty thousand were,
Who all upon their brows inscrolled
The Lamb's name and His Father's bare.
A shout then I heard from heaven there,
Like many floods met in pouring press;
And as thunder in darkling tors doth blare,
That noise, I believe, was nowise less.

74 But nonetheless, though it harshly roared,
And echo loud though it was to hear,
I heard them note then new record,
A delight as lovely to listening ear
As harpers harping on harps afford.
This new song now they sang full clear,
With resounding notes in noble accord
Making in choir their musics dear.
Before God's very throne drawn near
And the Beasts to Him bowed in lowliness
And the ancient Elders grave of cheer
They sang their song there, nonetheless.

75 Yet nonetheless were none so wise
For all the arts that they ever knew
Of that song who could a phrase devise,
Save those of the Lamb's fair retinue;
For redeemed and removed from earthly eyes,
As firstling fruits that to God are due,
To the noble Lamb they are allies,
Being like to Him in mien and hue;
For no lying word nor tale untrue
Ever touched their tongues despite duress.
Ever close that company pure shall sue
That Master immaculate, and never less." '

76 'My thanks may none the less you find,
My Pearl', quoth I, 'though I question pose.
I should not try your lofty mind,
Whom Christ to bridal chamber chose.
I am but dirt and dust in kind,
And you a rich and radiant rose
Here by this blissful bank reclined
Where life's delight unfading grows.
Now, Lady, you heart sincere enclose,
And I would ask one thing express,
And though it clown uncouth me shows,
My prayer disdain not, nevertheless.

77 I nonetheless my appeal declare,
If you to do this may well deign,
Deny you not my piteous prayer,
As you are glorious without a stain.
No home in castle-wall do ye share,
No mansion to meet in, no domain?
Of Jerusalem you speak the royal and fair,
Where David on regal throne did reign;
It abides not here on hill nor plain,
But in Judah is that noble plot.
As under moon ye have no stain
Your home should be without a spot.

78 This spotless troop of which you tell,
This thronging press many-thousandfold,
Ye doubtless a mighty citadel

Must have your number great to hold:
For jewels so lovely 'twould not be well
That flock so fair should have no fold!
Yet by these banks where a while I dwell
I nowhere about any house behold.
To gaze on this glorious stream you strolled
And linger alone now, do you not?
If elsewhere you have stout stronghold,
Now guide me to that goodly spot!'

79 'That spot', that peerless maid replied,
'In Judah's land of which you spake,
Is the city to which the Lamb did ride,
To suffer sore there for Man's sake.
The Old Jerusalem is implied,
For old sin's bond He there let break.
But the New, that God sent down to glide,
The Apocalypse in account doth take.
The Lamb that no blot ever black shall make
Doth there His lovely throng allot,
And as His flock all stains forsake
So His mansion is unmarred by spot.

80 There are two spots. To speak of these:
They both the name "Jerusalem" share;
"The City of God" or "Sight of Peace",
These meanings only doth that bear.
In the first it once the Lamb did please
Our peace by His suffering to repair;
In the other naught is found but peace
That shall last for ever without impair.
To that high city we swiftly fare
As soon as our flesh is laid to rot;
Ever grow shall the bliss and glory there
For the host within that hath no spot.'

81 'O spotless maiden kind!' I cried
To that lovely flower, 'O lead me there,
To see where blissful you abide,
To that goodly place let me repair!'
'God will forbid that', she replied,
'His tower to enter you may not dare.

But the Lamb hath leave to me supplied
For a sight thereof by favour rare:
From without on that precinct pure to stare,
But foot within to venture not;
In the street you have no strength to fare,
Unless clean you be without a spot.

82 If I this spot shall to you unhide,
Turn up towards this water's head,
While I escort you on this side,
Until your ways to a hill have led.'
No longer would I then abide,
But shrouded by leafy boughs did tread,
Until from a hill I there espied
A glimpse of that city, as forth I sped.
Beyond the river below me spread
Brighter than sun with beams it shone;
In the Apocalypse may its form be read,
As it describes the apostle John.

83 As John the apostle it did view,
I saw that city of great renown,
Jerusalem royally arrayed and new,
As it was drawn from heaven down.
Of gold refined in fire to hue
Of glittering glass was that shining town;
Fair gems beneath were joined as due
In courses twelve, on the base laid down
That with tenoned tables twelve they crown:
A single stone was each tier thereon,
As well describes this wondrous town
In apocalypse the apostle John.

84 These stones doth John in Writ disclose;
I knew their names as he doth tell:
As jewel first the jasper rose,
And first at the base I saw it well,
On the lowest course it greenly glows;
On the second stage doth sapphire dwell;
Chalcedony on the third tier shows,
A flawless, pure, and pale jewel;
The emerald fourth so green of shell;

The sardonyx, the fifth it shone,
The ruby sixth: he saw it well
In the Apocalypse, the apostle John.

85 To them John then joined the chrysolite,
The seventh gem in the ascent;
The eighth the beryl clear and white;
The twin-hued topaz as ninth was pent;
Tenth the chrysoprase formed the flight;
Eleventh was jacinth excellent;
The twelfth, most trusty in every plight,
The amethyst blue with purple blent.
Sheer from those tiers the wall then went
Of jasper like glass that glistening shone;
I knew it, for thus did it present
In the Apocalypse the apostle John.

86 As John described, I broad and sheer
These twelve degrees saw rising there;
Above the city square did rear
(Its length with breadth and height compare);
The streets of gold as glass all clear,
The wall of jasper that gleamed like glair;
With all precious stones that might there appear
Adorned within the dwellings were.
Of that domain each side all square
Twelve thousand furlongs held then on,
As in height and breadth, in length did fare,
For it measured saw the apostle John.

87 As John hath writ, I saw yet more:
Each quadrate wall there had three gates,
So in compass there were three times four,
The portals o'erlaid with richest plates;
A single pearl was every door,
A pearl whose perfection ne'er abates;
And each inscribed a name there bore
Of Israel's children by their dates:
Their times of birth each allocates,
Ever first the eldest thereon is hewn.
Such light every street illuminates
They have need of neither sun nor moon.

88 Of sun nor moon they had no need,
For God Himself was their sunlight;
The Lamb their lantern was indeed
And through Him blazed that city bright
That unearthly clear did no light impede;
Through wall and hall thus passed my sight.
The Throne on high there might one heed,
With all its rich adornment dight,
As John in chosen words did write.
High God Himself sat on that throne,
Whence forth a river ran with light
Outshining both the sun and moon.

89 Neither sun nor moon ever shone so sweet
As the pouring flood from that court that flowed;
Swiftly it swept through every street,
And no filth nor soil nor slime it showed.
No church was there the sight to greet,
Nor chapel nor temple there ever abode:
The Almighty was their minster meet;
Refreshment the Victim Lamb bestowed.
The gates ever open to every road
Were never yet shut from noon to noon;
There enters none to find abode
Who bears any spot beneath the moon.

90 The moon therefrom may gain no might,
Too spotty is she, of form too hoar;
Moreover there comes never night:
Why should the moon in circle soar
And compare her with that peerless light
That shines upon that water's shore?
The planets are in too poor a plight,
Yea, the sun himself too pale and frore.
On shining trees where those waters pour
Twelve fruits of life there ripen soon;
Twelve times a year they bear a store,
And renew them anew in every moon.

91 Such marvels as neath the moon upraised
A fleshly heart could not endure
I saw, who on that castle gazed;

Such wonders did its frame immure,
I stood there still as quail all dazed;
Its wondrous form did me allure,
That rest nor toil I felt, amazed,
And ravished by that radiance pure.
For with conscience clear I you assure,
If man embodied had gained that boon,
Though sages all essayed his cure,
His life had been lost beneath the moon.

92 As doth the moon in might arise,
Ere down must daylight leave the air,
So, suddenly, in a wondrous wise,
Of procession long I was aware.
Unheralded to my surprise
That city of royal renown so fair
Was with virgins filled in the very guise
Of my blissful one with crown on hair.
All crowned in manner like they were,
In pearls appointed, and weeds of white,
And bound on breast did each one bear
The blissful pearl with great delight.

93 With great delight in line they strolled
On golden ways that gleamed like glass;
A hundred thousands were there, I hold,
And all to match their livery was;
The gladdest face could none have told.
The Lamb before did proudly pass
With seven horns of clear red gold;
As pearls of price His raiment was.
To the Throne now drawn they pacing pass:
No crowding, though great their host in white,
But gentle as modest maids at Mass,
So lead they on with great delight.

94 The delight too great were to recall
That at his coming forth did swell.
When He approached those elders all
On their faces at His feet they fell;
There summoned hosts angelical
An incense cast of sweetest smell:

New glory and joy then forth did fall,
All sang to praise that fair Jewel.
The strain could strike through earth to hell
That the Virtues of heaven in joy endite.
With His host to laud the Lamb as well
Indeed I found a great delight.

95 Delight the Lamb to behold with eyes
Then moved my mind with wonder more:
The best was He, blithest, most dear to prize
Of whom I e'er heard tales of yore;
So wondrous white was all His guise,
So noble Himself He so meekly bore.
But by his heart a wound my eyes
Saw wide and wet; the fleece it tore,
From His white side His blood did pour.
Alas! thought I, who did that spite?
His breast should have burned with anguish sore,
Ere in that deed one took delight.

96 The Lamb's delight to doubt, I ween,
None wished; though wound he sore displayed,
In His face no sign thereof was seen,
In His glance such glorious gladness played.
I marked among His host serene,
How life in full on each was laid—
Then saw I there my little queen
That I thought stood by me in the glade!
Lord! great was the merriment she made,
Among her peers who was so white.
That vision made me think to wade
For love-longing in great delight.

97 Delight there pierced my eye and ear,
In my mortal mind a madness reigned;
When I saw her beauty I would be near,
Though beyond the stream she was retained.
I thought that naught could interfere,
Could strike me back to halt constrained,
From plunge in stream would none me steer,
Though I died ere I swam o'er what remained.
But as wild in the water to start I strained,

On my intent did quaking seize;
From that aim recalled I was detained:
It was not as my Prince did please.

98 It pleased Him not that I leapt o'er
Those marvellous bounds by madness swayed.
Though headlong haste me heedless bore,
Yet swift arrest was on me made,
For right as I rushed then to the shore
That fury made my dream to fade.
I woke in that garden as before,
My head upon that mound was laid
Where once to earth my pearl had strayed.
I stretched, and fell in great unease,
And sighing to myself I prayed:
'Now all be as that Prince may please.'

99 It pleased me ill outcast to be
So suddenly from that region fair
Where living beauty I could see.
A swoon of longing smote me there,
And I cried aloud then piteously:
'O Pearl, renowned beyond compare!
How dear was all that you said to me,
That vision true while I did share.
If it be true and sooth to swear
That in garland gay you are set at ease,
Then happy I, though chained in care,
That you that Prince indeed do please.'

100 To please that Prince had I always bent,
Desired no more than was my share,
And loyally been obedient,
As the Pearl me prayed so debonair,
I before God's face might have been sent,
In his mysteries further maybe to fare.
But with fortune no man is content
That rightly he may claim and bear;
So robbed of realms immortally fair
Too soon my joy did sorrow seize.
Lord! mad are they who against Thee dare
Or purpose what Thee may displease!

101 To please that Prince, or be pardon shown,
May Christian good with ease design;
For day and night I have him known
A God, a Lord, a Friend divine.
This chance I met on mound where prone
In grief for my pearl I would repine;
With Christ's sweet blessing and mine own
I then to God it did resign.
May He that in form of bread and wine
By priest upheld each day one sees,
Us inmates of His house divine
Make precious pearls Himself to please.

Amen Amen

SIR ORFEO

We often read and written find,
as learned men do us remind,
that lays that now the harpers sing
are wrought of many a marvellous thing.
Some are of weal, and some of woe,
and some do joy and gladness know;
in some are guile and treachery told,
in some the deeds that chanced of old;
some are of jests and ribaldry,
and some are tales of Faërie.
Of all the things that men may heed
'tis most of love they sing indeed.
In Britain all these lays are writ,
there issued first in rhyming fit,
concerning adventures in those days
whereof the Britons made their lays;
for when they heard men anywhere
tell of adventures that there were,
they took their harps in their delight
and made a lay and named it right.
Of adventures that did once befall
some can I tell you, but not all.
Listen now, lordings good and true,
and 'Orfeo' I will sing to you.

Sir Orfeo was a king of old,
in England lordship high did hold;
valour he had and hardihood,
a courteous king whose gifts were good.
His father from King Pluto came,
his mother from Juno, king of fame,
who once of old as gods were named
for mighty deeds they did and claimed.
Sir Orfeo, too, all things beyond
of harping's sweet delight was fond,
and sure were all good harpers there
of him to earn them honour fair;

himself he loved to touch the harp
and pluck the strings with fingers sharp.
He played so well, beneath the sun
a better harper was there none;
no man hath in this world been born
who would not, hearing him, have sworn
that as before him Orfeo played
to joy of Paradise he had strayed
and sound of harpers heavenly,
such joy was there and melody.
This king abode in Tracience,
a city proud of stout defence;
for Winchester, 'tis certain, then
as Tracience was known to men.
There dwelt his queen in fairest bliss,
whom men called Lady Heurodis,
of ladies then the one most fair
who ever flesh and blood did wear;
in her did grace and goodness dwell,
but none her loveliness can tell.

It so did chance in early May,
when glad and warm doth shine the day,
and gone are bitter winter showers,
and every field is filled with flowers,
on every branch the blossom blows,
in glory and in gladness grows,
the lady Heurodis, the queen,
two maidens fair to garden green
with her she took at drowsy tide
of noon to stroll by orchard-side,
to see the flowers there spread and spring
and hear the birds on branches sing.
There down in shade they sat all three
beneath a fair young grafted tree;
and soon it chanced the gentle queen
fell there asleep upon the green.
Her maidens durst her not awake,
but let her lie, her rest to take;
and so she slept, till midday soon
was passed, and come was afternoon.
Then suddenly they heard her wake,

and cry, and grievous clamour make;
she writhed with limb, her hands she wrung,
she tore her face till blood there sprung,
her raiment rich in pieces rent;
thus sudden out of mind she went.
  Her maidens two then by her side
no longer durst with her abide,
but to the palace swiftly ran
and told there knight and squire and man
their queen, it seemed, was sudden mad;
'Go and restrain her,' they them bade.
Both knights and ladies thither sped,
and more than sixty damsels fled;
to the orchard to the queen they went,
with arms to lift her down they bent,
and brought her to her bed at last,
and raving there they held her fast;
but ceaselessly she still would cry,
and ever strove to rise and fly.
  When Orfeo heard these tidings sad,
more grief than ever in life he had;
and swiftly with ten knights he sped
to bower, and stood before her bed,
and looking on her ruefully,
'Dear life,' he said, 'what troubles thee,
who ever quiet hast been and sweet,
why dost thou now so shrilly greet?
Thy body that peerless white was born
is now by cruel nails all torn.
Alas! thy cheeks that were so red
are now as wan as thou wert dead;
thy fingers too, so small and slim,
are strained with blood, their hue is dim.
Alas! thy lovely eyes in woe
now stare on me as on a foe.
A! lady, mercy I implore.
These piteous cries, come, cry no more,
but tell me what thee grieves, and how,
and say what may thee comfort now.'
  Then, lo! at last she lay there still,
and many bitter tears did spill,
and thus unto the king she spake:

'Alas! my lord, my heart will break.
Since first together came our life,
between us ne'er was wrath nor strife,
but I have ever so loved thee
as very life, and so thou me.
Yet now we must be torn in twain,
and go I must, for all thy pain.'
'Alas!' said he, 'then dark my doom.
Where wilt thou go, and go to whom?
But where thou goest, I come with thee,
and where I go, thou shalt with me.'
'Nay, nay, sir, words avail thee naught.
I will tell thee how this woe was wrought:
as I lay in the quiet noontide
and slept beneath our orchard-side,
there came two noble knights to me
arrayed in armour gallantly.
"We come", they said, "thee swift to bring
to meeting with our lord and king."
Then answered I both bold and true
that dared I not, and would not do.
They spurred then back on swiftest steed;
then came their king himself with speed;
a hundred knights with him and more,
and damsels, too, were many a score,
all riding there on snow-white steeds,
and white as milk were all their weeds;
I saw not ever anywhere
a folk so peerless and so fair.
The king was crowned with crown of light,
not of red gold nor silver white,
but of one single gem 'twas hewn
that shone as bright as sun at noon.
And coming, straightway he me sought,
and would I or no, he up me caught,
and made me by him swiftly ride
upon a palfrey at his side;
and to his palace thus me brought,
a dwelling fair and wondrous wrought.
He castles showed me there and towers,
Water and wild, and woods, and flowers,
and pastures rich upon the plain;

and then he brought me home again,
and to our orchard he me led,
and then at parting this he said:
"See, lady, tomorrow thou must be
right here beneath this grafted tree,
and then beside us thou shalt ride,
and with us evermore abide.
If let or hindrance thou dost make,
where'er thou be, we shall thee take,
and all thy limbs shall rend and tear—
no aid of man shall help thee there;
and even so, all rent and torn,
thou shalt away with us be borne." '

When all those tidings Orfeo heard,
then spake he many a bitter word:
'Alas! I had liever lose my life
than lose thee thus, my queen and wife!'
He counsel sought of every man,
but none could find him help or plan.
On the morrow, when the noon drew near,
in arms did Orfeo appear,
and full ten hundred knights with him,
all stoutly armed, all stern and grim;
and with their queen now went that band
beneath the grafted tree to stand.
A serried rank on every side
they made, and vowed there to abide,
and die there sooner for her sake
than let men thence their lady take.
And yet from midst of that array
the queen was sudden snatched away;
by magic was she from them caught,
and none knew whither she was brought.
Then was there wailing, tears, and woe;
the king did to his chamber go,
and oft he swooned on floor of stone,
and such lament he made and moan
that nigh his life then came to end;
and nothing could his grief amend.
His barons he summoned to his board,
each mighty earl and famous lord,

and when they all together came,
'My lords,' he said, 'I here do name
my steward high before you all
to keep my realm, whate'er befall,
to hold my place instead of me
and keep my lands where'er they be.
For now that I have lost my queen,
the fairest lady men have seen,
I wish not woman more to see.
Into the wilderness I will flee,
and there will live for evermore
with the wild beasts in forests hoar.
But when ye learn my days are spent,
then summon ye a parliament,
and choose ye there a king anew.
With all I have now deal ye true.'
  Then weeping was there in the hall,
and great lament there made they all,
and hardly there might old or young
for weeping utter word with tongue.
They knelt them down in company,
and prayed, if so his will might be,
that never should he from them go.
'Have done!' said he. 'It must be so.'

  Now all his kingdom he forsook.
Only a beggar's cloak he took;
he had no kirtle and no hood,
no shirt, nor other raiment good.
His harp yet bore he even so,
and barefoot from the gate did go;
no man might keep him on the way.
  A me! the weeping woe that day,
when he that had been king with crown
went thus beggarly out of town!
Through wood and over moorland bleak
he now the wilderness doth seek,
and nothing finds to make him glad,
but ever liveth lone and sad.
He once had ermine worn and vair,
on bed had purple linen fair,
now on the heather hard doth lie,

in leaves is wrapped and grasses dry.
He once had castles owned and towers,
water and wild, and woods, and flowers,
now though it turn to frost or snow,
this king with moss his bed must strow.
He once had many a noble knight
before him kneeling, ladies bright,
now nought to please him doth he keep;
only wild serpents by him creep.
He that once had in plenty sweet
all dainties for his drink and meat,
now he must grub and dig all day,
with roots his hunger to allay.
In summer on wildwood fruit he feeds,
or berries poor to serve his needs;
in winter nothing can he find
save roots and herbs and bitter rind.
All his body was wasted thin
by hardship, and all cracked his skin.
A Lord! who can recount the woe
for ten long years that king did know?
His hair and beard all black and rank
down to his waist hung long and lank.
His harp wherein was his delight
in hollow tree he hid from sight;
when weather clear was in the land
his harp he took then in his hand
and harped thereon at his sweet will.
Through all the wood the sound did thrill,
and all the wild beasts that there are
in joy approached him from afar;
and all the birds that might be found
there perched on bough and bramble round
to hear his harping to the end,
such melodies he there did blend;
and when he laid his harp aside,
no bird or beast would near him bide.

There often by him would he see,
when noon was hot on leaf and tree,
the king of Faërie with his rout
came hunting in the woods about

with blowing far and crying dim,
and barking hounds that were with him;
yet never a beast they took nor slew,
and where they went he never knew.
At other times he would descry
a mighty host, it seemed, go by,
ten hundred knights all fair arrayed
with many a banner proud displayed.
Each face and mien was fierce and bold,
each knight a drawn sword there did hold,
and all were armed in harness fair
and marching on he knew not where.
Or a sight more strange would meet his eye:
knights and ladies came dancing by
in rich array and raiment meet,
softly stepping with skilful feet;
tabour and trumpet went along,
and marvellous minstrelsy and song.

And one fair day he at his side
saw sixty ladies on horses ride,
each fair and free as bird on spray,
and never a man with them that day.
There each on hand a falcon bore,
riding a-hawking by river-shore.
Those haunts with game in plenty teem,
cormorant, heron, and duck in stream;
there off the water fowl arise,
and every falcon them descries;
each falcon stooping slew his prey,
and Orfeo laughing loud did say:
'Behold, in faith, this sport is fair!
Fore Heaven, I will betake me there!
I once was wont to see such play.'
He rose and thither made his way,
and to a lady came with speed,
and looked at her, and took good heed,
and saw as sure as once in life
'twas Heurodis, his queen and wife.
Intent he gazed, and so did she,
but no word spake; no word said he.
For hardship that she saw him bear,

who had been royal, and high, and fair,
then from her eyes the tears there fell.
The other ladies marked it well,
and away they made her swiftly ride;
no longer might she near him bide.
'Alas!' said he, 'unhappy day!
Why will not now my death me slay?
Alas! unhappy man, ah why
may I not, seeing her, now die?
Alas! too long hath lasted life,
when I dare not with mine own wife
to speak a word, nor she with me.
Alas! my heart should break,' said he.
'And yet, fore Heaven, tide what betide,
and whithersoever these ladies ride,
that road I will follow they now fare;
for life or death no more I care.'
His beggar's cloak he on him flung,
his harp upon his back he hung;
with right good will his feet he sped,
for stock nor stone he stayed his tread.
Right into a rock the ladies rode,
and in behind he fearless strode.
He went into that rocky hill
a good three miles or more, until
he came into a country fair
as bright as sun in summer air.
Level and smooth it was and green,
and hill nor valley there was seen.
A castle he saw amid the land
princely and proud and lofty stand;
the outer wall around it laid
of shining crystal clear was made.
A hundred towers were raised about
with cunning wrought, embattled stout;
and from the moat each buttress bold
in arches sprang of rich red gold.
The vault was carven and adorned
with beasts and birds and figures horned;
within were halls and chambers wide
all made of jewels and gems of pride;
the poorest pillar to behold

was builded all of burnished gold.
And all that land was ever light,
for when it came to dusk of night
from precious stones there issued soon
a light as bright as sun at noon.
No man may tell nor think in thought
how rich the works that there were wrought;
indeed it seemed he gazed with eyes
on the proud court of Paradise.

The ladies to that castle passed.
Behind them Orfeo followed fast.
There knocked he loud upon the gate;
the porter came, and did not wait,
but asked him what might be his will.
'In faith, I have a minstrel's skill
with mirth and music, if he please,
thy lord to cheer, and him to ease.'
The porter swift did then unpin
the castle gates, and let him in.

Then he began to gaze about,
and saw within the walls a rout
of folk that were thither drawn below,
and mourned as dead, but were not so.
For some there stood who had no head,
and some no arms, nor feet; some bled
and through their bodies wounds were set,
and some were strangled as they ate,
and some lay raving, chained and bound,
and some in water had been drowned;
and some were withered in the fire,
and some on horse, in war's attire.
and wives there lay in their childbed,
and mad were some, and some were dead;
and passing many there lay beside
as though they slept at quiet noon-tide.
Thus in the world was each one caught
and thither by fairy magic brought.
There too he saw his own sweet wife,
Queen Heurodis, his joy and life,
asleep beneath a grafted tree:
by her attire he knew 'twas she.

When he had marked these marvels all,

he went before the king in hall,
and there a joyous sight did see,
a shining throne and canopy.
Their king and lord there held his seat
beside their lady fair and sweet.
Their crowns and clothes so brightly shone
that scarce his eyes might look thereon.
 When he had marked this wondrous thing,
he knelt him down before the king:
'O lord,' said he, 'if it be thy will,
now shalt thou hear my minstrel's skill.'
The king replied: 'What man art thou
that hither darest venture now?
Not I nor any here with me
have ever sent to summon thee,
and since here first my reign began
I have never found so rash a man
that he to us would dare to wend,
unless I first for him should send.'
'My lord,' said he, 'I thee assure,
I am but a wandering minstrel poor;
and, sir, this custom use we all
at the house of many a lord to call,
and little though our welcome be,
to offer there our minstrelsy.'
 Before the king upon the ground
he sat, and touched his harp to sound;
his harp he tuned as well he could,
glad notes began and music good,
and all who were in palace found
came unto him to hear the sound,
and lay before his very feet,
they thought his melody so sweet.
He played, and silent sat the king
for great delight in listening;
great joy this minstrelsy he deemed,
and joy to his noble queen it seemed.
 At last when he his harping stayed,
this speech the king to him then made:
'Minstrel, thy music pleaseth me.
Come, ask of me whate'er it be,
and rich reward I will thee pay.

Come, speak, and prove now what I say!'
'Good sir,' he said, 'I beg of thee
that this thing thou wouldst give to me,
that very lady fair to see
who sleeps beneath the grafted tree.'
'Nay,' said the king, 'that would not do!
A sorry pair ye'd make, ye two;
for thou art black, and rough, and lean,
and she is faultless, fair and clean.
A monstrous thing then would it be
to see her in thy company.'
'O sir,' he said, 'O gracious king,
but it would be a fouler thing
from mouth of thine to hear a lie.
Thy vow, sir, thou canst not deny,
Whate'er I asked, that should I gain,
and thou must needs thy word maintain.'
The king then said: 'Since that is so,
now take her hand in thine, and go;
I wish thee joy of her, my friend!'
He thanked him well, on knees did bend;
his wife he took then by the hand,
and departed swiftly from that land,
and from that country went in haste;
the way he came he now retraced.
Long was the road. The journey passed;
to Winchester he came at last,
his own beloved city free;
but no man knew that it was he.
Beyond the town's end yet to fare,
lest men them knew, he did not dare;
but in a beggar's narrow cot
a lowly lodging there he got
both for himself and for his wife,
as a minstrel poor of wandering life.
He asked for tidings in the land,
and who that kingdom held in hand;
the beggar poor him answered well
and told all things that there befell:
how fairies stole their queen away
ten years before, in time of May;
and how in exile went their king

in unknown countries wandering,
while still the steward rule did hold;
and many things beside he told.
Next day, when hour of noon was near,
he bade his wife await him here;
the beggar's rags he on him flung,
his harp upon his back he hung,
and went into the city's ways
for men to look and on him gaze.
Him earl and lord and baron bold,
lady and burgess, did behold.
'O look! O what a man!' they said,
'How long the hair hangs from his head!
His beard is dangling to his knee!
He is gnarled and knotted like a tree!'
Then as he walked along the street
He chanced his steward there to meet,
and after him aloud cried he:
'Mercy, sir steward, have on me!
A harper I am from Heathenesse;
to thee I turn in my distress.'
The steward said: 'Come with me, come!
Of what I have thou shalt have some.
All harpers good I welcome make
For my dear lord Sir Orfeo's sake.'
The steward in castle sat at meat,
and many a lord there had his seat;
trumpeters, tabourers there played
harpers and fiddlers music made.
Many a melody made they all,
but Orfeo silent sat in hall
and listened. And when they all were still
he took his harp and tuned it shrill.
Then notes he harped more glad and clear
than ever a man hath heard with ear;
his music delighted all those men.
The steward looked and looked again;
the harp in hand at once he knew.
'Minstrel,' he said, 'come, tell me true,
whence came this harp to thee, and how?
I pray thee, tell me plainly now.'
'My lord,' said he, 'in lands unknown

I walked a wilderness alone,
and there I found in dale forlorn
a man by lions to pieces torn,
by wolves devoured with teeth so sharp;
by him I found this very harp,
and that is full ten years ago.'
'Ah!' said the steward, 'news of woe!
'Twas Orfeo, my master true.
Alas! poor wretch, what shall I do,
who must so dear a master mourn?
A! woe is me that I was born,
for him so hard a fate designed,
a death so vile that he should find!'
Then on the ground he fell in swoon;
his barons stooping raised him soon
and bade him think how all must end—
for death of man no man can mend.

King Orfeo now had proved and knew
his steward was both loyal and true,
and loved him as he duly should.
'Lo!' then he cried, and up he stood,
'Steward, now to my words give ear!
If thy king, Orfeo, were here,
and had in wilderness full long
suffered great hardship sore and strong,
had won his queen by his own hand
out of the deeps of fairy land,
and led at last his lady dear
right hither to the town's end near,
and lodged her in a beggar's cot;
if I were he, whom ye knew not,
thus come among you, poor and ill,
in secret to prove thy faith and will,
if then I thee had found so true,
thy loyalty never shouldst thou rue:
nay, certainly, tide what betide,
thou shouldst be king when Orfeo died.
Hadst thou rejoiced to hear my fate,
I would have thrust thee from the gate.'

Then clearly knew they in the hall
that Orfeo stood before them all.
The steward understood at last;

in his haste the table down he cast
and flung himself before his feet,
and each lord likewise left his seat,
and this one cry they all let ring:
'Ye are our lord, sir, and our king!'
To know he lived so glad they were.
To his chamber soon they brought him there;
they bathed him and they shaved his beard,
and robed him, till royal he appeared;
and brought them in procession long
the queen to town with merry song,
with many a sound of minstrelsy.
A Lord! how great the melody!
For joy the tears were falling fast
of those who saw them safe at last.
Now was King Orfeo crowned anew,
and Heurodis his lady too;
and long they lived, till they were dead,
and king was the steward in their stead.
Harpers in Britain in aftertime
these marvels heard, and in their rhyme
a lay they made of fair delight,
and after the king it named aright,
'Orfeo' called it, as was meet:
good is the lay, the music sweet.
Thus came Sir Orfeo out of care.
God grant that well we all may fare!

GLOSSARY

This glossary provides no more than the meanings of some archaic and technical words used in the translations, and only the meanings that the translator intended in those contexts (which in a very few cases may be doubtful). In the stanzas describing the breaking-up of the deer he employed some of the technical terms of the original which are debatable in meaning, and in such cases (e.g. *Arber, Knot, Numbles*) I have given what I believe was his final interpretation. References to *Sir Gawain* (G) and *Pearl* (P) are by stanza, and to *Sir Orfeo* (O) by line.

Arber Paunch, first stomach of ruminants, G 53.

Assay The testing of the fat of a deer, and the proper point at which to make the test, G 53.

Assoiled Absolved, G 75.

Baldric A belt passing over one shoulder and under the other, supporting a sword or a horn, G 100, 101; a strap to suspend the shield, G 27.

Barbican A strong outer defence of a castle, over a bridge or gate, connected with the main work, G 34.

Barrow Mound, G 87.

Beaver Moveable front part of a helmet, protecting the face, G 26.

Blazon Shield, G 27, 35.

Blear Dim, P 7.

Brawn Flesh, G 64, 65.

Buffet Blow, G 94.

Caitiff Boor, one of base mind and conduct, G 71.

Capadoce *This word is taken from the original; it apparently meant* a short cape, that could be buttoned or clasped round the throat, G 9, 25.

Caparison Ornamented cloth covering of a horse, G 26.

Carl Man, G 84.

Carols Dances accompanied by song, G 3; cf. *carol-dances* G 66, 75, and *they carolled* G 42.

Childermas The feast of the Holy Innocents, on the 28th of December, G 42.

Chine Backbone, G 54.

Churl Common man, G 84.
Cincture Girdle, G 98.
Cithern Stringed instrument, P 8.
Coat-armour Surcoat worn over the armour, embroidered with distinctive heraldic devices, G 25, 81.
Cognisance *literally* 'recognition', i.e. a personal badge by which the wearer could be known (referring to the Pentangle), G 81.
Coif Head-dress, G 69.
Corses Bodies, P 72.
Crenelles Battlements, G 34 (*strictly*, the indentations in the battlements, alternating with the raised parts, the 'merlons').
Crupper Leather strap passing round a horse's hindquarters and fastened to the saddle to prevent it from slipping forward, G 8, 26.
Cuisses Armour for the thighs, G 25.
Demeaned her Behaved, G 51.
Dolour Sorrow, P 28.
Doted Gone out of their wits, G 78.
Ellwand Measuring-rod an ell (45 inches) long, G 10.
Empery Absolute dominion, P 38.
Eslot Hollow above the breastbone at the base of the throat, G 53; = *neck-slot*, G 63.
Fain Glad, G 35.
Featly Neatly, G 34; deftly, skilfully, G 51.
Feigned Formed, fashioned, P 63.
Fells Skins, G 37, 69; *fox-fell*, G 77.
Finials Ornamental pinnacles on rooves or towers, G 34.
Flower-de-luce iris (*in the translation specifically* a white iris), P 17, 63.
Fore-numbles *The original has 'avanters', part of the numbles of a deer, see* Numbles; G 53.
Frore Very cold, frosty, P 90.
Gittern Stringed instrument, P 8.
Glair White of egg, P 86.
Glamoury Enchantment (enchanted being), G 99.
Gledes Live coals, G 64.
Gramercy Thank you, G 35, 42, 85.
Greaves Armour for the legs, G 25.
Greet Weep, O 104.
Grue Shuddering horror, G 95.

Guerdon Reward, recompense, G 72, 82; P 51, 52.
Guisarm Battle-axe, G 13, 15, 17, 91.
Gules Heraldic name for red, G 27, 28.
Halidom *In the oath 'So help me God and the Halidom', 'the Halidom' referred to* something of reverence or sanctity on which the oath was taken; G 85.
Handsels Gifts at New Year, G 4.
Hap Fortune, P 11.
Hastlets Edible entrails of a pig, G 64.
Heathenesse The heathen lands, O 513.
Hie Hasten, G 53.
Holt Wood, G 68.
Ingle Fire burning on the hearth, G 66.
Keep (*probably*) guard, protect, O 233.
Kerchiefs Head-coverings, G 39.
Kirtle A short coat or tunic reaching to the knees, G 73, P 17.
Knot *Technical term applied to* two pieces of fat in the neck and two in the flanks, G 53.
Latchet Loop, lace, fastening, G 26.
Lemman Lover, mistress, G 71.
Liever Rather, G 50, O 177.
Link-men Torch-carriers, G 79.
List Wished, G 61.
Loopholes Narrow slits in a castle-wall, G 34.
Ma fay! By my faith! G 59.
Marge Edge, G 87.
Margery-pearls pearls, P 17.
Margery-stones pearls, P 18.
Maugre In spite of; *maugre his teeth*, in spite of all he could do to resist, G 62.
Meed Reward, P 47.
Mellay Close hand-to-hand combat, G 63.
Molains Ornamented bosses on a horse's bit, G 8.
Numbles Pieces of loin-meat, *probably* the tenderloin or fillet, G 53.
Oratory Chapel, G 88.
Palfrey Small saddle-horse (especially for the use of women), O 156.
Pauncer Armour protecting the abdomen, G 80.
Pease Pea, G 95.
Pisane Armour for upper breast and neck, G 10.

Pleasances	Pleasure gardens, P 12.
Point-device	To perfection, G 26.
Poitrel	Breast-armour of a horse, G 8, 26.
Polains	Pieces of armour for the knees, G 25.
Popinjays	Parrots, G 26.
Port	Bearing, G 39.
Prise	*literally* capture, taking, G 64; notes blown on the horn at the taking or felling of the hunted beast, G 54.
Purfling	Embroidered border, P 18.
Quadrate	Square, P 87.
Quarry	Heap of slain animals, G 53.
Quest	Searching of hounds after game; *cried for a quest*, called for a search (by baying), G 57.
Rewel	Some kind of ivory, P 18.
Rood	Cross, P 54, 59, 68.
Ruth	Remorse, G 100.
Sabatons	Steel shoes, G 25.
Sendal	A fine silken material, G 4.
Sheen	Bright, P 4.
Slade	Valley, P 12.
Surnape	Napkin, *or* overcloth to protect tablecloth, G 37.
Tables	Horizontal courses, the stepped tiers of the foundation, P 83.
Tabour	Small drum, O 301.
Tabourers	Players on the tabour, O 521.
Tenoned	Closely joined, P 83.
Tines	Pointed branches of a deer's horn, G 34.
Tors	High hills, P 73.
Tressure	Jewelled net confining the hair, G 69.
Vair	Variegated (grey and white) squirrel's fur, O 241.
Weasand	Oesophagus, gullet, G 53.
Weed	Garment, G 95; *weeds*, P 64, O 146.
Welkin	Heavens, sky, G 23, P 10.
Wight	Being, G 84.
Wist	Knew, G 61.
Worms	Dragons, serpents, G 31.
Wrack	Drifting cloud, G 68.

APPENDIX

The Verse-forms of SIR GAWAIN AND THE GREEN KNIGHT and PEARL

I *Sir Gawain*

The word 'alliterative', as applied to the ancestral measure of England, is misleading; for it was not concerned with *letters*, with *spelling*, but with *sounds*, judged by the ear. The sounds that are important are those that *begin* words—more precisely, those that begin the stressed syllables of words. Alliteration, or 'head-rhyme', is the agreement of stressed syllables within the line in beginning with the same consonantal sound (sound, not letter), or in beginning not with a consonant but with a vowel. Any vowel alliterates with any other vowel: the alliterative pattern is satisfied if the words in question do *not* begin with a consonant.

'Apt alliteration's artful aid,' said an eighteenth-century writer. But to a fourteenth century poet in this mode three only of those four words alliterated. Not *alliteration* itself; for its first strong syllable is *lit*, and so it alliterates on the consonant *l. Apt, artful,* and *aid* alliterate; not because they begin with the same *letter, a*, but because they agree in beginning with no consonant; and that was alliteration enough. 'Old English art', where the words begin with three different letters, would be just as good.

But a line of this verse was not verse simply because it contained such alliterations; *rum ram ruf*, as Chaucer's parson mocked it, is not a line. It also had some structure.

The poet begins his poem with a very regular line, of one of his favourite varieties:

Siþen þe sege and þe assaut watz sesed at Troye

When the siege and the assault had ceased at Troy

This kind of line falls into two parts: 'When the siege and the assault' and 'had ceased at Troy.' There is nearly always a breath-pause between them, corresponding to some degree of pause in the sense. But the line was welded into a metrical unit by alliteration; one or more (usually two) of the chief words in the first part were linked by alliteration with the *first* important word in the second part. Thus, in the line above, *siege, assault; ceased.* (As it is the stressed syllable that counts, *assault* runs on *s*, not on a vowel).

Each of these parts had to contain two syllables (often whole words, like *siege*) that were in their place sufficiently stressed to bear a 'beat'. The other syllables should be lighter and quieter. But their number was not counted, nor in this medieval form was their placing strictly ordered. This freedom has one marked effect on rhythm: there might be no intervening light syllable between the stresses. It is of course an effect far easier to produce in English than to avoid, being normal in natural speech. Verse that uses it can accommodate easily many natural phrasings. The medieval poets used it especially in the second part of their lines; examples from the translation are

Tirius went to Tuscany   and tówns fóunded   (stanza 1)

Indeed of the Table Round   all those tríed bréthren   (stanza 3)

The alliteration may be at a minimum, affecting only one word in each part of the line. This is not frequent in the original (and in some places of its occurrence mistakes in the manuscript may be suspected); it is somewhat more so in the translation. Far more often, the alliteration is increased. Mere excess, when both of the stresses in the second part alliterate, is seldom found; two examples occur in consecutive lines in stanza 83:

Þay *b*oȝen bi *b*onkkez   þer *b*oȝes ar *b*are,
Þay *c*lomben bi *c*lyffez   þer *c*lengez þe *c*olde

and are preserved in the translation. This is an excess, a rum-ram-ruf-*ram*, that soon cloys the ear.

Increased alliteration is usually connected with increase in weight and content of the line. In very many verses the first part of the line has three heavy syllables or beats (not necessarily, nor indeed usually, of equal force). It is convenient to look at this sort of rhythm in this way. Natural language does not always arrange itself into the simple patterns:

the siege and the assault   had ceased at Troy

Tirius to Tuscany   and towns founded

There might be more 'full words' in a phrase. 'The king and his kinsman/and courtly men served them' (see stanza 21, line 16) is well enough and is a sufficient line. But you might wish to say: 'The king and his good kinsman/and quickly courtly men served them.' As far as the second half of the line went, you restrained your wish and did not allow the language to have its head; you kept the ends of lines simple and clear. At most you would venture on 'and courtiers at once served them'—avoiding double alliteration and putting the adverb where in natural narration it could be subordinated in force and tone to *court-* and *served*, leaving them plainly as the beats. But in the first part of the line 'packing' was much practiced.

In 'The king and his good kinsman' *good* is not of much importance, and can be reduced in tone so as hardly to rise up and challenge the main beats, *king* and *kin*. But if this element joins in the alliteration, it is brought into notice, and then one has a triple type: 'The king and his kind kinsman'. This variety, in which there is a third beat inserted before the second main beat, to which it is subordinated in tone and import, but with which it nonetheless alliterates, is very common indeed. Thus the second line of the poem:

And the *f*ortress *f*ell in *f*lame   to *f*irebrands and ashes

But the added material may come at the beginning of the line. Instead of 'In pomp and pride/he peopled it first' (see the 9th line of the poem) you may say: 'In great pomp and pride'. This will lead easily to another variety in which there is a third beat before the first main stress, to which it is subordinate, but with which it alliterates; so in the eighth line of the poem:

Fro *r*iche *R*omulus to *R*ome   *r*icchis hym swyþe

When *r*oyal *R*omulus to *R*ome   his *r*oad had taken

Less commonly a full but subordinate word may be put instead of a weak syllable at the end of the first part of the line; thus in stanza 81:

Þe gordel of þe grene silke,   þat gay wel bisemed

That girdle of green silk,   and gallant it looked

If this is given an alliteration, one gets the type:

And *f*ar over the *F*rench *f*lood *F*elix Brutus (stanza 1)

Further varieties will then develop; for example, those in which the third beat is not really subordinate, but either phonetically, or in sense and vividness, or in both, a rival to the others:

But *w*ild *w*eathers of the *w*orld a*w*ake in the land

Thc *r*ings *r*id of the rust on his *r*ich byrnie (both from stanza 80)

It may sometimes occur that the added beat bears the alliteration and the phonetically or logically more important word does not. In the translation, this type is used in order to provide an alliteration when a main word that cannot be changed refuses to alliterate. Thus in the first line of stanza 2 the translation has:

And when *f*air Britain was *f*ounded by this *f*amous lord

for the original

Ande quen þis *B*retayn watz *b*igged bi þis *b*urn rych(e)—

since 'Britain' was inescapable, but neither *bigged* (founded) nor *burn* (knight, man) have any modern counterparts to alliterate with it.

As was said earlier, alliteration was by ear, and not by letter; the spelling is not concerned.

*J*usted ful *j*olilé þise *g*entyle kniȝtes (stanza 3, line 6)

alliterated, despite the spelling with *g* and *j*. Quite another matter is 'licence'. The poet allowed himself certain of these: where neither the spelling nor the sound were the same, but the sounds were at least *similar*. He could occasionally disregard the distinction between voiced and voiceless consonants, and thus equate *s* with *z*, or *f* with *v*, and (often) words beginning with *h* with words beginning with a vowel. In the translation the same licences are allowed when necessary—a translator needs even more help than one composing on his own. Thus:

Quen Zeferus syflez hymself on sedez and erbez

When Zephyr goes sighing through seeds and herbs (stanza 23)

and:

Though you yourself be desirous   to accept it in person   (stanza 16)

where the second stress is the 'zire' of *desirous*, and the third is the 'sept' of *accept*.

The cases where the alliteration is borne not by the first but by the second element in a compound word (such as *eyelid* or *daylight* in lines alliterating on *l*) are really not different metrically from those in which a separate but subordinate word usurps the alliteration. For example:

And unlouked his yȝe-lyddez,   and let as him wondered

He lifted his eyelids   with a look as of wonder   (stanza 48)

One variety is frequently used in the translation which is not often found in clear cases in the original; that is 'crossed alliteration'. In this, a line contains two alliterative sounds, in either the arrangement *abab* or *abba*. These patterns are used in the translation because they satisfy the requirements of simple alliteration and yet add more metrical colour to make up for the cases where triple or quadruple alliteration in the original cannot be rivalled in modern English. Thus:

All of *g*reen were they *m*ade,   both *g*arments and *m*an (stanza 8)

Towards the *f*airest at the *t*able   he *t*wisted the *f*ace (stanza 20)

In the following line the pattern is *f/s/z/f*:

And since *f*olly thou hast *s*ought,   thou de*s*ervest to *f*ind it (stanza 15)

The frequent occurrence in the translation of 'Wawain' for 'Gawain' follows the practice of the original. Both forms of the name were current; and of course the existence of an alternative form of the name of a principal character, beginning with another consonant, was a great help to an alliterative poet.

But in *Sir Gawain* there is end-rhyme as well, in the last lines of each stanza. The author had the notion (so it may probably be said, for nothing quite like it is found elsewhere) to lighten the monotony and weight of some 2,000 long alliterating lines on end. He broke them up into groups (hardly really 'stanzas', as they are very variable in length), and at the end of each he put a patch of rhyme. This consists of four three-beat lines rhyming alternately (now known as the 'wheel') and a one-beat tag (known as the 'bob') to link the 'wheel' with the preceding stanza. The bob rhymes with the second and fourth lines of the wheel. There is no doubt of the metrical success of this device; but since the rhymed lines had also to alliterate, and there is not much room to move in the short lines of the wheel, the author set himself a severe technical test, and the translator a worse one. In the translation, the attempt to alliterate as well as rhyme has had to be abandoned a little more often than in the original. As an example of the bob and wheel both in the original and in the translation, this is the end of stanza 2:

If ze wyl lysten þis laye bot on littel quile
I schal telle hit astit, as I in toun herde,
        with tonge,
    As hit is stad and stoken
    In stori stif and stronge,
    With lel letteres loken,
    In londe so hatz ben longe.

If you will listen to this lay but a little while now,
I will tell it at once as in town I have heard
        it told,
    as it is fixed and fettered
    in story brave and bold,
    thus linked and truly lettered
    as was loved in this land of old.

II *Pearl*

In *Pearl* the author adopted a twelve-line rhyming stanza in which alliteration is used as well. The line in *Pearl* is a French line, modified primarily (a) by the difference of English from French generally, and (b) by the influence of inherited metrical practices and taste, especially in the areas where the alliterative tradition was still strong. The essential features of the ancient English alliterative practice are wholly unlike, in effect and aim, what is found in *Pearl*. In the old alliterative verse the 'line' had no repeated or constant accentual rhythm which gave it its metrical character; its units were the half-lines, each of which was independently constructed. The line was internally linked by alliteration; but this linking was deliberately used *counter* to the rhetorical and syntactic structure. The chief rhetorical or logical pauses were normally placed (except at the end of a verse period of several lines) in the middle of the line, between the alliterations; and the second half-line was most frequently more closely connected in sense and syntax to the following line.

In complete contrast to all this, there is in *Pearl* a basic and model accentual rhythm of alternating strong/loud—weak/soft syllables; the poem being written to a scheme:

x / x / x / x (x)
Þay songen wyth a swete asent (line 94 of the original).

'Model' lines of this kind make up about a quarter of the lines in the poem; but if those lines are included in which there occurs the simple variation of allowing one of the 'falls' to contain *two* weak syllables, the proportion rises to about three-fifths, and higher still if two such two-syllable falls are allowed. In all these cases (since only those in which the metrically unstressed elements are genuinely 'weak' are counted) the metrical pattern of alternating strong-loud and weak-soft syllables is clearly maintained. And in spite of the 'variations' that are used, and of the doubt concerning the presence or absence of final *-e*, this pattern remains indeed so frequent and insistent as to impart to the metrical effect of the whole a certain monotony, which combined with the emphasis of alliteration can (at any rate to a modern listener) become almost soporific. This is increased by the poet's preference for making the last beat, which is a rhyming syllable, share in the alliteration.

In *Pearl* the *total line* is the unit, and is usually 'locked up in itself'; in the vast majority of cases, the major marks of punctuation must be placed at the line-ends. Even 'commas', when phonetically used (that is, when not used simply by custom, to mark off phrases which are not naturally marked off even by light pauses in speech) are infrequent within the line; while 'run-ons' from one line to the next are extremely rare.

And finally, alliteration in the verse-form of *Pearl* plays *no* structural part in the line at all. It may be divided among the four stresses in any order or amount from two to four, and where there is only one pair these may be placed together as AB or as CD, leaving the other half alliteratively blank. And it may be absent altogether; in the 1,212 lines of the poem, over 300 are quite blank. Moreover, unless the number of blank lines is to be made even larger, syllables may assist in alliteration that do not bear the main metrical stresses, or are in the structure of the line relatively weak. In other words, alliteration is in *Pearl* a mere 'grace' or decoration of the line, which is sufficiently defined as such, and as being 'verse', without it. And this decoration is provided according to the skill of the poet, or linguistic opportunity, without guiding rule or other function.

Each stanza of *Pearl* has twelve lines, containing only three rhymes, always arranged *ab* in the first eight and then *bcbc* in the last four. The whole poem would contain 100 stanzas in twenty groups of five, if the fifteenth group (which begins with stanza 71) did not contain six. It has been argued that a stanza has been included in the manuscript which the author meant to strike out; but against this is the fact that the extra stanza in *Pearl* gives the poem a total of 101, and there are 101 stanzas in *Sir Gawain*.

The groups of five stanzas (which are indicated in the manuscript by an ornamental coloured initial at the beginning of each group) are constituted in this way. The last word in each stanza reappears in the first line of the following one (so stanza 1 ends in the original 'Of Þat pryuy perle wythouten *spot*', and stanza 2 begins 'SyÞen in Þat *spote* hit fro me sprange'). This link-word reappears in the first line of the first stanza of the following group (so stanza 6 begins 'Fro *spot* my spyryt Þer sprang in space'), and the new link-word appears at the end of that stanza (so stanza 6 ends 'Of half so dere adubbemente', and stanza 7 begins '*Dubbed* wern alle þo downez sydez'). As this last instance shows, the link need not be precisely the same, but may be constituted from different parts of the same verb, from noun and adjective with the same stem, and so on. The linkage fails in the original at the beginning of stanza 61, as it does in the translation.

Thus not only are the stanzas linked together internally as groups, but the groups are linked to each other; and the last line of the poem, 'And precious perlez vnto his pay' (where *pay* means 'pleasure') echoes the first, 'Perle, plesaunte to prynces paye.' This echoing of the beginning of the poem in its end is found also in *Sir Gawain*, and in *Patience*.

This form was not easy to compose in, but very much more difficult to translate in; since the rhyme-words used by the poet rarely still fit in modern English, and the alliterating words fit as seldom. In the translation, satisfaction of the rhyme-scheme is of course given the primacy, and the alliteration is less rich than in the original. But the effect of the translation on the modern ear is probably that of its original on a contemporary ear in this respect, since we no longer habitually expect alliteration as an essential ingredient in verse, as the people of the North and West of England once did.

GAWAIN'S LEAVE-TAKING

Now Lords and Ladies blithe and bold,
  To bless you here now am I bound:
I thank you all a thousand-fold,
  And pray God save you whole and sound;
  Wherever you go on grass or ground,
    May he you guide that nought you grieve,
  For friendship that I here have found
    Against my will I take my leave.

For friendship and for favours good,
  For meat and drink you heaped on me,
The Lord that raised was on the Rood
  Now keep you comely company.
  On sea or land where'er you be,
    May he you guide that nought you grieve.
  Such fair delight you laid on me
    Against my will I take my leave.

Against my will although I wend,
  I may not always tarry here;
For everything must have an end,
  And even friends must part, I fear;
  Be we beloved however dear
    Out of this world death will us reave,
  And when we brought are to our bier
    Against our will we take our leave.

Now good day to you, goodmen all,
  And good day to you, young and old,
And good day to you, great and small,
  And grammercy a thousand-fold!
  If ought there were that dear ye hold,
    Full fain I would the deed achieve—
  Now Christ you keep from sorrows cold
    For now at last I take my leave.